Ordinary Saints

"In *Ordinary Saints*, Devenish reminds us that we are citizens of heaven and not of this earth any longer. After joining the Jesus community, a new spirit-power is available to enable us to love our neighbor, forgive our enemy, and give away our lives—none of which are natural tendencies. The author makes it clear that the task of ordinary saints is to live for others and not for ourselves. He challenges the church to nurture this form of Christlikeness as a compelling personal and communal calling. He echoes the Apostle Paul's message that our lives are living proofs of the reality of God at work in the world. This book is a must-read for anyone wishing to educate future Christian leaders, and for ordinary Christians who desire to orient their heart towards what God loves."

—**Judy TenElshof**, Professor of Spirituality, Marriage and Family, Institute for Spiritual Formation, Talbot School of Theology and Biola University, California

"The current climate of the Christian church is dry. It needs the enlivening of a new spiritual current to awaken our dry bones. In this pioneering book, Stuart Devenish advances our understanding of what it means to be a saint today. He exegetes saintly lives to highlight their features so we can grasp the deeper dynamics of devotion. This book will fan into flame a desire to be a person whose life demonstrates the heat of godly desire. We need more books like this one to encourage, instruct, and guide those saints who devote their lives to knowing God and becoming like his son Jesus. How hilarious of God to renew the world on the back of the weakness and witness of the saints—many of whom are lurking among us, awaiting fresh instructions."

—**Sue Whiteley**, Retreat Facilitator and Trainer; previously Associate Dean of Formation, Australian College of Ministries

"Many of the great exemplars of the Christian spiritual life live under the radar. They do not seek the spotlight, and most are surprised to see themselves described as 'saints.' It is precisely for this reason that Stuart Devenish's book is so valuable. He calls saints out from their extraordinarily ordinary vocations and introduces us to them as the friends of God. Without decrying the importance of doctrines and beliefs, Devenish makes a compelling case for the power of the gospel to make itself known in the everyday world through the beautiful lives of God's holy people. Christianity with its sleeves rolled up is not to be underestimated, especially when seasoned with genuine love and grace. *Ordinary Saints* will be a helpful and encouraging resource for those saints/holy people who are called to live out their faith in these paradoxical times."

—**Tim Harris**, Assistant Bishop, Anglican Diocese of Adelaide; Vice Principal, Saint Barnabas Theological College, Adelaide

"From the desert father Anthony, to the gentle Saint Francis, from the firebrand John Wesley, to the social activist Dorothy Day, to ordinary Christians known personally to the author, *Ordinary Saints* explores what it means to be a saint. Wonderfully, the author does not leave the saints as some unattainable icon to admire, but rather presents them as an invitation through whose example you and I can grow in holiness to embrace God's gift of sainthood. I plan to use this text as a timely book in my teaching of Christian spirituality to university students, because it is academically sound. It is also a book I will recommend to my friends, because it is such an encouragement to me in my own personal growth in Christ."

—**Steve Emery-Wright**, Hyupsung University, South Korea; previously at Cliff College, Sheffield, UK

"In *Ordinary Saints*, Stuart Devenish invites us into an internal discussion and reflection about sainthood. He shows that sainthood is not something esoteric and divorced from our lives but that it embraces all of the complexities and conflicts of what it means to be human. He paints portraits of saints to build questions to help our reflections, and to inspire us. By connecting with God, others, and one's deepest self, sainthood is seeded and encouraged to grow. As the title says, saints can be ordinary. But saints can also be extraordinary. They have shaped the world in the past, and can do so again. The message that comes through is full of delight, hope, and power. Overall, this is a generous, creative, and educational book, worthy of careful and repeated reading."

—**Maxine Green**, Principal and CEO, George Williams College, YMCA London

Ordinary Saints

Lessons in the Art of Giving Away Your Life

Stuart C. Devenish

FOREWORD BY
Tim Costello

CASCADE Books • Eugene, Oregon

ORDINARY SAINTS
Lessons in the Art of Giving Away Your Life

Copyright © 2017 Stuart C. Devenish. All rights reserved. Except for brief quotations in critical publications or reviews, no part of this book may be reproduced in any manner without prior written permission from the publisher. Write: Permissions, Wipf and Stock Publishers, 199 W. 8th Ave., Suite 3, Eugene, OR 97401.

Cascade Books
An Imprint of Wipf and Stock Publishers
199 W. 8th Ave., Suite 3
Eugene, OR 97401

www.wipfandstock.com

PAPERBACK ISBN: 978-1-62564-746-7
HARDCOVER ISBN: 978-1-4982-8571-1
EBOOK ISBN: 978-1-5326-1427-9

Cataloguing-in-Publication data:

Names: Devenish, Stuart C. | Foreword by Costello, Tim.

Title: Ordinary saints : lessons in the art of giving away your life / Stuart C. Devenish.

Description: Eugene, OR: Cascade Books, 2017 | Includes bibliographical references and index.

Identifiers: ISBN 978-1-62564-746-7 (paperback) | ISBN 978-1-4982-8571-1 (hardcover) | ISBN 978-1-5326-1427-9 (ebook)

Subjects: LCSH: 1. Christian saints. | 2. Saints' Attributes. | 3. Holiness. | I. Title.

Classification: BX4662 .D45 2017 (print) | BX4662 (ebook)

Manufactured in the U.S.A.   04/03/17

for Ros,

kindred spirit and resident saint,
on the occasion of our 40th wedding anniversary

September 2016.

"As for the saints who are in the land, they are the glorious ones in whom is all my delight."

(Ps 16:3)

Abstract

IN THE POST-CHRISTIAN AGE, after the death of institutional religion, is there any place left for holy people to live as lovers of God? Yes! God's favorite way of making himself present in the world is through the righteous lives of his holy people. This is a book about *saints* (defined as activated disciples) who are alive now, and whose everyday goodness announces that God is at work in the world.

Saints are blood-bought, love-steeped, twice-born, remade people who are Christianity's living witnesses. Like Jesus, their Master, they are the message, the messenger, and the working model of the kingdom of God. In following Jesus, ordinary saints are invited to give away their lives and spend out of their resources to convey the substance of their faith to a waiting and watching world. They know that, "Whoever wants to save their life will lose it, but whoever loses their life for me and the gospel will save it" (Mark 8:35).

If ever there was a time when saints need to live courageously for Christ in the world, it is now. But it will take conviction, credibility, and a great deal of audacity. *Ordinary Saints* explores what it means to be a saint in the twenty-first century, by exploring the depth-dimensions of saints' lives, bodies, emotions, values, and relationships.

It offers the simple recipe that if God exists, if the Bible is true, if Jesus saves ... what's going to prove it are the lives of ordinary saints. Thinking of the great saints of the early era of Christian history, St. Augustine asked himself, "If they, why not I?—If those men and women could become saints, why cannot I with the help of Him who is all-powerful?"

Contents

Acknowledgements | xiii

Foreword by Tim Costello | xv

Introduction: The Parable of the Healing Water | 1

1. After Church | 13
    a. The Convent Becomes a Gallery | 13
    b. The Post-Christian Age | 14
    c. Why Saints? | 16
    d. The History of Christianity is the Story of Its Saints | 19
    e. Saints in the Post-Christian Age | 22

2. The Imperfections of Saints | 24
    a. Saints Behaving Badly | 25
    b. Literary Saints | 28
    c. Saints in the Local Church | 30
    d. Saints in Devotional Literature | 32
    e. But Saints Nonetheless | 34
    f. Sinning Like a Christian | 36
    g. A Spirituality of Imperfection | 38

CONTENTS

3. The Perfections of Saints | 42
   a. Saint Damian of Molokai | 42
   b. The (Im)possibility of Speaking about Saints | 44
   c. Saintliness as Call and Response | 48
   d. More Literary Saints | 51
   e. Saints in Devotional Writings | 53
   f. The Everyday Goodness of Ordinary Saints | 56

4. The Qualities Embedded in Saintly Lives | 61
   a. The Qualities Embedded in Saintly Lives | 61
       1. Love for humanity | 63
       2. Overflowing joy | 63
       3. Generosity of spirit | 64
       4. Willingness to suffer | 64
       5. Deep humility | 65
       6. Essential goodness | 65
       7. Profound wisdom | 66
       8. Holiness of life | 67
       9. Practice of prayer | 67
       10. An eternal perspective | 68
       11. Readiness to resist evil | 68
       12. Forgiving one's enemies | 69
   b. In Praise of Saints | 69
   c. Poem: In Praise of Saints | 71

5. Saints as Persons | 72
   a. Nadia's Face | 72
   b. Christianity and Persons | 74
   c. On Being Human Persons | 79
   d. The Testament of Saints | 86

Contents

- e. The Faith of Etty Hillesum | 89
- f. Invitation to Humanity from St. Clements' Church | 93

6. Bodies of Evidence | 94
   - a. Madam Linda Watson | 94
   - b. Christianity and "Dubious" Matter | 96
   - c. God and Flesh | 101
   - d. Saints as Christ's Agents | 104
   - e. Performing Saints' Bodies | 108
   - f. Geoff and Di Hall Go to China | 112

7. Holy Wounds | 116
   - a. Suffering Humanity | 116
   - b. The Fellowship of His Sufferings | 117
   - c. Holy Sadness | 119
   - d. The Pattern of Ministry | 122
   - e. The Thorn in the Flesh | 124
   - f. The Dark Night of the Soul | 126
   - g. Voluntary Vulnerability | 128
   - h. Saints and the Averted Face | 130
   - i. Saints and Suffering | 132

8. (Extra)ordinary Saints on Parade | 138
   - a. Introduction | 138
   - b. The Vocation of Holiness | 146

9. The Laughter of Saints | 149
   - a. People Who Laugh at Saints | 150
   - b. God and Holy Joy | 152
   - c. Sarah Laughed | 155
   - d. A Litany of Holy Laughter | 156
   - e. The Laughter of Saints | 159

Contents

10. The Evocation of Saints | 162
    a. The Chapel of the Insurrection | 162
    b. The Evocation of Saints | 164
    c. A World in Need of Saints | 166
    d. Why Saints Have Currency Today | 167
    e. You Will Be My Witnesses | 168
    f. Saints as Radical Christians | 170

Bibliography | 175
Index | 183

Acknowledgements

IT TAKES A WHOLE village to raise a child. And it takes a good many people to write a book. I want to say a heartfelt "thank you" to the many people who have played a part with me in this writing project. Writing about saints has given me the opportunity to speak with many truly amazing people in order to get the "inside" story on their faith journeys. It has been a privilege listening to their life stories firsthand. Frequently I knew I had a front row seat on the pilgrimages of modern-day saints.

I begin by offering a special thank you to my wife Ros. Her support in the many ministries and travels we have shared together over the past fifteen years (in particular) has been generous and unstinting. Living away from "home" and at a distance from family and friends is part of the significant personal cost she has willingly paid. She has patiently put up with my frantic dashes to the desk at all hours of the day and night to capture some thought or insight. I simply couldn't have done any of this without you sweetheart.

I want to thank my publishers, Wipf and Stock, for exercising faith in me as a writer, and for publishing this, my second book as a solo author. I want to thank my local editor, James Cooper, for doing such a fine job of preparing the manuscript for public consumption. I want to thank the people who comprised the four Melbourne-based focus groups that met with me in 2012 to discuss the key themes that now form the substance of this work. The focus groups belonged to the Mooroolbark Baptist Church, Eastern Hills Community Church, Syndal Baptist Church, and the Churches of Christ Victoria/Tasmania State Office. Hopefully the fruit of their wisdom has made the leading ideas in the book more accessible to readers.

I want to thank the people who have entrusted their life stories to me, and allowed me to retell them here. Each story makes an extraordinary

Acknowledgements

contribution to this project. The book would not be what it is without the retelling of real-life stories of real-life saints. From the very beginning I knew that a book about saintliness constructed at arm's length from warm blooded people would be a dismal failure. Your stories have brought this book alive. And speaking of warm blooded people . . . I want to say a special thank you to David and Gina McGregor with whom I boarded in 2014. Their welcome was warm and their hospitality was gracious. From the beginning I was made to feel welcome into their home, their family, and the beautiful city of Adelaide. I wrote nearly half the book during those long quiet evenings in their home. And I benefited from many long discussions with David, clarifying my thinking by drawing from his extensive theological knowledge and pastoral intelligence. More than a few choice ideas found their way into the book. Thank you David and Gina!

I am grateful to the faculty and staff at Tabor College of Higher Education in Adelaide where I serve on the faculty of the School of Ministry Theology and Culture. Thank you for your warm welcome into your learning community. Thank you to my Head of School, Dr. Aaron Chalmers, for allowing me time to write. I also wish to acknowledge the support and sponsorship of the Centre for Contemporary Spirituality here at Tabor, which is led by Dr. Phil Daughtry. The Centre exists to make the resources of Christian spirituality available to a Christian and a non-Christian audience.

And last but not least, I'm also grateful to you—the reader—for the openness and curiosity you bring to this book.

Stuart Devenish
Easter, 2017

Foreword

Tim Costello

IN THE EVANGELICAL CHURCHES of the 1960s and '70s where Stuart and I grew up, saints were rarely discussed. That was not merely to preserve a self-consciously Protestant "distance" from the taint of ritualism and sacramentalism. It also reflected the cultural space where Christians were contending at the time, seeking to make the Jesus story new and modern, reconciling its essence with the age of mass communications, radical social change, and an assertive, youth-centred popular culture. Saints and sanctity felt like relics from an age long gone, no longer relevant to the challenges we face in our times.

That was an age of ecumenical ferment. Across the spectrum of the churches, people were experimenting with emergent ideas, some of which would have surprised earlier generations. Who would have thought that the Catholic Church would not only embrace a certain degree of modernity and liberalism, but that Catholics would be exploring both rock masses and charismatic worship? And at the same time, many Evangelicals, steeped in an individualist mind-set, were thirsting for community and even ritual, reflected in new thinking about "being church" and a new energy around curated worship.

The last thing I would have predicted back then was that several decades on, a new generation would be looking to such things as *saints, sainthood* and the concept of *sanctity* to inform them on their spiritual journeys. The thing we sometimes fail to grasp about faith, is that while its truth and essence are unchanging, the language and practice of faith needs to be "updated" in every age by each new generation. We are all conditioned by our culture, which pours out an endlessly shifting context that is forever challenging our foundations. We may keep thinking we have heard the last word, but then something comes along to make us think again.

And this is where saints come in. *Saints*—defined in this book as righteous, faith-filled people, who are willing to "give up" their lives to serve the needs of humanity in our troubled world—are a remarkably "up-to-date" subset of society. Against the culturally mandated consumer culture rampant in the West, saints represent a counter-movement that has the potential to significantly influence the kind of values, life choices, and practical priorities people in our cities, towns, and villages embrace. It seems to me that saints can no longer be seen as "relics" from a lost era. Saints, sainthood, and sanctity may just be the new cultural "currency" the world needs in order to step back from the brink of war, poverty, injustice, and social/ecological disaster.

It is clear that Stuart is writing for a Western audience, and so his language of the "post-Christian" age works in that environment. But I think things are more complicated than that. Our "times" are not so readily divisible. I spend much time located in the developing world, and in conversation with people who live and work in situations of poverty and dire need. In those contexts, religious faith continues to play a much greater role, both in individual consciousness and as a social and cultural organizing force, than it does in the West. The language of the "post-Christian" age works for us at home: but in the majority world, it is clear that a "Christian age" continues to maintain a presence in many places as an urgent necessity. What connects the dots is the saints and holy people who ply their trade of goodness, mercy, and generosity in whichever corner of God's vineyard they find themselves. Wherever I go, I meet saints. They are more ubiquitous than you think. Their presence in rich and poor, black and white, developed and underdeveloped cultures and communities, is a source of great encouragement to me personally, and to the cause of good around the world.

There are a number of concepts that are leading contributors to the discourse of human well-being in the twenty-first century. Notions such as human rights, social justice and agency, community and mutual responsibility. Many of these are tightly bound up with Jewish and Christian notions of the human person, human dignity, and physical, social, and spiritual flourishing. The nature of good and evil, and the possibility of and need for redemption also belong in this list. Religious saints—living and deceased—take their inspiration from Jesus, who fed the hungry, healed the sick, clothed the naked, and befriended the sinner. And so-called secular

Foreword

saints—living and deceased—also contribute much to our society through their generosity, active altruism, and a deep love for humanity. Culturally and spiritually, we are not all in the same space, but all of us are compelled to embrace the present and the future, and to make sense of it through the wisdom and revelation of the present and the past.

Ordinary sainthood is a brilliantly useful concept because it joins present reality to transcendent possibility. It joins the heroic possibility of individual lives to the God-given seed of sanctity that lies within everyone. Stuart is an explorer, combining restless intellectual curiosity and courage with a deep well of hope. He has mapped some challenging terrain in this book, and marked out some important landmarks that will encourage and enable many to follow, continuing their own faith journey of being and becoming.

Tim Costello is Chief Advocate for World Vision Australia after serving as its CEO.

Introduction

The Parable of the Healing Water

ONCE UPON A TIME there was a village set on the edge of a forest at the foot of a mountain. The ancient landscape contained much beauty and many dangers, but the wise elders chose to settle their families in that place for good reason. A river flowed through the village, fed by snow-capped peaks above. It watered the vegetable gardens, provided transport to the markets downriver, and cooled the air in the heat of the summer. But what made the village unique was the healing properties of the water. The people in the village lived longer, happier, and healthier than those in neighboring villages. It was the water that set the village apart and gave life to the community that lived there.

The villagers had long known about the benefits of drinking and bathing in the water, and generously invited passing travelers to partake of its soothing properties. As the news of the healing waters grew in reputation, more and more pilgrims came seeking to be cured of their ailments. As they came the sick grew well, the anxious were consoled, the old and infirm felt younger, and fewer infants succumbed to illness and death. Many visitors who made short visits chose to stay longer. Many moved into the village permanently, building houses and planting gardens of their own. And so the village grew beyond its ancient boundaries as people continued to benefit from drinking the water.

At first, the old residents welcomed newcomers and enjoyed their new fame. They prospered as prices for their food, produce, and land went up. Dignitaries and high-ranking officials came to live in the village. But over time the markets became crowded, the ancient forests were chopped down for housing and firewood, the farms struggled to provide enough food, and the streets became mired in mud and traffic. And curiously, as more and more people arrived, demanding to be healed, the life-giving properties of the water began to diminish. It seemed the mysterious quality of mercy that came unseen when gently invited, withdraw when people demanded to be healed without the humility of asking.

Slowly but surely, resentment grew between the old residents of the village and the newcomers. Anger and misunderstanding arose as the old residents tried to dam the river, and as greedy merchants began to sell the once-free healing water at inflated prices. And when the cost of rent also increased, the new residents began to steal in order to pay for the expensive water. Soon, the peaceable village was wracked by violence. What began as a healing stream became a river of sorrows. And so it continued for a long time, until the mystery of the healing waters became lost in the mists of memory, the people of the village now preoccupied with their bad-tempered neighbors, and their many illnesses and ailments. Misery settled like a pall on the land.

Few continued to believe in the power of the water or expected it to change their lives or make them well. But there were some among the residents—old and new—who found silent eddies where the water still contained its healing properties. They also discovered it in wells, in side tributaries, on the banks on the far side of the river, and—on occasion—in the vegetables that drew up moisture from the water table below. Over time, however, the story of the healing waters became, for most people, no more than old wives' tales. But those who sought quietly for the healing water, who asked for it in humility and gentleness and who continued to drink it and bathe in it, knew the power of the water was more than a fairy story ... it was *real*.

Christianity Today

In the early part of the twenty-first century, Christianity has become old before its time. Under the weight of its 2,000-year-long history and its incredible vitalizing influence across time and continents, the "Way" of Jesus is now itself in need of revitalization. The parable of the healing water illustrates how Christianity's life-giving gospel began to lose its strength when it became swallowed up by big-R institutional religion. When long-time Christians (the old villagers) assert ownership over the gospel (the healing

INTRODUCTION

water in the parable), that does not belong to them alone but was given on trust for everyone, Christianity loses its genius. When new pilgrims who have believed in recent years (the new villagers in the parable) benefit from receiving the good news of Jesus for themselves, but learn that if they are to continue in the faith they must fight for their place in the "sheepfold," Christianity's integrity as a "host" to newcomers, strangers, and outsiders grows faint. When unbelievers observe Christianity's leaning towards destructive intramural wars over doctrine, sacraments, liturgy, and worship styles, this—more than anything else—has become the greatest deterrent to non-believers accepting the Christian message. Too often Christianity's message has been rejected not because it is false but because it has been delivered by untrustworthy messengers.

In the parable, the water (which equates to Christianity's gospel) began to lose its life-giving powers when it became the subject of bitter wrangling between institutional interests and the vested interests of time-honored groups and their leaders. Note that it was not a matter of the water losing its healing powers intrinsic to its nature. Instead it was a matter of greedy people muddying the waters, making its healing properties secondary to their own self-interest. With the passing of time, even gold loses its luster. So with enough distraction and infighting, the true value of the Christian gospel has become tarnished, its light hidden under a bushel (Matt 5:15). Its capacity to offer the forgiveness of sins through faith in Christ and deliver people into a right relationship with God, has been seriously undermined.

But there is one group of people that has not rejected Jesus' teaching. Unlike others who have relegated the good news that Jesus saves to the domain of myth, folklore, and legend, this group continues to make the Christian message their primary point of reference, their *true north* for the way they "live and move and have their being" in the world (Acts 17:28).[1] It is this group of people who have not resorted to blaming God for his failure to meet their demands for salvation at discount prices. Neither have they resorted to stoning their fellow Christians because their doctrine is wrong, because their practice is imperfect, or because they fail to meet the impossible standards believers expect of one another. Instead, this group of people continues to believe in the saving power of Christ's gospel, and to practice the ancient traditions of worship, prayer, service, and sanctification as their primary mode of existence. It is these habits of humility that graciously afford them access to God's loving presence and life-changing power.

1. Unless otherwise indicated, all Biblical references are from NIV.

This group of people continues to drink the water and to bathe in it, believing it has miraculous power to make them whole. For them, Christ's message is not some decaying myth that belongs to a dead religion whose power has passed it use-by date. For them the "Way" of Jesus is the key that unlocks God's powerful salvation for all who choose to believe. "For in the gospel, a righteousness from God is revealed, righteousness that is by faith from first to last, just as it is written: 'The righteous will live by faith'" (Rom 1:17). In today's world these people are called *Christians*, but they have also been known by many other names such as disciples, believers, followers of the "Way," the brothers, those who are faithful, the baptized . . . and *saints*. I have chosen to refer to them generically as *saints* . . . adding the descriptor "ordinary" saints because these people don't live behind the safety of cloistered walls or between the pages of sacred books—but in the rough-and-tumble world of relationships, work, family, children, mortgages, love, disappointments, life and death. It is here in the real world that saints are called to live out their allegiance to Christ. Here is what the Apostle Paul tells us to do:

> So here's what I want you to do, God helping you: Take your everyday, ordinary life—your sleeping, eating, going-to-work, and walking-around life—and place it before God as an offering . . . . Don't become so well adjusted to your culture that you fit into it without thinking. Instead, fix your attention on God. You'll be changed from the inside out (Rom 12:1-2, *The Message*).

It is out there in the everyday world that the unremarkable lives of saintly people tell the story of God's love for them, how they have been healed from their old lives of sin and wickedness, and have become a part of the new humanity Christ came to establish on earth as the forerunner to his eternal kingdom.

This is a book about saints who are alive right now, whose everyday holiness demonstrates the continuing power and relevance of the Christian message in today's world. Such people follow Christ out of a deep-seated conviction that their own lives have been changed in some fundamental way by their encounter with him. They function out of the overwhelming conviction that Jesus' teachings offer the most authentic, credible, and trustworthy instruction for people who are serious about fulfilling God's call to honor their parents and families, to resist evil and do good, and to become the men and women they were created and destined to be.

Introduction

And this is no surprise to God. There are many ways in which he makes himself known in the world, e.g., through his written revelation in the texts of the Old and New Testaments. Through the coming of his Son Jesus into the world as God's Messiah to "save his people from their sins" (Matt 1:21). Through the message of the gospel that invites people to participate in God's redemptive work in human history. And through the miraculous power of God's Holy Spirit to alter the direction of people's lives, and the course of history. But one of the most amazing displays of God at work in the world is through the extraordinary lives of ordinary saints. It is there, in the changed, renovated, transformed lives of ordinary Christians, that God's work can be most clearly observed. Against the backdrop of greed, lust, ego, wickedness, and selfishness that characterizes our twenty-first-century consumer culture, ordinary saints are called to exhibit lives that are exactly the opposite. Their lives are to be characterized by humility, purity, generosity, goodness, and servant-heartedness—all qualities that first originate in and emanate from Jesus, their Master.

Jesus taught that a tree is recognized by the fruit it produces. "No good tree produces bad fruit, nor on the other hand, does a bad tree produce good fruit" (Luke 6:44). In the same way, the lives of holy people are recognized by their actions. Holy is as holy does. According to the book of James (who tradition says was the brother of Jesus, and the leader of the Jerusalem Council), "Faith by itself, if it is not accompanied by action, is dead" (Jas 2:17). Saints demonstrate the quality of their inner lives through the actions of their outer lives. They put their faith into practice, becoming living models of what it means to be a follower of Christ, whose words, lives, and actions spell out the substance of the Christian faith for the world to see. C. S. Lewis called this kind of people "carriers." Lewis wrote, "Men are mirrors, or 'carriers' of Christ to other men. Sometimes unconscious carriers."[2] Lewis uses the word "carriers" to depict Christian faith as something like an infection, albeit a "good infection." This infection, he says, is the result of catching a dose of God-likeness, that ultimately changes the way we live, think, and act in our own skin and in the world. According to Lewis, Christians are carriers of a kind of godly infection that remakes, reforms, and re-mints them into a new form of humanity, which is of ultimate significance to the Christian faith. Clearly, there are many images and metaphors we may apply to represent what Christians become as a result of their encounter with Jesus, such as those who carry the divine "infection,"

---

2. Lewis, *Mere Christianity*, 159.

or bearers of the "light" of Christ into a darkened world, or as those who have been "healed" as a result of drinking the healing water (as in the parable that opens this book). In each case, I'm calling *saints* the people who have benefited from and been deeply changed by their reception of the Christian gospel into their lives.

What I Mean by Saints

Christianity has been around for 2,000 years, during which time much of the language used to express Christianity's most indispensable concepts has either changed or been lost. For example, in today's world, people are sometimes confused about what the word *saint* means. Because saints are central to everything I want to talk about in this book, it is important for me to tell you what I mean by saints so there is no confusion when I use the word. So, I'm going to make five statements that will provide you with a working definition of sainthood. These five statements will come in the following shape: First, what I *do not* mean by the word saint. Second, what I *do* mean by the word saint. Third, how I think a saint and a disciple are the same but different. Fourth, why I think saints are important at this particular moment in history. And fifth, I'm going to talk about saints as people who have a vocation to live holy and selfless lives that represent an extension of Jesus' own life.

First, what I *don't* mean by saints. I am not taking saints to mean only those people who have been canonized by the church, or saints in heaven. Rather, I prefer to stick closer to the biblical concept of saintliness as meaning those who have been "set apart," and nominated as real believers in Jesus. What I am *not* referring to when I use the word *saints* are dead people who have the prefix "St." supplied before their name, who are canonized, beatified, venerated, or consecrated by the historical Christian church. I have no wish to promote a new "cult of the saints" where people from the past who have lived extraordinary lives receive the veneration of those still living. Of course, I want to offer the dear departed who are our mothers and fathers in the faith the proper honor and respect we owe to the dead in Christ. Along with the biblical writer, we recognize that "we are surrounded by a great cloud of witnesses" (Heb 12:1) who cheer us on from the bosom of God, and who represent the trophies of the church from times past. The beauty of their holy lives, their willingness to lay down their lives as martyrs for Christ and his church, and other qualities of their saintly

INTRODUCTION

obedience provide endless examples for us to celebrate. But my preference is to reserve my veneration and intercession for Christ alone, and not make such large requests to the saints.

Second, I want to tell you what I *do* mean when I refer to saints. What I mean by saints is anyone who has responded to Jesus' invitation to "Come, follow me" as a voluntary and intentional act of the heart. What sets these people apart and makes them worthy of the name "saints"—regardless of whether they are living or dead, male or female, black or white, rich or poor, Protestant, Catholic, or Orthodox, educated or illiterate—is the deep conviction that they are loved by God, that Christ's death and resurrection has brought them into a right relationship with God, that their destinies have been altered, and their submission to Christ means that their highest calling in life is to reproduce his life in their own lives. Saints, then, are sanctified people whose citizenship is in heaven, who set their compass by Christ's "true north," and who set their watch by heaven's clock. Essentially, my use of the word *saints* returns to the biblical language for people who have been made righteous through their faith in Christ and who subsequently adjust their mode of living to reflect Christ's life in the world. Their lives are marked by holy living, a singular devotion to Christ, a commitment to live for others and not for themselves.

Third, how saints and disciples are the same but different. When I was preparing to write this book, I asked a number of people whose opinions I trust to help me conceptualize the book more clearly. The question they most frequently asked was why am I talking about saints and not disciples? Here is my answer. At its simplest level, Jesus addressed himself to a group of twelve young men he had invited to become his disciples. The word *disciple* means follower or student. Essentially, Jesus was inviting them to enroll as students in his school. With the exception of Judas—who reneged on his promise to follow Jesus—those first disciples were to become Jesus' apostles (meaning "sent ones") whose task it was to preach the gospel where it had not previously been preached, to establish new congregations where there previously were none, and to lay the foundations of Christian life and truthfulness in a world where there were many religions but no "light" of Christ. Under Jesus' guidance and instruction, these young men were to undergo intensive training in what it meant to be a follower of Jesus the Christ. The word *disciple* has particular relevance to the relationship *between* Jesus and the one who follows him. It is the Jesus-to-follower relation which is in focus.

But when it comes to saints, something different in is focus. Whereas the word *disciple* highlights the obedience that the disciple offers to Jesus, the word *saint* highlights the kind of life that the Christian disciple lives before the watching world, to represent him- or herself as a member of Christ's kingdom and as a follower of his "Way." What is in focus here is the disciple-to-world relationship. Saints live out their relationship with Jesus by putting their newfound holiness to work in a world that is anything but holy. So in summary: I use the word *disciple* to refer to the Jesus-to-follower relationship, and I use the word *saint* to refer to the disciple-to-world relationship. I'm putting forward the idea that Christlike disciples live lives that are acts of countercultural testimony to the world. This is the distinction I make between disciples and saints.

Fourth, why I think saints are so important for the Christian church at this particular time in history. The basic premise of this book is that Christianity's trophies are not its theological formulations, its architecture, or its moral teachings (as important as these are)—rather, Christianity's trophies are to be found in the exceptional quality of the lives and characters of its saints. In this regard, perhaps Christianity's most compelling challenge is not to build large churches but to grow *great* people! The Christian gospel invites people into a spiritual encounter with Christ that promises to "re-mint" ordinary people into saints so that their lives may become walking billboards, offering the most compelling "proofs" for the relevance and power of Christ's gospel. Extending and defending this basic idea will be my task throughout the remainder of this book.

And fifth, what is the distinctive calling of the ordinary saint? One of the reasons why saints are so misunderstood in today's self-centered culture is that saints insist on living for others, not themselves. One of the most noticeable characteristics of saints is that they choose to give away their lives for the sake of others. Feeding the hungry, clothing the naked, housing the homeless, providing for the poor, visiting the sick, educating the illiterate, advocating for those who suffer injustice, and overcoming evil with good—all these things lie at the center of the vocation of saintliness. Saints do these things not because they have been sent as God's policemen to tell the world what it can and cannot do. Saints value goodness because God is goodness itself, and because he created the world for his own good pleasure. The onus is on his creatures—and in particular his redeemed and re-created sons and daughters in the form of his saints—to love God by loving their neighbors. To fulfill Jesus' command to love as he has loved, is

Introduction

to dispense with the worldly wisdom of self-centered greed and acquisition (whose primary purpose is to get, grasp, consume, keep, control, possess) in favor of the heavenly principles of giving away their lives, and "doing to others as we would have done to ourselves" (Matt 7:12).

I'm hoping you can see the sense in me returning to the Apostle Paul's language of saints found in the New Testament, to explore in this book what is in effect a discipleship theme. Eugene Peterson supports this approach.

> 'Saint', as it turns out, is Paul's noun of choice for the people of God—men and women who, no longer lost, follow Jesus in the cosmos. Throughout every letter Paul wrote, 'saint' is his word for us. In subsequent centuries 'Christian' came to supplant 'saint' as the common designation.[3]

So my choice to return to the language of saints has biblical precedence, and it equates to what we call today genuine Christians, or activated disciples. My working definition of what it means to be a saint—then—comes in three parts. First, *submission*. Saints are people who have heard Jesus' call to "Come, follow me" and who have made a deep-level, all-encompassing, life-changing decision to submit their lives to Christ and to follow him no matter what the cost. Second, *gratefulness*. Saints are people who recognize that Jesus' voluntary death on the cross destroyed the power of sin, removed the burden of guilt, and replaced it with a new way of living in the world. They know themselves to be loved by God generously and without condition. That is why they worship Christ as their Lord, their savior and their friend. And third, *generosity*. Having received the generosity of God's overwhelming love for them in Jesus, saints find their greatest pleasure in performing their calling as citizens of God's kingdom by "selling all" (Mark 10:21) and giving away their lives and their worldly possessions to the poor and the needy. Saints have a deep-level conviction that when they "give up" their lives, they find them again, and when they spend their lives in service of others in the name of Christ, they are given the treasures of heaven in return. On the last day, these people can expect to hear Jesus' welcome and invitation, "Well done, good and faithful servant. Come and share your master's happiness!" (Matt 25:21 and 23).

---

3. Peterson, *Practise Resurrection*, 77.

Ordinary Saints

Three Central Arguments

I want to offer three central arguments that form the substance of the book. Providing them here early in the book will provide the reader with an overview of the whole book in seed form, and enable you to grasp the significance of my overall argument, and therefore to know what to look for in the pages that follow.

- Saints need to be reminded how to be saints: The post-Christian age represents a new and challenging environment for saints. Despite its 2,000-year-long occupation at the center of Western history, it is safe to say that the Christian church has never been in this place before. The twenty-first-century post-Christian context represents a complex and ever-changing environment that is uncomfortable for many Christians who no longer instinctively know how to be spiritual. It may just be that this place of "discomfort" provides a renewed challenge to Christians to "remember" the significance of Christ's call on their lives. The British author John Drane asked the rhetorical question, "Do Christians know how to be spiritual?"—observing that after a century of secularism and a lifetime of consumerism, many have forgotten what it means to be a saint.[4] Hence, the need to be reminded of the sacred calling to be "salt and light" in a world that is rapidly changing. And that rapidly changing world calls for saints to engage in their ministries of seasoning the world with beauty, simplicity, and generosity outside the ministries often assigned inside the church in the form of pastor/priest, worship leader, prayer group leader, and administrator. In the new post-Christian environment where saints find themselves, the natural habitat of saints will be in the rough-and-tumble world of the public square, in the spheres of the media, politics, industry, education, medicine, the food industry, the arts and entertainment, and more.

- Saints' lives are revelatory: Saints are 3D living gospels that reveal the substance of the Christian message through their words and deeds. Some people may question the wisdom of studying the lives of holy people. "Why not just preach the gospel?" they may ask. I agree they have a point. But the New Testament is full of examples of ordinary saints whose lives serve to showcase the grace of God. The end

---

4. Drane, *Do Christians Know How to Be Spiritual?*

product of biblical Christianity is redeemed people who have turned from their sin, who have repented and embraced Christ, who have become faith-filled disciples, whose lives are changed, and who have accepted the call to live countercultural and holy lives as members of the kingdom of God. It is always the case that the old old story is intended to produce new new lives.

- Saints' lives are living proofs of the gospel: At a time when the authenticity of the Bible has been called into question by secular humanist scholarship, when the teachings of Christianity are no longer believable in the minds of many punters, and when the institutional church is no longer seen as credible because of the actions of some of its leaders—I will argue in this book that one of the only convincing proofs that verify the teachings of Christianity is the lives of its ordinary saints. If God exists, if Jesus saves, if the Bible is true, if Christianity is real . . . it needs saints' lives to *prove* it!

These three central arguments form the substance of the book. They will be developed and further augmented in the following chapters.

Intended Readers

This book is intended for an educated lay readership among a predominantly Christian audience. In particular, the book is addressed to three groups of readers I will refer to as *saints, servants,* and *instructors.* First, *saints*: As previously indicated, my use of the word *saints* returns to the biblical usage of the word. I'm using the word *saints* to refer to faithful people who live in the everyday world, and who make their countercultural confession that "Jesus Christ is Lord, to the glory of God the Father" (Phil 2:11). Saints are believers who belong to and participate in the worshipping communities of Christian congregations around the world, and who express their faith through engagement with the burning issues of their host culture.

Second, *servants*: Servants are ministry leaders who lead and serve congregations. Whether we refer to them as pastors, priests, elders, or by another title, they have been charged by Christ to "Feed my sheep" (John 21:17). Through teaching, mentoring, and modeling, servants are charged with the responsibility of embedding in the lives of those under their spiritual care, something of the life, grace, and truth of Christ. To be a saint is effectively to "copy a life"—the life of Christ—and so the role of servants (as I speak of them here) is to support others in endeavoring to do just that. Servants fulfill their calling as spiritual overseers by providing a form of cure of souls that is both a nurturing form of pastoral *care* of saints through the rough-and-tumble of everyday life, and through spiritual direction which is an essential part of pastoral leadership. In our day, spiritual direction is often thought to be too intrusive or too time-consuming a task for pastoral leaders. Yet ministry leaders are charged with the responsibility of providing opportunity for spiritual growth. It is servants who make *godfaring* the priority for their lives, and who offer spiritual guidance and direction to the saints under their care.

And third, *instructors*. I think of instructors as people who offer training to servants of all kinds. We might find instructors in a variety of offices and roles such as bishops, priests, pastors, theological educators, counselors, spiritual directors, abbots, retreat leaders, confessors, and catechists. Whereas in earlier times the role of the *catechist* (Greek, meaning "instructor, teacher, or guide") was highly valued, such spiritual guides have in our own day been sidelined and ignored. They deserve more recognition than they are presently given, and—I suggest—will need to be given an increasingly important part to play into the future.

The scene is now set for our exploration of the lives of ordinary saints, who live out the spiritual life of Christ in our post-Christian age. Let's begin the adventure.

1

After Church

*believing in the
post-Christian age*

"Some things that should not have been forgotten were lost" (J. R. R. Tolkien).

The Convent Becomes a Gallery

The idyllic township of Daylesford in regional Victoria, Australia, boasts a world-class art gallery. Built in the 1860s, the historic three-story stone mansion served as the private residence of a mining magnate during the gold rush era, then as a convent for members of the Roman Catholic Holy Cross Presentation Sisters, as a girls' school in the 1970s, and, since 1988, as an art gallery. Located on the crest of Wombat Hill Botanical Gardens, the gallery has a wonderful view across the historic town. The heritage-listed buildings are framed by leafy gardens and crowned by a charming copper belfry. The whole scene conveys a sense of deep tranquility and lightness of spirit in the observer. Today, the gallery is a vibrant and creative space that includes a restaurant, a range of sassy fashion outlets, several display areas for contemporary art pieces, and the swanky Chapel Bar which features prominently in the gallery's advertising.

But there is a major disconnect between the avant-garde spirit promoted by the new owners—whose intention is to attract the younger tourist "set"—and the quiet devotion of the nuns who lived and worshipped on the site for eighty years. The deep-seated faith of those God-fearing women persists in the soul of the building. A tangible sense of the spiritual lingers in the chapel, the prayer benches, and the infirmary. It is easy to imagine the nuns singing their matins, canticles, and prayers of *misericordia* ("Lord, have mercy!") at the set hours. But in jarring contrast to the chaste and virtuous faith of the nuns—the artwork that adorns the walls of what was once the nuns' chapel, dining, and living rooms, is far from chaste and devout. Provocative homoerotic images, depicting naked women in various inflammatory erotic poses, and homosexual men carousing during a fashion shoot, adorn the walls as framed paintings and prints, and in painted frescoes. The virtuous and uncorrupted faith of the nuns, and the degenerate and dissipated lives depicted in the artwork displayed in the gallery, could not provide a greater contrast. When the convent becomes a gallery, something very important is lost. Meet the new "normal" in our post-Christian society.

The Post-Christian Age

In recent years the expression *post-Christian* has entered our language. Not everyone is comfortable using that kind of language, but I'm afraid it's here to stay. For people who have spent much of their lives inside the church, it seems intimidating. But the benefit of such language is that it reminds us not everything is as it once was. What I understand by the term "post-Christian" is the arrival of the end of the era of Christendom. Christendom was a time from an earlier period in history when Christianity was the dominant cultural-shaping force and religious system in the Western world. In contrast, Christianity has been forced from the center to the margins of mainstream culture. The term *post-Christian*, then, reminds us that a significant shift has taken place in the Western world. Whereas Christianity was once the religion of the masses, it now holds a minority status in the broader culture. Ours is a post-Christian age, a new season that is "after church."

There was a time when Christianity was the religious tradition of Western society. Children were given birth names belonging to biblical heroes, marriages were conducted in God's name, the faithful were baptized into Christ, adherents were instructed in the ways of righteousness, and the dead were buried in expectation of the hope of the resurrection and the life of the world to come. Of course, not all people were professing Christians during that time, and even those who were may have exhibited their faith with woeful inconsistency. Even so, up until the mid-twentieth century there existed a settled consensus throughout the West that Christianity was the only real option in matters of religious faith. Families generally "signed up" to one or another of Christianity's "sub-franchises," calling themselves Anglicans or Episcopalians, Roman Catholics, Lutherans, Presbyterians, Methodists, Baptists, Congregationalists, Brethren, Foursquare, or whatever brand was available. Everyone who was anyone was a communicant member of their church and thought it normal to attend Sunday school, Christian Endeavour, Boys' Brigade, Girl Guides, harvest festivals, musical cantatas, evangelistic rallies, and missionary prayer meetings. Religious life was firmly integrated with the life of the culture and society, and only the black sheep and the *avant-garde* thought it either necessary or possible to suggest or behave otherwise.

In those times, the influence of the Christian gospel could be seen in the way people thought about and ordered their lives, individually and as a society. For centuries, the Christian church had pronounced the forgiveness of sins, the possibility of a right relationship with God, the comfort of faith as a hedge against the terrors of the night, and provided a sanctioned and convincing way of reading human history . . . including the promise of life after death and the gift of eternal life to those who held firm in their faith. Not surprisingly, therefore, the statutes of the State were often underpinned by the certainties of Christian belief, and so we prayed, "God save the Queen," people swore to tell the truth on the Bible in court, and governments prayed openly for God's blessing on their legislative agendas. Indeed, the language of faith was foundational when devising and defending all manner of social, economic, and political endeavors, such as the partnership between the free market economy and the responsibility of governments to uphold the interests of the most vulnerable in society. It seemed that the State, the marketplace, and society rested on an unshakable foundation. "In God we trust," we said to ourselves.

But at some undefined point, the page of history turned. The baptized forgot their vows, the taught were dissuaded from the teaching, and Christianity went from nurturing mother to homeless orphan in the space of a few short generations. The end result is that, for the majority of people in the Western world, Christianity is now no longer regarded as the true fount of blessing, or a trustworthy arbiter of our private and communal lives. On the contrary, the ever-present influence of secular humanist education, postmodern relativism, and skepticism towards formal religion has ensured that the twenty-first century has been declared the post-Christian age. As the post-Christian age, Christianity's appeal is in decline, and people are progressively open to novel spiritual options. In today's society, people are less likely to express their spiritual beliefs in Christian terms, and are more likely to express no faith at all (as in atheism), or a faith other than Christianity (such as Buddhism, Islam, Hinduism, or adherence to any of the new spiritualities on offer in our culture). What is noticeable in the majority population is the growing intolerance towards the teachings of Christianity. Sometimes this goes to the extreme and becomes *christophobia*, meaning a fear of or even hatred toward Christians.

The present moment presents a unique challenge to Christians across the Western world. It is a moment when the resolve of saints to follow Christ anywhere, anytime, under any circumstances, is being sorely tested. The post-Christian age is a time when people can be and do anything—gangsters and rappers, artists and musicians, dopeheads and dropouts, lesbians and leprechauns, sports stars and porn stars—yet still retain the admiration of the dominant culture. But to be a committed Christian is frowned upon as unwarranted, unbecoming, and indecorous. We need to ask whether there is any place left for Christian believers to practice their faith in the public square, and to live a "public faith" that contributes to the wider social dialogue about matters relating to the human condition, and how best to live the good life. If Christian institutional religion in the public square is out of fashion, what place remains for ordinary saints who continue to believe that Christ's teachings are true? And what of their claims that those same teachings have lasting relevance for the whole world?

Why Saints?

If you had told me five years ago that I would write a book about saints, I would have been astonished beyond belief! Saints have never been part of my upbringing, my faith formation, or my belief system. What mattered most to me throughout my life as a Christian believer was the person of Jesus, the truths contained in the Bible, the life-changing power of the gospel, and the new life to which Christ had called me as his disciple. I freely admit that until fairly recently, I had a somewhat limited understanding of the full implications of my Christian faith, and felt that any talk of saints reeked of popish hocus-pocus, or worse, meant entering into the dark realm of pre-Christian devilry. According to the teaching I had received, Roman Catholics, saints, and holy water represented the "dark side" of Christianity.

So you can understand why anything relating to the saints in the form of praying to the saints, saintly relics, beatification, indulgences, stigmata, and veneration, produced an allergic reaction in me.

Yet here I am, five years on, now deeply convinced that saints form an important foundation of the Christian faith and cannot be dispensed with. So what changed my mind and made me "fall in love" with saints? How was it that this good Protestant disciple, pastor, missionary, and teacher underwent such a radical journey of discovery that resulted in me becoming a *hagiophile* (a "lover of saints")? How was it that I experienced an awakening to their significance? Perhaps that two-dollar token of St. Jude I bought at a community fair several years ago put a hex on me. St. Jude is known as the patron saint of "hopeless causes." What does it say about me that I now possess a cast metal pendant bearing his name? Perhaps reading all those Catholic books about saints has warped my thinking. Or maybe the many friendships I've developed with Catholic and Eastern Orthodox disciples over the years have clouded my judgment. Somehow I don't think so. Then why this newfound affinity for saints?

I would like to think I have finally come to my senses, and discovered something which the historic church—including the saints of old—has always known. I have discovered that the history of Christianity is the story of its saints. I can now argue with clarity and conviction that I'm standing on very safe ground when I suggest to you—my readers—that in the new set of conditions that pertain in the post-Christian context, Christianity stands or falls on the quality of the saints it produces. Perhaps nothing has changed. Dark times demand great saints, but then nothing produces great saints quite like dark times. Here, then, are some important reasons why saints can be considered the backbone of the Christian faith.

First, the "communion of saints" forms an important part of the historic confession of the Christian Church as contained in the Apostles' Creed:

> I believe in God, the Father Almighty, creator of heaven and earth.
> I believe in Jesus Christ, God's only, Our Lord . . . I believe in the Holy Spirit, the holy catholic Church, the *communion of saints*, the forgiveness of sins, and the resurrection of the body, and the life everlasting. Amen.[1]

---

1. McGinlay, *Uniting in Worship*, 122, emphasis added.

The communion of saints is an idea central to the Apostle Paul's teachings in 1 Corinthians 12, where believers manifest the life of the Spirit in the world through their confession that "Jesus is Lord," by possessing such "gifts of the Spirit" as wisdom, faith, healing, prophecy, and speaking in tongues, and through their unity in diversity, just as Christ's body, the church, is said to be one body with many members. Because we belong to Jesus' *ekklesia* (Greek for "called out community"), there is a unity and cohesion among us in terms of shared doctrine, shared devotion, shared worship, shared experience, shared practice, and shared testimony. We need to value those saints who have gone before us, and who—according to Hebrews 12—are even now cheering us on. But we also need to value the holy lives of saintly people in the present moment, whose consecration represents a faithful and worthy testament to the love of God, "poured into our hearts by the Holy Spirit" (Rom 5:5).

Second, Christianity is not a set of abstract doctrines to be believed, but a life to be lived. Undoubtedly there is a set of truth-claims that form the substance of classical, biblical, orthodox Christianity concerning God, Jesus Christ, the Holy Spirit, the church, and the kingdom of God. We give thanks to God for the great doctrines that detail the substance of our faith. Yet it is only when these great truths are realized through the lives of faithful believers that Christianity becomes properly grounded in the world. The realities of the new birth, a changed allegiance, and a new Spirit-guided and empowered life are evidence of where Christianity's great truths "connect" with the real world. It was a central premise of the theologian Karl Barth that "No knowledge of God exists in the world save in the hearts of regenerate believers."[2] It is only on the basis of the passionate spiritual experiences of redeemed, remade, and re-minted disciples (aka *saints*) that proper theology makes any sense or has any relevance in the world.

Third, the gospel of Jesus Christ is a powerful, life-changing, history-altering message. In the words of the English hymn writer Katherine Hankey (1834–1911) it is "The old old story of unseen things above, of Jesus and his glory, of Jesus and his love." But in every case the old old story of the love of God made known to us through the death and resurrection of Christ, was always intended to produce new new people. The gospel is a message intended to turn sinners into *saints*, orphans into sons and daughters, and dead people into living souls.

---

2. Baillie, *Our Knowledge of God*, 17.

Fourth, the Bible has much to say about the importance of *saints*. The word *saint* (Greek *hagios* meaning "holy, devout, or sanctified") is used thirty-nine times in the New Testament, and as such the concept of saints and saintliness is integral to the Christian Scriptures. The biblical use of the term indicates that saints are those men and women who have been made holy by their faith in Christ, who live their lives by the power of the Spirit, and live out of the resources of heaven even as they live here on earth. Lists of saints form a substantial part of the New Testament. Let's take Romans 16, for example. The Apostle Paul addresses himself to "All in Rome who are loved by God, and called to be saints" (Rom 1:7). At the end of that same letter, he addresses himself to members of the congregation there in Rome. He lists the names of twenty-seven people, and refers indirectly to many more. Although he had not been to Rome, Paul knew many of those people personally and was actually related to some of them. And what's more, he says those people were "worthy of the saints" (16:2), and referred to the "community of the saints" to which they belonged (16:15). Hebrews 11, the famous "faith" chapter, also provides powerful examples of what faith looks like in the lives of ordinary human beings—illustrations that have proved enormously inspiring and influential to Christian disciples in every generation.

Fifth, in this post-Christian age, *saints* have a particularly important function to play. In a time when secular scholarship has called the Bible into question, when evidence-based science demands proof before it will accept any truth claims, and when society has marginalized the church for consistently failing to live up to its calling . . . it is the lives of authentic saints that form the most credible "proofs" for the power of the gospel and the existence of the kingdom of God. If God exists, if Jesus saves, if the Bible is true, if Christianity is real . . . it needs living saints to *prove* it!

The History of Christianity is the Story of Its Saints

The history of Christianity is the story of its saints. Out from the pages of the Bible there marches a vast procession of people who found themselves as actors in God's historical drama. Anyone who has grown up in the Christian tradition is familiar with their stories. They have shaped our lives in more ways than we can say. We cannot see their faces, but their names and deeds have come down to us through the chronicles of time, as living messengers from God. Representatives from the Hebrew Bible include the naked Adam and Eve, the obedient Abraham, the beautiful Rebecca, the redneck Esau, the leader Moses, the prostitute Rahab, the kingly David, the suffering Job, the sensuous Solomon, the weeping Jeremiah, the fearless Daniel, and the questioning Habakkuk.

Representatives from the New Testament are the diminutive Zacchaeus, the surprised Samaritan woman at the well, the candid Nathanael, the blind Bartimaeus, the laughing children who approached Jesus, the disloyal Judas, the doubting Thomas, the passionate Mary Magdalene, the thunderbolt Paul, the believing merchant Lydia, the intellectual Apollos, and the unfamiliar (to us) Epenetus, who was the first convert in the East and who represents a kind of first fruits for the kingdom of God from the Gentile world.

Subsequently, out from the pages of human history there has marched a vast procession of people who have found themselves as actors in God's historical drama. Anyone who believes that the past has significance for the present will agree we ought not pass them by without a second look. These are our forebears in the faith, who faced life-and-death choices and determined that life without God was not really life at all. They have shaped our lives in more ways than we can know. We cannot see their faces, but their names and deeds have come down to us through the chronicles of time, as living messengers from God. Two thousand years of faith-filled, costly, tearful, glorious, depressing, and exhilarating life experience is wrapped up in their life stories. Although they may have lived long ago and very often far away, we find ourselves able to connect with them because their all-too-human lives resonate with our own fractured humanity. Here is just a tiny representative sample, chosen from between the close of the biblical canon onwards: the saintly Anthony (c. 251–355) who was the founder of monasticism, the gifted Augustine (354–430) whose conversion to Christ changed the course of history, the loving Francis of Assisi (1181–1226) who abandoned the world for the riches of the spiritual life, the mystically inclined Julian of Norwich (1342–c. 1420) who saw God in all things, the firebrand John Wesley (1703–1791) whose heart, strangely warmed, helped Christianity rediscover itself, the social activist Dorothy Day (1897–1980) who launched the Catholic worker movement, the deeply compassionate Archbishop Desmond Tutu (1931–) who lead South Africa's Truth and Reconciliation Commission, and the Christian missionary Graham Staines (1942–1999) who was burnt to death for his faith with his two sons in India. Christianity does not exist apart from such heroes of faith. Rather, it is in their lives, and in the lives of saints throughout all time, that Christianity—the work of heavenly salvation in human history—makes its appearance.

And so in our own day, out from the pages of present-day life, there marches an equally impressive procession of people who find themselves actors in God's historical drama. Without our necessarily being aware of them, they surround us on every side. Their lives are so ordinary, and we are so preoccupied with the demands of our own lives, that they may easily pass us by unnoticed. We see their faces, and we know some of their names and parts of their stories. Although they shape our lives in more ways than we can know, we often do not truly "see" them for who and what they are. Often they are too close for us to recognize that they are heroes of faith. We may doubt they have anything to teach us, or that we have anything to learn. In any case, we feel we do not have time enough to stop and sit at their feet to behold the wisdom they carry inside their lives. Instead we rush on to the next appointment—we have no time to stop, look, and listen.

But there *are* moments in our lives when people reveal to us things of ultimate significance, through their personal example. If we are awake and alert, if we are able to listen carefully, the gift of faith in holy "others" sparks a spiritual connection with God and enlivens our hearts too. There are many such people whose lives have touched my own life, whose humanity and deep spirituality have taught me that my life is not entirely my own, and that it is too important a gift to be squandered on worldly passions and trifling ambitions. It is my privilege, here, to offer their names as those who have been "taught by God" (1 Thess 4:9), and whose love of Christ shows them to be true citizens of heaven. In other words, *saints*.

At various times in my life I have gotten to know people in whose lives I have seen Christ set before me in flesh and blood. People like the effervescent Bill Gaunson, who invited me to consider baptism as the entry point to a life of commitment to Christ. Like the saintly Saboad Sahu, who visited Australia from India on a speaking tour, and told me God had a purpose for my life. Like the loving and smiling Eric Evans, who showed me what living for Jesus looked like and who suggested I should read C. S. Lewis. Like the loving Sister Ella, whose soul smiled out through her wrinkled face. Like the blind physiotherapist Graham Laycock, who saw things in the spiritual realm. Like the magnetic life of Phil Bowring, whose public example of godliness was seen and known by everyone. Like the sagacious Noel Vose, who opened books and worlds to me. Like the grounded Don Byrne, who put mission on the map for me. Like the polymath Keith Hinton, who knew much about everything. Like the live wire Barbara Alison, who gave Christian discipleship a joyous and credible face. Like Keith and Val Butler, who introduced community and spiritual direction into our vocabulary. And like Deirdre Madden, who poured out her life so that the women in disadvantaged communities across Australia and the Pacific could receive an education. In each case, Christian discipleship was commended to me as something inspiring, wonderful, and exceedingly good. Of course I realize that the faith experience of many people has been negative, hurtful, and damaging. But my experience of faith has on the whole been warm, nurturing, and wonderfully consistent with Jesus' teaching. Because of the examples of godliness and goodness I saw lived out in the lives of these people in front of my eyes, I found it difficult to resist its allure.

Each of these people have played an important part, serving as messengers from God to me. They have spoken into my life when I was in need of guidance, or reminded me of God's call on my life. God has used such people to speak to each of us. We have read eternity in the lives of such people, who are heaven's calling cards wrapped up in flesh. Saints' lives are of inestimable significance to God, and in the post-Christian times in which we find ourselves, their significance is becoming even more important. Christianity is indebted to them and their faithful example of what it means to follow Christ in the times in which they lived . . . including our own post-Christian times.

Saints in the Post-Christian Age

Christianity is the religion of witnesses. Throughout its 2000-year-long history, Christianity has placed a high priority on its saints, mystics, martyrs, and seers. These men and women have carried in the fragile containers of their persons the substance of the teachings of Jesus. In their holy lives there can be found the genius of the Christian faith, which has the power to transform sinners into saints, and where ordinary people are raised to extraordinary heights of Christlikeness.

But in the post-Christian age, saints and sages are not valued. While a "cult of the hero" has an important part to play in twenty-first-century culture, our heroes and heroines are not likely to be saints, but wicked anti-heroes. "The modern (scientific, materialist) world has abolished the figure of the saint or at least dismissed it as some sort of primitive throwback."[3]

3. Meltzer and Elsner, *Saints*, ix.

The label of *saint* is more likely to be given to a football team, a finance company, or a hospital than it is to be given to virtuous people who have set their hearts on *godfaring*.[4]

The resulting confusion means that in our own time saints are becoming an endangered species. Our task in this book is to focus once again on the role of holy people as God's agents of change. Saints remind us that the rumor of God is true, that goodness is still an active force in the world, and that repentance, faith and, new beginnings are the foundations for the "good life."

---

4. Clark, *Godfaring*, xiv.

2

The Imperfections of Saints

"The friends of God are not superhuman...
they are flesh and blood, just like you and me"
(James Howell).

Introduction

THERE WAS A TIME long ago when pilgrimage was not so much a journey to visit holy places as it was to make a visit to holy people. In times gone by when pilgrimage played a much greater role in peoples' lives, saints were understood to be "living monuments"[1] in whose persons were held the substance of the divine image in concrete form. In the exemplary lives of saints, faithful pilgrims were able to observe how frail and impermanent creatures could overcome the limitations of sinful humanity in order to draw near to God.

One memorable story of pilgrimage took place in the deserts of North Africa during the early fourth century. It concerns the novice monk, Paphnutius, who went on pilgrimage into the farthest reaches of the desert in search of counsel for his soul.[2] After a long and perilous journey into the wastes of the wilderness, without food or water, he came upon the cave dwelling of a saintly anchorite. Approaching the entrance to the cave, Paphnutius called a greeting to the occupying saint. On receiving no reply, he called again . . . this time a little more loudly. Again he received no reply. So he ventured into the cave, and peering through the darkness was able to

---

1. Frank, *Memory of the Eyes*, 30.
2. Ibid., 79–80.

see the outline of a man seated in the repose of prayer. Taking the saint by the arm, he shook him. To his horror, the saint's arm came off in his hands and crumbled to dust. Instead of grasping the splendor of the holy as he had expected, the saint had disintegrated in his hands. The moral of the story is that when scrutinized too closely, saints tend to fall apart. Ultimately, what makes a saint is not so much the "rule of faith" by which they live, or the force of their character as a holy person. What makes a person a saint is the God they dedicate their lives to and whom they worship. Any saint worth their salt knows that the source of their sanctity and their growth in holiness belongs to God, and not themselves. Their growth in the spiritual life to possess righteousness only has worth because the God whom they worship offers it as a gift to those who seek and find him.

Saints Behaving Badly

The Apostle Paul began his epistle to the church in Rome by addressing himself "To all in Rome who are loved by God and called to be saints: Grace and peace to you from God our Father and the Lord Jesus Christ" (Rom 1:7). It is likely there were few holy people living in that violent and power-hungry city. Yet a revolution was about to take place when these holy people—*saints*—were about to fulfill Jesus' promise that the "meek . . . would inherit the earth" (Matt 5:5) and the "peacemakers . . . would become sons of God" (Matt 5:8). Within 400 years, Rome was to become the center of the Christian world. Saints are living, breathing subjects of sanctity whose every prayer to God is that "Thy Kingdom come," and whose every action strives to answer that prayer by seeking to align their will with that of their heavenly Father—"Thy will be done." If there were no saints, there would be no Christianity. And understood from a certain vantage point, if Christianity no longer existed, then the world would cease to exist: "What the soul is in the body, the Christians are in the world."[3] But sanctity is not a *fait accompli*. Sanctity does not come prepackaged, ready-made, and fully guaranteed. Instead, sanctity is the free gift of God, that comes to us through intentional striving, long-suffering, and hard-won victories. Saints are always saints-in-formation. As the fourth-century theologian and Christian apologist Tertullian put it, saints are not born—they are made. Whatever else we might say about saints, they are always imperfect, unfinished, and in the process of being forged. Certainly, we can see the likeness of Christ

3. Arnold, *Early Christians*, 115.

in them, but it is always a faint image by comparison with the heavenly template of Jesus the second Adam. True saints are the first to admit that their attempts to manifest the life of heaven through their lives, words, and intentions . . . are imperfect and misshapen.

Every generation of people finds itself in possession of a unique assortment of strengths and foibles peculiar to it. So infants and children are known for their playfulness and lovable qualities. They are said to possess a purity and innocence almost unknown among adults. Mischievousness and curiosity are the noticeable traits of children, yet such childish antics can easily turn sour. Instead of reflecting beauty and goodness, children's behavior can give rise to the worst kinds of petulant emotion and tantrums. The same can be said of teenagers and youth. Teenagers are best known for their strength and beauty, their idealism and optimism. But, as if to offset these agreeable qualities, these same young people must wrestle with fits of depression, envy of others, and murderous rage.

Similarly, adults bear responsibility for raising their children, providing stable and loving homes for their families, putting food on the table through their hard work and generosity. But there are many adults whose marriages fall apart, whose children resent them, whose jobs provide little satisfaction, and who are easily distracted by frivolous pleasures, addictive behaviors, and other kinds of relationship-destroying habits.

And then there are the elderly. In their best moments, the elderly are sweet, loving beacons of morality who—because of their long life experience—are invested with wholesome wisdom and virtue. We value their courage in the face of their mortality and frequent illnesses. But we also know that many elderly people can be irritable, cantankerous, and incorrigible. Of course, we not only see these behavior traits in the elderly (or in the young) . . . we also recognize them as regrettable but hard-to-remove stains in our own lives. Whatever failures we attribute to any particular generation, we recognize that those same failings also represent ingrained universal negative qualities that afflict every generation of the human race and which demonstrate our human brokenness. The Apostle Paul's perturbed cry represents the frustration of us all: "What a wretched man I am! Who will rescue me from this body of death?" (Rom 7:24).

It was Dante, in his *Inferno*, who described every human creature as being "smudged by Adam's ink."[4] And saints are no different. As Paphnutius discovered in his encounter with the anchorite saint, when scrutinized too

---

4. Dante, "Inferno Canto 1," 14.

closely saints tend to fall apart. What foibles and frailties belong uniquely to saints? The "sins that so easily beset" believers (Heb 12:1) continually surround the company of the holy. The very things that the goodly company of the saints is known for, such as holiness, purity, reverence, and mercy, are all too easily reversed. In that instance, holiness becomes hypocrisy, reverence becomes rudeness, sanctity becomes sanctimoniousness, and piety becomes profanity. We know that love is the most tender and beautiful of all human affections. But we also know that with the smallest amount of provocation love can become deep loathing. Marriages that begin in romance and kindheartedness can soon end in bitterness, resentment, and seething rage. So the piety of good people can, through falling headlong into temptation without a thought for the consequences, or lack of attention to maintaining the golden thread of faith that joins us to God, quickly degenerate into the most outrageous human behavior. All too often the failures of irreligion, profanity, apostasy, blasphemy, legalism, and carnality accompany saints like a shroud of insects on a summer's night.

And so Peter denied Jesus, Judas betrayed him, the apostles distrusted Paul, who called himself the "worst of sinners" (1 Tim 1:16), Euodia and Syntyche where at each other's throats (Phil 4:2), the early church splintered into factions, the first Jewish Christians resented the Gentile believers, the Eucharist deteriorated into a drunken farce (1 Cor 11:27ff.), false apostles arose in opposition to the apostles, and the first missionary team was marred by conflict between Paul, Silas, and John Mark.

And this is only the beginning of Christian history! In subsequent centuries, the early Jesus community distorted the teachings of Jesus. Instead of repeating the invitation Jesus gave to his first-century audience in their own time, the Christian church—in God's name—committed simply terrible acts. The persecution of heretics, the oppression of the Jews, the exclusion of women, the centralization of power in the hands of the clergy, the amassing of enormous wealth to the detriment of the poor, the Inquisition, the curtailing of religious freedoms, the condemnation and trial of Galileo, the Crusades in the Middle East, the sexual abuse of the children under its care, and the list goes on.

The tragedy is that, in the name of righteousness, Christians have committed all kinds of unrighteous deeds such as idolatry, greed, adultery, intolerance, bigotry, high-mindedness, and puritanical prejudice. If the Apostle Paul could accuse the Jews of dishonoring God's name because of their idolatry and law-breaking (Rom 2:24), we ought not be surprised that there is today a growing peal of voices opposed to a Christianity, whose devotees are seen to break their own creed, misconstrue Jesus' teaching, and so discredit the gospel. God help us when saints behave badly!

It is easy to understand that before they were converted to Christ, many people who later became saintly and passionate disciples of Christ, lived as "cutthroats, crooks, trollops, conmen and devil-worshippers."[5] This is the stuff of testimony, the powerful retelling of stories in which once drunken, selfish, untrustworthy, good-for-nothing people get saved, and turn, over time, into precious jewels of heaven whose saintly character mirrors that of Christ himself. Wonder of wonders: "heaven came down and glory filled my soul." But no one can excuse the person who deliberately chooses to remain in sin after they have turned to Christ, been baptized, joined the Christian community, and pitched themselves to the world as people of faith. The Apostle Paul is clear about the disingenuous nature of this position when he refutes the possibility of "doing evil that good may come" (Rom 3:8). And the writer to the Hebrews says that those who go on sinning after they have repented are "crucifying the Son of God all over again and subjecting him to public disgrace" (Heb 6:6).

Literary Saints

Church history is full of saints behaving badly. As if mirroring this sad history, there is also no limit to the number of "false" saints one finds depicted in fictional literature. Some might argue that misrepresenting real-world saints via invented characters concocted by authors in their fictional writing is unwarranted. But as we are often told, art simply imitates life, and fiction does no more than reproduce in stylized form what we see in everyday life. Thus, the "types" and "counter-types" of saints and sinners we meet in fictional literature do no more than remind us of what we have already seen in the lives of the people around us—or, heaven help us, in our *own* lives. A couple of examples may help illustrate this point.

The Whisky Priest

Graham Greene's unnamed "whisky priest," from his novel *The Power and the Glory*, is a vivid example of a saint who falls victim to evil, even as he

---

5. Craughwell, *Saints Behaving Badly*.

sets about trying to do good in the world.⁶ On the "deficit" side, he is alcoholic, he is an outlaw from the officials in southern Mexico, where Catholic services were forbidden and practicing priests condemned to death, he has fathered an illegitimate daughter, and he finances his liquor by overcharging his parishioners to baptize their infants. But on the "credit" side, he is principled insofar as his own conscience troubles him deeply. He is committed to his calling as a priest to the extent that he genuinely cares for the people under his ministerial care, and he is courageous despite the danger of arrest as he negotiates the country back roads at night in order to administer the last rites to a dying gangster. Eventually, he is caught and executed for having a bottle of contraband whisky in his possession. Alone, outcast, anguished, addicted, and abandoned by anyone who ever knew him, the whisky priest seeks to remain faithful to his calling, and earns the undying love of the poor people in the *barrio* (district), to whom he continues to offer the mass and his genuine pastoral care during his final days. "Greene seems to be indicating that, even though the whisky priest is no spiritual luminary, his simple courage and trust in the world helps to bring some rays of the light of spirituality into the lives of those he encounters."⁷ The moral of the whisky priest is that one cannot fight evil alone, without the moral and spiritual support of others. To do so is to become a victim of evil yourself.

Elmer Gantry

Elmer Gantry, a novel by Sinclair Lewis, explores the life of the main character, whose name serves as the title of the book.⁸ In 1930s America, the book ranked as a number-one best seller. It tells the story of a young, athletic college student who abandoned his earlier career plans of becoming a lawyer in favor of becoming a Christian minister. He is ordained first as a Baptist evangelist and then as a Methodist minister. But at his core, Elmer Gantry is a self-serving alcoholic letch, who knows how to whip a congregation up into a frenzy with the "rapture of salvation" in his soul on Sunday, but whose own life for the remainder of the week is characterized by lust, greed, and animal appetites. He might be a "salesman of salvation," but secretly he is a religious phony who does not live for God but for "his girl,

---

6. Greene, *Power and the Glory*, 1946.
7. Gordon, *Fighting Evil*, 73.
8. Lewis, *Elmer Gantry*.

his work, his fame, and his power over other people."[9] Combining Sinclair Lewis's own cynicism towards the Christian faith and the worst aspects of saints behaving badly, Elmer Gantry manages to capture the worst kinds of religious misbehavior imaginable. "Elmer Gantry is like a man struggling to wake up from a deep sleep but to no avail. Despite his best intentions, he cannot escape the slumber of his unregenerate state. As a result, his entire life and career are compromised."[10] The novel begins with a scene in a bar where Gantry is rolling drunk. The middle of the book is preoccupied with Gantry's liaisons with his female manager, Sharon Falconer. While the conclusion—predictably—describes his coming to an unhappy end. The moral of the story is that there is no place to hide for a religious huckster and shyster. "Your sins will find you out" (Num 32:23).

Saints in the Local Church

Anyone who belongs to a local church soon discovers that churches are practice pitches for saints behaving badly. I have been a pastor, missionary, and Christian leader for over thirty years, and if I had taken the trouble to record their antics, I could have written the book on the imperfections of saints. But that does not mean the local church of itself is a bad place to be. It simply reflects the ongoing story of humanity's sinfulness since creation and the fall. As the prophet Jeremiah well understood, "The human heart is the most deceitful of all things, and desperately wicked. Who really knows how bad it is?" (Jer 17:9, KJV). But in a certain kind of way, this diagnosis applies uniquely to saints who ought to know better.

The Man They Call Moses

In a town in regional Australia there lives a man everyone calls "Moses." He has long, white, flowing hair and a generous beard down to his chest. He drives a colorful hand-painted Kombi van that often has loud Christian music blaring from its speaker system. The bumper bars and side windows are plastered with stickers that, along with everything else, give the impression that Moses belongs to a 1970s-style flower power or Jesus revolution movement. He distributes gospel tracts in people's letter boxes, and accuses

---

9. Ryken, Ryken, and Wilson, *Pastors in the Classics*, 42.
10. Ibid., 47.

longtime believers in the town of being "false" witnesses. When he goes down the main street, Moses bears witness to his Christian faith by asking questions like, "If you died tonight, would you go to heaven or hell?" and "Will you be ready when Jesus comes again?" There is nothing wrong with believers sharing their faith in Christ. In fact, it is the obligation of every Christian to testify to the new life that is theirs through faith in Christ. But because Moses is so confrontational, instead of drawing people's attention to the beauty and truth of the gospel, he tends only to succeed in reinforcing their already negative opinions against Christians as angry, moralistic, dogmatic, opinionated, and nosy. Because of his behavior as a counter-witness, Moses has managed to convey precisely the opposite meaning to the one he intended. Had he been less aggressive, more pastoral, more caring of others in the town, he might have managed to be more winsome and to present a more compelling case for Christ to his audience. But as it stands, all he has managed is to drive people who were already suspicious of the Christian faith further away from it. The next time these people encounter a Christian, they'll be less inclined to engage with them (on any level) and so less receptive to what may be a more Christlike example of the faith.

Jimmy Swaggart's Fall from Grace

Jimmy Swaggart (born 1935 in the small rural Louisiana town of Ferriday) in a poor rural background came to fame as a teenage evangelist and a red-hot gospel preacher. A cousin to rock and roll flame Jerry Lee Lewis and country music star Mickey Gilley, Swaggart married his fifteen-year-old girlfriend when he was only seventeen. Due to his authoritative stage presence and powerful preaching, Swaggart became an influential Christian leader not only in America but worldwide. Swaggart was lead pastor of a large Assemblies of God congregation in Baton Rouge, Louisiana. He had an international television ministry that reached viewers in 100 nations around the world, and attracted donations in the order of the $150 million per year. Swaggart was outspoken in his opposition to adultery and homosexuality, pouring fire and brimstone on fellow evangelist Jim Bakker for committing adultery with his secretary, and accusing rival televangelist Martin Gorman of moral indiscretions in 1986. But in 1988 Swaggart found himself sitting at the penitents' bench when a picture of him taking a prostitute into a Louisiana motel was released to the media. In the days that followed, Swaggart preached his "Apology Sermon," in which he tearfully confessed his sin to his congregation, the world, his Lord, his wife, and his family. Subsequently, Swaggart was defrocked by the Assemblies of God denomination, and—one might have assumed—was destined to suffer the ignominy of disappearing into the pages of history. However, since 2009 Swaggart has recommenced television broadcasting and boasts of reaching millions of viewers in the US, UK, Asia, Africa, and the Middle East. It would appear that after his downfall, Jimmy Swaggart is making a comeback.

Saints in Devotional Literature

Devotional literature records a continual stream of the many ways in which saints have behaved badly, and offers instruction on how to return to the bosom of Christ through repentance and faith. It should come as no surprise that one of the chief means of spiritual instruction is through the lives of men and women who have wandered far from God, but who have been humbled and returned to God through tearful repentance. The point for discovery is not why or how they abandoned God, or even how far they travelled from God, but the fact that God did not abandon them. Such a fall from grace can prove a necessary journey, when the wanderer realizes they have become the prodigal son, and begins the journey of repentance to recover their lost identity as followers of Christ.

Thomas Merton

Renowned Trappist monk Thomas Merton (1915–1968) was born in France to an American mother and a New Zealand-born father. At six years of age, Merton's life was turned upside down when his mother died, prompting his father, an artist, to travel restlessly throughout Europe and beyond. Merton attended an English boarding school called Oakham, and completed his university education at Clare College, Cambridge. During his formative years he received love and support from a staunch Catholic family, and this was to impact his later life in a big way. While at Cambridge, Merton lived a rather degenerate life and managed to father an illegitimate child to a young woman. Tragically, it seems that both the mother and the child were killed in German air raids over England during the Second World War, and were never heard from again. While completing his higher education at

The Imperfections of Saints

Columbia University in New York, Merton wrote for a campus magazine and lived the dissipated life of a carousing socialite.

One day, in 1938, he surprised his friends by announcing that he was to be baptized as a Catholic. Having read the work of Jesuit poet Gerard Manley Hopkins, Merton had decided—as if on impulse—to become a Roman Catholic. After completing his masters degree he attempted to join the Franciscan order, but was turned away because he had fathered a child out of wedlock. After teaching for several years, he went on retreat to a Trappist monastery in Kentucky, called the Abbey of Our Lady of Gethsemane, to which he was eventually admitted. During his twenty-plus years as a Trappist monk, living under the vows of poverty, chastity, and obedience, Merton wrote many books including his own autobiography entitled *The Seven Storey Mountain* (1948), which became a runaway best seller. We will have more to say concerning Merton's life story later, but the point here is that during a stay in hospital in 1966, as a result of his lifelong poor health, he fell in love with one of the nurses and embarked upon a tumultuous six-month affair. This entailed breaking his vow of chastity, and in so doing, breaking his vows of obedience to his Trappist Order. However, after a season of discernment and repentance, Merton returned to his calling as a monk, a writer, and a spiritual teacher. Falling in love as a monk was not the wrong thing to do. But abandoning his calling as a follower of Christ was. Although painful, he found his way "home" to faith and returned to his vocation as a monk. Since his untimely death by accidental electric shock in Thailand in 1968, Thomas Merton has been acclaimed as one of Christianity's spiritual "masters." Without doubt, Merton's life is a story of contradictions, yet following his death he remains one of the most widely read and respected authorities of the Christian spiritual life.

All these descriptions of saints behaving badly provide a sobering inventory of the many ways in which saints have sought to overcome temptation (only to succumb), to resist evil (only to be overpowered by it instead), and to work out their salvation (beset, just like anyone else, by fear and trembling). Discussing the way in which even great saints have shared in fallen human nature, Phyllis McGinley wrote: "They lost their tempers, got hungry, scolded God, were egotistical or testy or impatient in their turns, made mistakes and regretted them . . . they went on doggedly blundering their way toward heaven."[11] Similarly, the historian of Christian mission Stephen Neill referred to Christian missionaries as

---

11. McGinley, *Saint-Watching*, 5–6.

those who, on the whole, are "feeble folk, not very wise, not very holy, not very patient. They have broken most of the commandments and fallen into every conceivable mistake."[12]

As we observe the two millennia that separate the apostolic period and the contemporary twenty-first-century, post-Christian age, we are forced to admit that the redeemed community has not always looked very redeemed, and the way Christians have behaved has not always reflected the teachings of Jesus, or borne witness to the presence of the indwelling Spirit of holiness, or testified to the unseen realm of God's kingdom. Divisions within the church, conflict between leaders, marriage breakdowns, the exclusion of women from leadership, the sexual abuse of children under church care . . . all reinforce the point I have been making in this chapter, that even saints have a habit of behaving badly. Heaven help us!

But Saints Nonetheless

As we have seen, there is a "shadow" side to saints. But that is not all there is to saints. Our discussion so far has not shown them in their best light. Furthermore, it has not depicted them in their true light, as God sees them—as men and women who have given their hearts to Christ and who subsequently enjoy the favor of God, but whose lives are still in the process of being formed as saints. At worst, they are sinners whose lives dishonor God because of their failure to live up to their baptism, making them unworthy of his Name. Certainly, there are times when they seem more at home in the world than they are devoted to their prayers, to worship, or the service of others. But, at their best, they remain *saints*, whose undying affection for God, devotion to Christ, and love for their neighbor marks them out as a people set apart by God for his name and for his purposes.

Saints and Sinners

Martin Luther (1483–1546) was the German monk whose rediscovery that the "righteous will live by faith" (Rom 1:17), launched the Protestant Reformation. Luther's favorite saying was (in Latin) *simul justus et peccator*. In English this reads, "Christians are simultaneously *sinners and saints*." Christian discipleship is the ongoing process of attending to Christ's call on our

---

12. Neill, in Bosch, *Transforming Mission*, 519.

lives to "Come, follow me" (Mark 1:17), even as other siren voices clamor for our attention. Christian disciples are never more saints than when they consciously and intentionally prioritize obedience to Christ. Conversely, Christian disciples are never more sinners than when they ignore the rule of Christ in their lives, and choose instead to direct their own steps. And as saints, retaking control of our own lives inevitably means "selling out" to a range of less worthy priorities, usually associated with our own appetites and self-interest.

Robert E. Webber was right to point out that Jesus' submission to God did not come without struggle. "Even as Jesus struggled to surrender his will to the Father, so also, in our spiritual life, Jesus is the model not only for the victory but also for the struggle."[13] For saints, who are always caught between good and evil, between obedience and willfulness, remembering that Jesus' obedience to the Father required him to sweat "drops of blood" (Luke 22:44), is of great importance. Obedience for Jesus was not a simple, automatic fact. It came through struggle. It was built on relationship with God. It grew out of character and resulted in commitment to a new way of living. But struggle was the basis on which the new life was achieved. The Apostle Paul best described that struggle when he wrote, "The good I want to do I cannot do, and the evil that rises up within me I cannot resist" (Rom 7:14–20). The life of holiness to which saints are called does not in the first instance alleviate temptation and the desire for sin, but heightens it. Paul describes the life lived in the power of the Spirit as a life that continues to be characterized by deep groaning. Regarding the "new life" that is ours in Christ, the Apostle Paul writes, "The groaning of the created order represents the birth-pangs of something new, and the sons and daughters of God feel the same groaning in their spirits as they await the arrival of God's kingdom"(Rom 8:22–24). As sanctified sinners, therefore, saints are not immune to suffering and struggle. Rather, these things are the testing ground where authentic faith is hammered out. The choice between life and death, light and darkness, hope and despair, proximity to God or exclusion from his presence, is costly, binding, and ongoing.

> A [good] power, if we obey it, blesses and helps us; but the same power, if we disobey it, curses and ruins us . . . . Saul is obedient, and all is brightness, courage, hope, happiness. Saul disobeys, and his soul becomes melancholy, gloomy, irritable, suspicious, envious, distracted . . . . There is no privilege which you cannot turn

---

13. Webber, *Divine Embrace*, 174.

into a curse. God does love you, and will never cease to love you, no matter what you are, no matter where you go . . . but His love shall be to you either a spirit of help or a spirit of harm, according to your obedience or disobedience to Him.[14]

But once chosen, the choice is total and complete. On the other side of the call to follow Christ comes the decision to submit. And out of the decision to submit comes consecration and surrender, which is the deepest level of Christian sanctity.

Sinning Like a Christian

William Willimon wrote a book with the strange title *Sinning Like a Christian*.[15] In it he says something quite amazing—he says it's not so much that Christians don't sin, but rather that when they do sin they know where to go and who to talk with in order to find forgiveness for their sins. For Christians, the first thing to say about sin is that *everyone* sins. As the old saying has it, "To err is human, to forgive is divine." That is why confession is so important in Christian life and practice. Whereas the "wicked . . . are inept, crippled, deficient people who never really get the hang of human existence,"[16] the righteous are only too aware of what separates them from God and the pathway to authentic existence. Confession entails naming the cause of our brokenness, and pleading with God for forgiveness in the name of his Son, Jesus Christ. It is the first act of the penitent sinner. So the Apostle Peter can say, "Go away from me Lord; I am a sinful man!" (Luke 5:8), and the Apostle Paul can describe himself as the "worst of sinners" (1 Tim 1:15). St. Augustine, after he had prayed, "Thou hast made us for thyself and restless is our heart until it comes to rest in Thee,"[17] went on to pray:

> The house of my soul is too narrow for Thee to come in to me; let it be enlarged by Thee. It is in ruins; do Thou restore it. There is much about it which must offend Thine eyes; I confess and know it. But who will cleanse it? Or, to whom shall I cry but to Thee? "Cleanse Thou me from my secret faults," O Lord, "and keep back

---

14. Brooks, *Visions and Tasks and Other Sermons*, 307-8.
15. Willimon, *Sinning Like a Christian*.
16. Eagleton, "The Nature of Evil," 11.
17. Augustine, *Confessions*, 1.

Thy servant from strange sins." . . . "If Thou, Lord, shouldst mark iniquities, O Lord, who shall stand?"[18]

Catholic novelist and short story writer Flannery O'Connor observed that, "Sin is sin whether it is committed by the Pope, bishops, priests or lay people. The Pope goes to confession like the rest of us."[19] Saints continue to wrestle with sin because they know its destructive effects. Sinners don't know they're sinning and mistakenly believe their rebellious lives are the normal state of human existence.

At first the phrase "sinning like a Christian" seems like a collision of opposites—like mixing sugar and salt. But on taking a second look, something previously unnoticed comes into view. Basically, says Willimon, Christians know they are sinning, whereas unbelievers don't. In the Christian tradition, the "Prayer of Humble Access" forms a central part of the preparation for the Eucharist or the Lord's Supper. The "Prayer of Preparation" reads:

> Almighty God, to whom all hearts are open, all desires known, and from whom no secrets hidden: cleanse the thoughts of our hearts by the inspiration of your Holy Spirit, that we may perfectly love you, and worthily magnify your holy name, through Christ our Lord. Amen.[20]

It prepares worshippers for the hearing of the gospel, the confession of the creed, the prayers of intercession and penitence, and leads to the "Prayer of Humble Access."

> Father eternal, giver of light and grace, we have sinned against you and against our neighbor, in what we have thought, in what we have said and done, through ignorance, through weakness, through our own deliberate fault. We have wounded your love, and marred your image in us. We are sorry and ashamed, and repent of all our sins. For the sake of your Son Jesus Christ, who died for us, forgive us all that is past; and lead us out from our darkness to walk as children of light. Amen.[21]

What follows is the "Prayer of Absolution":

---

18. Ibid., 5.
19. O'Connor, *Spiritual Writings*, 84.
20. *Australian Anglican Prayer Book*, 114.
21. Ibid., 122.

Almighty God, our heavenly Father, who in his great mercy has promised forgiveness of sins to all those who with heartfelt repentance and true faith turned to him: have mercy on you, pardon and deliver you from all your sins, confirm and strengthen you in all goodness, and bring you to everlasting life, through Jesus Christ our Lord. Amen."[22]

In his book *People of the Lie*, Scott Peck suggested that if one is looking for genuine evil, one ought to look first within the synagogue and the church.[23] It is the nature of evil to "hide among the good," he tells us. And this is largely because since evil, as a nonentity having no capacity to create anything by itself, must draw its substance from something larger, something good. Evil only has the power to destroy and of itself cannot create anything. It must affix itself to something "real" in order to deceive its customers into believing sin to be a worthwhile activity. In the twenty-first century, we blithely polarize evil and goodness as if their two separate essences can never be mixed, but Jesus knew otherwise. The wheat and the tares must mingle in this world, in order to demonstrate the benefit of the one and the waste of the other. And likewise, the sheep and the goats must mix, before being sorted into their proper categories for reward and judgment. To sin like a Christian is not the end of the story. It is a recognition that we are in need of salvation now and into the future, must confess our sins, and receive the salvation that Christ makes available to us so freely and so graciously.

A Spirituality of Imperfection

There is something deeply troubling about saints who are depicted as over-perfect—what many might call "plaster saints" who are so heavenly minded they are of no earthly use. Their standard of holiness is so high it can seem impossible for the average person to achieve. As a result, the aspiring disciple feels they might as well attempt to fly to Mars and back, as attempt the unattainable task of becoming a saint. Yet we have discovered in this chapter that many—if not most—saints suffer from clay feet, and at the center of their lives there is often a deep brokenness. The Christian faith represents an invitation to frail and imperfect human creatures to share in the life of God. Like Israel before it, the church is called to live up to the standard of

---

22. Ibid., 122.
23. Peck, *People of the Lie*, 263.

The Imperfections of Saints

God's righteous character: "Be perfect, therefore, as your heavily Father is perfect" (Matt 5:48): . . . even as it is aware that perfection is a divine—not a human—attribute. The church understands itself, without exception, to be an "imperfect company." As such, we can only begin to approach the perfection of God after the righteousness of Christ has been graciously given to us, through repentance, as a gift. In this new state of grace, when God looks at us, it is the perfections of Christ he sees—not the stumbling imperfections of individual saints and corporate Christian communities.

Henri Nouwen (1932–1996) was a Dutch-born Roman Catholic priest and writer in the field of spirituality (among other areas). Will Hernandez wrote a book entitled *A Spirituality of Imperfection*, exploring how Nouwen felt himself to be a deeply broken and needy human being, whose sense of incompleteness fashioned a central part of his ministry throughout his life. Writing of his own life, Nouwen spoke of being "broken with psychological wounds, physical limitations, and emotional needs."[24] Recognizing this strange disconnect between the Christian's call to minister out of God's perfection while remaining in their own imperfect state, Nouwen wrote *The Wounded Healer*, which has since become a Christian classic. There, Nouwen reminds us that, like the saint:

> . . . the minister is called to recognize the sufferings of his [sic] time in his own heart and make that recognition the starting point of his service. Whether he tries to enter into a dislocated world, relate to a convulsive generation, or speak to a dying man his service will not be perceived as authentic unless it comes from a heart wounded by the suffering about which he speaks.[25]

In Christian terms, spirituality is not so much about perfection as it is about connection, and specifically a connection with God. This is the whole point of the Christian faith—that humanity is broken and needs fixing, and only God in Christ is capable of doing the fixing. As Kurtz and Ketchum offer:

> The core paradox that underlies spirituality is the haunting sense of incompleteness . . . . For to be human is to be incomplete, yet yearn for completion; to be imperfect, yet long for perfection; to be broken, yet pray for wholeness. All these yearnings remain necessarily unsatisfied . . . . Because we are imperfectly human—or

---

24. Hernandez, *Henri Nouwen*, 76.
25. Nouwen, *Wounded Healer*, xvi.

better, because we are perfectly human, which is to say humanly imperfect.[26]

If incomplete, broken, yet-to-become-whole saints are the disgrace of Christianity, it is only in Christ that we are able to continue in the faith as sinners without being evicted. It is only in Christ that grace can be found to overcome our *disgrace*—that we can transition from the defeated humanity of Romans chapter 7, to the redeemed humanity of Romans chapter 8. If Paul can say, "O wretched man that I am! Who will rescue me from this body of death?" (Rom 7:24), the saint, the true believer, can say, "Thanks be to God—through Jesus Christ our Lord!" (Rom 7:25), and "Who shall separate us from the love of Christ?" (Rom 8:35). The answer to this question is, quite simply, *nothing and no one can!* For since Christ has rescued us from sin, willful disobedience, the judgment of the law, and ultimately death, nothing and no one can separate us. Such a thing is not possible.

Conclusion

In anticipation of the Jubilee Year 2000 anniversary of the commencement of the Christian church, Pope John Paul II called for that same church to undertake an examination of its own conscience:

> . . . it is appropriate that as the second millennium of Christianity draws to a close the Church should become ever more fully conscious of the sinfulness of her children, recalling all those times in history when they departed from the Spirit of Christ and His Gospel and, instead of offering to the world the witness of a life inspired by the values of her faith, indulged in ways of thinking and acting which were truly forms of counter-witness and scandal. Although she is holy because of her incorporation into Christ, the Church does not tire of doing penance. Before God and man, she always acknowledges as her own her sinful sons and daughters.[27]

The Danish philosopher Søren Kierkegaard made the astute observation that "God creates out of nothing. Wonderful you say. Yes, to be sure, but he does what is still more wonderful: he makes saints out of sinners."[28] Ironically, it is our very brokenness, incompleteness, and imperfection that

---

26. Kurtz and Ketchum, *Spirituality of Imperfection*, 18–19.
27. John Paul II, *Tertio Millennio Adveniente*, § IV-33.
28. Kierkegaard, *Journals*, 59.

invites us to seek the completeness, healing, and perfection that can only be found in Christ. Looking beyond themselves to that higher life that is their eventual inheritance, faithful saints take seriously the words of their Lord and Savior: "For whoever wishes to save his life will lose it; but whoever loses his life for My sake will find it" (Matt 16:25).

3

The Perfections of Saints

"There is only one sadness, not to be a saint"
(Leon Bloy).

Saint Damien of Molokai

THE MAN WHO WAS to become famous as the "leper priest" did not begin his life as anyone special. Father Damien (as he became known) was born in Belgium in 1840 as Josef de Veuster, to humble farming parents. Josef and his older brother Auguste believed they had a religious vocation from God and entered holy orders with the Congregation of the Sacred Hearts of Jesus and Mary. Josef took the name of Brother Damien in memory of an early Christian saint who was known for performing miracles. Following their training and ordination, the older brother was to join a mission to the Hawaiian islands. But when it came time for the expedition to depart he was too sick to travel, so his brother Damien took his place. Hawaii in the 1860s was experiencing a major public health crisis, with many villagers being afflicted by diseases brought to the islands by Europeans in the form of influenza, syphilis, and leprosy. When Hawaii's King Kamehameha IV relocated victims of leprosy to an isolated settlement on the island of Molokai, to stop it spreading across the archipelago, it was decided that the leper colony should have a priest to care for its spiritual needs. Of the four brothers who volunteered, Damien was the first to go.

So in May 1873, Father Damien arrived on Molokai and was presented to the community of 600 lepers who were to become his congregation. They not only suffered from the rigors of leprosy, but also knew the privations of separation from their families, the pangs of starvation, and the threat of death. From the beginning, Damien busied himself in the community. He set up gardens and farms to feed the hungry, and constructed buildings and roads to give order and dignity to the ramshackle community. He organized horseback riding, a band, a choir, and a hospital where he and others could dress the ulcerated limbs of the afflicted. He built a parish church known as St. Philomena, where he taught the (Catholic) Christian faith, and taught people to read and write. He described himself as "one who will be a father to you, and who loves you so much that he does not hesitate to become one of you; to live and die with you."

For sixteen years Father Damien was the community's spiritual father, healer of souls, builder of houses, mender of relationships, dresser of ulcers, and undertaker who built coffins and dug graves. He was also the community's advocate to church authorities who were far away and who did not fully understand the plight of the people, and fundraiser among the world community in order to meet the urgent medical needs of the leper colony on Molokai. In 1885, after prolonged exposure to patients with the disease, Father Damien announced that he too had leprosy. "I am one of you," he said. "Without the constant presence of our Divine Master (Jesus) upon the altar of our poor chapels, I never could have persevered casting my lot with the afflicted of Molokai; the consequence of which begins now to appear on my skin and is felt throughout the body." Although he was given a dispensation to leave the island to seek medical care, Damien chose to remain and continued to care for his beloved community, building churches, hospitals, clinics, and over 600 coffins. He lived a remarkable life characterized by openness to the needs of others, and to people who were different from himself. "Among his best friends were Meyer, a Lutheran, the superintendent of the leper colony, Clifford, an Anglican, and Moritz, a painter, a free-thinker who was the doctor on Molokai and Dr. Masanao Goto, a Japanese Buddhist and leprologist."[1]

Father Damien died on the island of Molokai on April 15, 1889. He was forty-nine years old, and described himself at that time in his life as "the happiest missionary on earth." From the time of his death and to this day, he has received the undying love of the Hawaiian people. Although buried on the island of Molokai, the Belgian government subsequently applied for, and was given, permission to repatriate his remains to Belgium. On the request of the Hawaiian people, Damien's right hand was later returned to

---

1. Vatican News Service, "St. Josef de Veuster."

Molokai. Pope John Paul II beatified Damien on June 4, 1995. Today he is believed to be the patron saint of outcasts, those with HIV and AIDS, leprosy, and the state of Hawaii.

The (Im)possibility of Speaking about Saints

Saints and saintliness are unlikely topics for discussion in today's world. Most people find it difficult if not impossible to know what to do with saints, because twenty-first-century culture offers no category for essential goodness. To a self-obsessed culture that makes a virtue out of living selfish and self-centered lives, the appearance of holy men and women who make a practice of giving away their lives on the scene is something truly outrageous. The very idea of signing up to vows of poverty, chastity, and obedience, comes as a shock in an age that has fallen in love with wealth, sexuality, and unbridled freedom. Who in their right mind would want to do such a thing? As a result, "The modern (scientific, materialist) world has abolished the figure of the saint, or at least dismissed it as some sort of primitive throwback."[2] It is no wonder that saints are an embarrassment to the dominant culture, calling them "holy fools" who contradict the core values of a world that has lost not only its direction but its soul.

But there are instances where the disregard for saints has gone beyond merely misunderstanding the true nature of saints, to become a blatant attack on the calling of holy people, and the very notion of holiness as a possible ideal. Although not going so far as to attack saints physically and to cause their martyrdom, many modern thinkers have nevertheless sought to deliberately discredit the very idea of Christian holiness.

One such example is the case of Frederick Nietzsche (1844–1900) who wanted to steal what properly belonged to the saints in order to reappropriate it to another purpose altogether. Nietzsche is well known for his rage against God, which is foretold in the madman's announcement concerning the "death of God" in his philosophical essay, *Thus Spake Zarathustra*. In Nietzsche's estimation, ordinary mankind, who looked upward to worship God, was weak and despicable and deserved to be overthrown. In place of God as our one true object of worship, he offered up what he called the *übermensch* (the "overman" or "superman"), who was Nietzsche's symbol for the new humanity, whose duty it was to rise to the level of its proper destiny. Nietzsche's aim was to replace religious observers—whom

2. Meltzer and Elsner, *Saints*, ix.

he called a laughing stock and a painful embarrassment, "poison-mixers" and despisers of life—with a new and thoroughly secular humanism strong enough to overcome the struggles of life without kowtowing to the demands of (what he called) an interventionist God. They could do this, he proposed, by exercising a potent life force he called the "will to power." But in order to locate this will to power, Nietzsche first had to find it. He did so in the lives of the very saints he tried to disparage.

> The mightiest men have hitherto always bowed reverently before the saint, as the enigma of self-subjugation and utter voluntary privation—why did they thus bow? They divined in him . . . . The superior force which wished to test itself by such a subjugation; the strength of will, in which they recognized their own strength and love of power, and knew how to order it; they honored something in themselves when they honored the saint . . . . The mighty ones of the world learned to have a new fear before him, they divined a new power, a strange, still unconquered enemy; it was the "will to power" which obliged them to halt before the saint.[3]

Thus, in an attempt to find a foundation on which militantly atheistic humans could shake their fists at God, Nietzsche tried to steal something that belonged rightfully to holy people. Why did he do this? Because the saints were not afraid of death and dying. The great saints and martyrs did not shrink from the threat of imprisonment, exile, decapitation, or some other grizzly fate, but affirmed their faith in God's unfailing love. Nietzsche mistook this extreme confidence and self-effacement for a complete lack of fear in the face of death (which originated from their belief that death must give way to resurrection), and as a new form of "power" that the saints—he wrongfully assumed—somehow possessed in themselves is a function of their own power base. But every true saint knows another truth altogether: "When I am weak, then I am strong" (2 Cor 12:10). "Unless a grain of wheat falls into the earth and dies, it remains alone, but if it dies, it bears much fruit" (John 12:24). The axiomatic moment of Christian discipleship is a willingness to lay down one's life, to embrace the cross, and to follow Christ wherever he leads.

The irony of Nietzsche's mistaken project was to identify the power by which he intended to transform the individual human will into the supreme good, with the purest form of love that can only be found in the lives of the saints—those who have surrendered completely to Christ. Ironically,

---

3. Nietzsche, *Beyond Good and Evil*, 48.

Nietzsche wanted the resurrection power of Christ without following Christ to the cross, and became distressed when he was unable to possess it for himself. Yet from the point of view of Christian theology, there is no resurrection without the crucifixion—Christ's redeeming act of self-sacrifice that arose of necessity out of his direct and specific obedience to God. We cannot rise to new life with Christ without first denying ourselves, taking up our cross, and following him.

Another example is the philosopher Susan Wolf, who derided and belittled righteous people in her treatment of moral saints.[4] Wolf asserted that saints cannot be what they claim to be, but are instead "sick souls" whose decision to forego their own self-interest for the sake of serving others is contrary to acceptable standards of mental health and sanity in today's world. On these grounds, Wolf vilified and maligned saints as dangerous, unreasonable, and impractical. She wrote:

> I don't know whether there are any moral saints. But if there are, I am glad that neither I nor those about whom I care most are among them. By moral saint I mean a person whose every action is as morally good as possible . . . . A moral saint will have to be very, very nice. It is important that he not be offensive. The worry is that, as a result, he [sic] will be dull-witted, humorless or bland.[5]

In pitting a saint's duty to God and neighbor against their duty to their own well-being and self-preservation, Wolf sees the potential for self-destructive forces to dominate the lives of would-be saints. But she mistakenly identifies the saint's motive for charitable acts as a pathological fear of damnation before—what she claims—an angry and judgmental God. Wolf misses completely the substance of Christian teaching in the form that questions saints being called to mimic the pattern of divine self-effacement. The truth is that saints find their greatest fulfillment in prioritizing the needs of others over against themselves.

Wolf's attack on moral saints on the grounds that they are "diseased souls" wracked by pain is a misnomer. It is likely she was blinded by her own culturally shaped convictions that people are predisposed towards the instinct for self-preservation, and that there is no possibility for altruism in the human spirit. She condemned saints for not conforming to Western culture's narcissistic tendencies . . . forgetting that saints have always been know for subverting the values of the dominant culture. In light of the

---

4. Wolf, "Moral Saints."
5. Ibid.," 419–20.

increase of philanthropy on the part of wealthy citizens across the Western world—many of whom function out of secular humanist convictions, and to whom we might assign the title of "secular saints" because of the good deeds they do—it is clear that people do good things because the circumstances call for it, or because helping other people makes them feel good about themselves. Altruism can be its own reward. Such actions are carried out against the values of the culture and sometimes perhaps against their better judgment . . . but they nevertheless contribute to the well-being of others. This is not the stuff of insanity, but rather of human conscience awakened to the needs of others. The timely arrival of Martin Seligman's "positive psychology" as a leading contributor to human well-being, demonstrates that everyone—not just the saint—flourishes in their own souls when they act generously towards others.[6] And as they do so, the giver demonstrates his or her own inward maturity and happiness by seeking the well-being of their neighbor. Thus, Jesus' encouragement to "love our neighbor as ourselves" is not a command simply for holy people, but for persons everywhere if they are to achieve the level of humanity to which they rightly aspire.

Understood through the lens of classical and redemptive Christianity—instead of through the lens of nineteenth-century godless ideology (as in the case of Nietzsche) and twentieth-century misplaced humanist self-confidence (as in the case of Wolf)—there is much to be said in favor of saints. It ought not to be so difficult to speak of saints and their significance for the world. The purpose of this book is to invite readers to consider that over against the ever-increasing number of villains, gangsters, pawns, rogues, idiots, and clowns, society needs saints, benefactors, martyrs, seers, and wise ones if goodness is to prevail. The most basic thing to say about saints is that they are God's appointed agents in the world, and that the truth of Christianity can be recognized most plainly by observing saints at work in the world. "Next to Holy Scripture there certainly is no more useful book for Christians than that of the lives of the saints, especially when unadulterated and authentic."[7] True, saints don't fit easily in a secular age. But the reason for their "difference" is because they have pledged allegiance to Christ and the redemptive values of the biblical narrative, and they have found the audacity to act with the courage of their convictions. Their doing

---

6. Seligman, *Flourish*.
7. Kieckhefer, *Sainthood*, 5.

so keeps the rumor of God alive, and reminds unbelievers there is more to the world than the faithless eye is capable of seeing.

> [Saints] aren't misfits at all. Holiness only appears to be abnormal. The truth is, Holiness is normal; to be anything else is to be abnormal. Being a Saint is simply being the person God made me to be. Saints at the end of the day are not really strange or odd or misfits. They are simply real, or normal. They actually are what we are all made to be, what we can be.[8]

As von Balthasar says, "It is not dry manuals (full as these may be of unquestionable truths) that plausibly express to the world the truth of Christ's Gospel, but the existence of the saints, who have been grasped by Christ's Holy Spirit. And Christ himself foresaw no other kind of apologetics."[9] Therefore it ought to be entirely possible to speak of saints in the twenty-first-century world. When we are surrounded by so much evil, and when we go to such great lengths to imagine a just society and the "good life" is the right of all—the goodness of saints must surely be the building block needed to produce that to which we universally aspire.

Saintliness as Call and Response

The spiritual life is primarily a life of call and response.[10] Jesus called his disciples to "Come, follow me" (Matt 4:19). It is a "call" that repeats God's summons found in the Old Testament for humanity to attend to his covenant and his teaching. In Genesis, God called to Adam and Eve in the garden, "Where are you?" (Gen 3:9). God called Abraham to leave his country and his father's household and made him a promise: "I will give you many descendants and they will become a great nation. I will bless you and make your name famous, so that you will be a blessing" (Gen 12:2). God called Moses to lead Israel out of Egypt into the land he had promised to give them. While in the desert of Sinai, the angel of the Lord called Moses from within the burning bush. "Take off your sandals, because you are standing on holy ground. I am the God of your ancestors, the God of Abraham, Isaac and Jacob" (Ex 3:4–6). Throughout the history of Israel, we find this pattern of call and response. Name who you will: Joshua, Samuel, David,

---

8. Howell, *Servants, Misfits, and Martyrs*, 31.
9. Von Balthasar, *Glory of the Lord*, 494.
10. Chrétien, *Call and the Response*.

Ruth, Elijah, Gideon, Daniel, Nehemiah, Sampson, Isaiah, Jeremiah, and Daniel... this pattern of God calling men and women to participate in his cosmic drama continues, through the New Testament, and onwards right up to the present time.

We pick up the story where Jesus called the first disciples to follow him, to "be with him" (Mark 3:14). They were to "learn of me"—a process that would variously require them to take his yoke upon them (Matt 11:28-30), and to "take up their cross daily" (Luke 9:23). Jesus' call to "Follow me" includes the call to participate in his mission by going and doing likewise. In its simplest formulation, Jesus' teaching can be broken into three "moments." The first is the Great Commandment (Mark 12:28-31), which describes the necessity to love God with all one's heart, mind, soul, and strength—and to love our neighbors in the same way. The measure of our love for God is the extent to which we truly love our human neighbor. The second is the Sermon on the Mount (Matt 5-7), where Jesus describes the attributes of people who belong to the kingdom of God. It is the humble, the merciful, the pure in heart, and the peacemakers who enter the kingdom, who see God's face, and who are called sons and daughters of God. The third is the parable of the Good Samaritan (Luke 10:25-37), where Jesus called his followers to "really" love their neighbors, even when they are altogether different from them. Jesus identified our neighbor as anyone in need. Often our prejudices and cultural conditioning prevent us from reaching out to these people, but according to Jesus, lepers, wounded strangers, "unclean" others—people not like us—are the very people whose lives we are to touch. After telling the story of the Good Samaritan, Jesus commanded his audience to "Go and do likewise" (Luke 10:37). Throughout the Gospels, following Jesus is a completely down-to-earth thing, putting into practice the same kinds of habits, generosity of spirit, and life choices we see Jesus making. Following Jesus means adopting his mode of life, and joyfully choosing to "Go and do likewise."

And Jesus' call to "Come and follow me" and "Go and do likewise" extends to his disciples in the twenty-first century, whom we are calling saints in this book. Saint Damien of Molokai (whose story opened this chapter) spent his life among the lepers of the Hawaiian Islands as a direct response to Christ's call on his life. Damien's life is an object lesson in faith in action, a picture of flesh-and-blood Christianity *par excellence*. The same can be said of anyone whose life is spent in service of the gospel, whoever they may be, wherever they are from, however and wherever they are called to serve, and whatever their particular God-given *charism* (spiritual gift) happens to be.

At least some of those who are called to be saints belong to monastic orders and so find themselves engaged as contemplatives through lives of prayer, community service, and participating in the life of God. The Roman Catholic priest Raimon Panikkar (1918–2010), in his book *Blessed Simplicity*, argued that monks represent a kind of "universal archetype."[11] Panikkar is wary of suggesting that men and women who join religious orders in any sense "own" the mystery of the spiritual life. Access to that mystery, he says, belongs to everyone who seeks to achieve the highest level of integration and maturity available to the human person. Monkhood is the structured and communal approach to the mystery of the spiritual life that organizes itself intentionally around the point of intersection between ordinary and extraordinary life. Monks and nuns do by ordination what average Christians do by their baptism . . . they make vows of commitment that exercise a character and commitment-shaping power over their lives. "After . . . consecration . . . there is no more 'life as usual.'"[12] This is the depth of the commitment that Christian discipleship represents, and the heights of the response that saintly submission and consecration calls for. It is a whole-person response that invites every fiber in a saint's being to resonate with the divine will and purpose.

The consecrated life, with its total commitment to living a God-saturated life, invites us to build on the threefold understanding of the life of faith as submission, gratefulness, and generosity identified earlier, and so to deepen our understanding of the shape of the saintly life in practice. Here we draw from the work of James McClendon, to help us focus on the Christian spiritual life as a life that has a particular form.[13] First, McClendon identifies the primacy of lived experience over our tendency to rationalize and formularize it into a set of discrete doctrines. He uses the phrase "a theology of life"[14] to ensure we understand that deeply held convictions are to be "lived out" through our lives. And second, McClendon speaks of the "radical" nature of Christian discipleship. Sainthood is neither a shallow nor a part-time endeavor. It asks everything of us in our totality . . . the

---

11. Panikkar, *Blessed Simplicity*.
12. Ibid., 91.
13. McClendon, *Biography as Theology*.
14. Ibid., 142.

whole of us without any reservations or exceptions. Christianity is not a creed to be confessed, but a life to be lived.

More Literary Saints

Prince Myshkin

The Russian novelist Fyodor Dostoevsky (1821–1881) is one of history's most compelling writers. He is best known for such blockbuster novels as *Notes from Underground* (1864), *Crime and Punishment* (1866), and *The Brothers Karamazov* (1880). In *The Idiot* (1869), Dostoevsky set out to represent innocence in the life of a human person. But it is not an easy task because in a world that was far from innocent and which bore its shame like a badge of honor, innocence is cast as weakness, purity as naiveté, and beauty begins to look like vulnerability. In the case of Myshkin, we discover a young man of uncertain parentage who returns to his home city of St. Petersburg after spending a season abroad under professional medical treatment for a mysterious malady. As the story unfolds, it seems increasingly likely that the illness was a serious form of epilepsy. But in this case, the epilepsy is sometimes accompanied by "a blinding light which floods his soul." Such language is commonly used to describe ecstatic religious experience. Dostoevsky would have us understand that, although not wise in the ways of the world, Myshkin is attuned to spiritual realities in a way that most ordinary people are not. While he describes himself as both a child and an idiot, he nevertheless has peculiar insight into the impulses, fears, failings, and sufferings of the regular people around him. His ability to intuit deeper relational (including spiritual) dynamics is the cause of his ability to overcome people's repulsion to his sickness and his ability to obtain their trust. There are times when his luminous insight into the characters of other people is prophetic, even if his discomfort in social settings is sometimes pathetic. But ultimately he cannot prevent suffering: the mistreated Maria dies, and the reckless and free-spirited Natasha also. But he is only able to empathize with and travel alongside them out of some inner resource of essential goodness which is the mark of the saintly person.

How do we understand what Dostoevsky was trying to do in representing the saintly qualities through the awkward and obviously flawed life of Prince Myshkin? Dostoevsky himself judged that his attempt was a failure, and there are critics aplenty who would agree with him. According to Mochulsky, "Sanctity is not a literary theme. In order to create the image of a Saint, one has to be a Saint oneself. Sanctity is a miracle; the writer cannot be a miracle worker. And Christ only is holy, but a novel about Christ is impossible."[15] The idea of the holy "fool" is embedded as an archetype in both Scripture as well as general literature.[16] Few if any so-called holy fools ever make a name for themselves, because of the extent of the social disapproval they experience. Yet holy fools are the subjects of divine approval and the objects of God's abiding love. Ultimately, we must return to Jesus' teaching in the Gospels where he teaches that the children of this generation are more "shrewd" than the "children of the light" (Luke 16:8-9), thus reminding us that the challenge for godly people is always to be "as wise as serpents and as harmless as doves" (Matt 10:16).

The Bishop in *Les Misérables*

In addition to the main characters of Jean Valjean (the fugitive) and Javert (the policeman), one of the first characters Victor Hugo introduces to his readers is the bishop of the town of Digne in rural France. On the surface, *Les Misérables* appears to be a story of dramatic struggle and unjust oppression, but it is the character and actions of the bishop that ultimately makes the story redemptive. In a world characterized by violence and bloodshed, oppression and rough justice, the bishop's merciful act towards Jean Valjean is what ultimately transforms the fugitive from villain to model citizen, and from a selfish man into a man who fears God.

First, the bishop welcomes Valjean into his home. The bishop lives not in the resplendent bishop's residence, but a humble servant's quarters adjacent to it. He welcomes Valjean with the words, "This house is not mine but Christ's. It does not ask a man his name but whether he is in need. You are in trouble, you are hungry and thirsty, and so you are welcome. You need not thank me for receiving you in my house. No one is at home except those seeking shelter."[17] It is while in the bishop's residence receiving food, hospitality, and welcome, that Jean Valjean, in a moment of spite, relapses to the moral dissoluteness of his early upbringing—he steals the bishop's silverware and runs away into the night. He is soon captured by the policeman Javert and brought face-to-face with the bishop to be confronted with

---

15. Mochulsky, *Dostoevsky*, 346.
16. McCarthy, *Sharing God's Good Company*.
17. Hugo, *Les Misérables*, 87.

his crime. But instead of accusing Jean Valjean of theft, the bishop informs the diligent Javert that the silverware was given as a gift. Thereafter the narrative of *Les Misérables* explores Jean Valjean's journey towards redemption, seen in his protection of Cossett and his care for the women who work in his factory. By contrast, we witness the slow disintegration of Javert, whose unwavering dedication to the principle of law means he cannot cope with the idea that the fugitive, Valjean, is a better man than he is. Ultimately, Javert takes his own life in a desperate attempt to redeem himself... an act that is all the more pitiable because it is motivated by selfishness and bitter rage.

The real Bishop of Digne was Charles François Bienvenu Myriel. He belonged to a French aristocratic family who possessed wealth and privilege. After he married and moved to Italy, his wife died, and for reasons that are not clear, he entered the priesthood. He lost his fortune in the upheavals surrounding the French revolution, and was reduced to a priest's salary. However, as a bishop, he was in effect clerical royalty and could have lived in the lap of luxury in the Episcopal Palace adjacent to the Digne church. But he did not. Instead, he chose to live a humble life. What money he had he gave to the poor. He seems to have had great compassion towards the faults of humanity and was indignant at injustice. Victor Hugo thought him to be a man of unimpeachable Christian character and so modeled his literary bishop on him.

Saints in Devotional Writings

St. Julian of Norwich (1342–ca. 1423)

Julian is one of England's best-known mystics and teachers of the Christian faith. She was a Benedictine nun, a solitary anchoress whose life was given over to prayer and asceticism. Although not formally canonized as a saint by the Roman Catholic Church, "Blessed Julian of Norwich" is widely venerated among Catholics (she even has her own feast day on May 13 each year), and is well known and much loved among Protestants and especially Anglican Christians. Little is known about Julian's life, partly no doubt because she was a woman living in a man's world, and partly because she was not given to self-promotion. Yet we know enough about her to recognize her value as a teacher and exemplar of the Christian faith and spiritual life, both to the age in which she lived, and for us today.

Julian was born in and lived most of her life in the city of Norwich, 200 km northeast of London. In its day, Norwich was a kind of second city to London, and a center for libraries and literature, education and learning, innovation and the arts. Julian herself was well educated, and became the first ever woman to have written a book published in English (*Revelations of Divine Love*, 1395). Her knowledge of the Latin Vulgate Bible was extensive, and her writing style rivaled that of the well-known English poet Martin Chaucer. Julian's spirituality is focused on her life of prayer, and in particular on her oft-repeated request to experience Christ's passion in her own body. On May 30, 1373—with her mother and her minister present in her room—she did in fact undergo a vivid experience of suffering that was akin to Christ's passion. It occurred at a time when she was extremely ill, and involved great physical and spiritual pain. Judged to be near to death, Julian was administered the Last Rites, and was thought to have actually died. However, she roused, and although her body felt "dead" she went on to receive sixteen visions that were delivered in the form of "bodily," "bodily and yet more spiritual" (or sensory), and "spiritual" revelations.[18]

The shorter version of the record of her visions is called *Showings*, and the longer called *Revelations of Divine Love*, that appears to have been written later. Together, they describe the universe as filled with light, and speak of God's overflowing love for humanity. Julian described God not only as Father, but also as Mother. For Julian, the end product of prayer practiced in a right manner was to be united with the Lord. Everything exists simply because God loves it and has called it into being. At the core of Julian's spirituality is the goodness of God, who allows sin to besmirch the human condition in order to prepare us for repentance and submission to Christ.

Due to her renown as a healer and a counselor, people came from the surrounding countryside to visit Julian, giving accounts of the benefits from their encounters with her. Essential to her teaching was that knowledge of God and knowledge of self are inseparable, that God is nearer to us than our own souls, and that the love of God conveys its own value, meaning, and purpose. In her own case, Julian submitted herself to the authority of the church, stating: "I yield me to our mother Holy Church, as a simple child ought." It was she who penned the well-known phrase, ". . . but all shall be well, and all shall be well, and all manner of things shall be well"—that was repeated and made famous by the twentieth-century English poet T. S. Eliot in the fourth of his "Four Quartet" poems.

18. Guiley, "Julian of Norwich," 198–99.

The Perfections of Saints
Dietrich Bonhoeffer (1906–1945)

Born in Breslau, Germany, Bonhoeffer was the sixth of eight children. His father was a professor of neurology and psychiatry, and his mother the granddaughter of a distinguished church historian. Bonhoeffer was educated at the University of Tübingen, and in 1927, at the age of twenty-one, was awarded a doctorate for his thesis on the topic of the communion of saints. His research brought into focus his central convictions: namely that Christian discipleship is not simply an individual, interior, and religious practice, but has a communal, external, and political component to it. As with most of Bonhoeffer's thought, the idea of being a silent witness to the gospel of Christ was anathema. In addition to his work as a pastor and a theologian, Bonhoeffer was heavily involved in social justice and political action in the face of rising Nazi aspirations to exert control over Germany and its expansionist military aspirations across Europe. As a committed pacifist, Bonhoeffer registered his opposition to the persecution of Jews in 1933. He opposed the State Church's collaboration with the Nazi regime, and along with others organized the birth of the Confessing Church. The Barmen Declaration was largely written by the theologian Karl Barth, but had the full participation and support of Bonhoeffer. The Barmen Declaration rejected the Reich's subordination of the church to the state, and rejected the State Church's weak capitulation to rising German nationalism, and its claims that the Reich was the "agent" of God in the world.

In *The Cost of Discipleship* Bonhoeffer wrote, "When Christ calls a man, he bids him come and die."[19] Such total commitment is repeated in Bonhoeffer's rejection of what he called "cheap grace," and his call for believers to practice "costly grace" instead. His early visit to Union Theological Seminary in New York, where he met Reinhold Niebuhr, and his exposure to the social gospel preached by some leaders of the black churches in America, influenced him greatly. Further travels throughout Europe, the United States, Mexico, and Cuba convinced him of the growing importance of ecumenism among Christians. In particular, Bonhoeffer's two-year pastoral appointment among German-speaking churches in England, and his return to Union Theological Seminary to teach in 1939 were really significant for him. However, soon after arriving in New York for the second time, Bonhoeffer realized his true calling was to return to Germany, which he did almost immediately. His work setting up underground seminaries at

---

19. Bonhoeffer, *Cost of Discipleship*, 79.

Finkenwald and Sigurdshof is well-known. Also well-known is his cooperation with a plot to assassinate Hitler, which ultimately failed.

Bonhoeffer was arrested in April, 1943, and imprisoned in Tegel military prison awaiting trial. During the long and difficult waiting period, he wrote his *Letters and Papers from Prison*. Bonhoeffer was executed by hanging on April 9, 1945, just weeks before the end of the Second World War. Bonhoeffer's legacy is one of unrelenting faith in God, made manifest in his strenuous engagement with the world. Like Dorothy Day, the American Christian convert and founder of the Catholic Worker movement who protested, "Don't call me a saint; I don't want to be dismissed so easily," it is unlikely that Bonhoeffer would want to have been called a saint. But given the extent of his influence, and the courage he expressed in living out his convictions in the face of such powerful enemies, it is hard to think of a more fitting title.

The Everyday Goodness of Ordinary Saints

Pastor Ronnie Williams (1940–2003)

Ronnie was a well-known and respected Noongar Aboriginal leader and Christian pastor in Australia. Born in 1940 in Albany on the south coast of Western Australia, he never knew his father and was raised instead by his grandparents. Along with many other Aboriginal people, Ronnie faced a great deal of discrimination and injustice throughout his life. He was unable to attend school until age eight because Aboriginals were prevented from receiving an education. When Ronnie was fourteen, his grandfather invited him to go on a trip. Ronnie turned him down. But while he was away, his grandfather was killed in a fight. Plagued by guilt, Ronnie turned to drinking, and lived a dissolute life on the edges of townships. He played guitar and sang country and western songs to raise money for beer and liquor. But during a chance meeting with a missionary at the Gnowangerup Agricultural Show, he was given a Bible and a picture of Jesus holding a lamb. To Ronnie, the lamb symbolized his own helplessness and simplicity. He became a follower of Jesus Christ, and spent the remainder of his life visiting outback communities, sharing the gospel with people in prison, and caring for lost and lonely people.

Ronnie trained for the ministry at the Gnowangerup Bible Training Institute in Western Australia's southern districts, and joined United

Aborigines Mission (UAM) as a cross-cultural missionary to the community of Warburton Ranges, where the aboriginal men initially called him "white fella" because his skin was lighter. But soon, because of his obvious love for them, he became known as "kuta" (brother).[20] He preached in aboriginal settlements and in established churches, in family homes, and on street corners. With a ready smile and a mischievous sense of humor, Ronnie was always ready to offer pearls of wisdom (both practical and spiritual) and to pray for and help anyone in need without a shadow of reproach. Ronnie's Aboriginal wife died after a long illness. He eventually met and married Diana, an educated white American professional who left her job as an executive at Chase Manhattan Bank in New York to come to Australia to work among Aboriginal people. They "roughed it" for the better part of twenty years, living in tents, out of the back of their car, and staying with Ronnie's extended family and their many friends throughout Australia.

One of the most notable things about Ronnie was his disarming smile and his ability to connect with people wherever he found them. This openness and friendliness stemmed from his own sense of struggle in his early life. He said, "I know what it's like to be on the outside, where nobody wants to know you, so I try to help those wherever I can." He became a bold Aboriginal man who had grown from a timid child, his brown face pressed against a window pane, looking in at white society, never being invited in, but having something important to say. As an adult he invited himself in.

In 1999 Ronnie and Diana moved to Canberra, Australia's national capital, so Diana could lecture in the Christian Missionary and Alliance College. Not one to lose an opportunity, Ronnie frequented Parliament House to talk with and pray for the nation's leaders. He also spent time with his own people in the "tent embassy" outside Parliament House, which had become the protest capital for Aboriginal Australians. "Whether he met with the heads of State, business executives, fatherless children or prostitutes, he accorded them all the same respect."[21] Ronnie died of cancer in 2003, leaving his wife Diana and his daughter Lydia, along with thousands of friends and family members, to mourn his loss and celebrate his life.[22]

---

20. Milnes, Milnes, and Truscott, "Aboriginal Pastors Interpret Forgiveness," 3.
21. Moyes, "New South Wales Parliament Hansard."
22. Williams, *Horizon is Where Heaven and Earth Meet*, tells the story in detail.

Ordinary Saints

Sister Ella Williams (1915–1998)[23]

Ella Williams was born to Methodist parents in Fremantle in Western Australia during the First World War. She spent the better part of fifteen years working in an office as a secretary. But she became dissatisfied with her life, sensing that God had something more for her to do than to shuffle paper. She joined the Order of the Sisters of the People in 1956. The order was started by the Perth Central Methodist Mission in response to an outbreak of typhoid fever during the Kalgoorlie gold rush. After joining, Ella's first appointment was to the East Perth district, where a large low socioeconomic community lived with poor health, high rates of crime, and unemployment. Her duties involved pastoral work in the homes of the people, delivering food parcels, advocating for the families with the legal authorities, and presenting Christ through her many acts of mercy and kindness.

Ella served as a member of the order for twenty-eight years in many different roles . . . visiting the homeless, caring for the sick in hospitals, taking the initiative in planning for and delivering aged care,[24] acting as a chaplain at the Bandyup Women's prison, serving as a frontline pastoral carer in the Perth, Fremantle, and Adelaide City Missions, as well as a frequent visitor to the Mogumber Aboriginal Mission in the Moore River district to the north of Perth. But Sister Ella's ministry was only just beginning. In 1976 she read Malcolm Muggeridge's book, *Something Beautiful for God* (1971), and was deeply moved by his account of Mother Teresa's work among the poor in Calcutta, and her ability to "see" God in the faces of the people among whom she worked. Consequently, Sister Ella made seven trips to Calcutta to work with Mother Teresa and her Sisters of Charity. Working alongside Mother Teresa in the Kalighan slum was both the most difficult and the most thrilling thing Sister Ella ever did. During her visits to the rubbish dumps, where she found discarded babies and starving naked children, she saw humanity at its lowest and humblest. There were many times when she was shaken to the core and wondered if she had made the right decision in going to India, yet she remembered Jesus' promise: "I will never leave you nor forsake you." Sharing in the physical and spiritual care of the terribly poor and lowly was overwhelming, and yet enormously fulfilling. "The biggest problem for these people," Sister Ella would say, "is

---

23. My thanks to Sheena Hesse of Uniting Church Archives Office in Perth, Western Australia, for her assistance in researching Sister Ella's life.

24. The Ella Williams Hostel was named in her memory.

not the threat of leprosy or tuberculosis but the feeling of being unwanted, uncared for, unloved."[25]

During her years of ministry in India, Sister Ella was known for two things. The first was that she was willing to do anything that needed doing—washing bodies, scrubbing beds, feeding anybody that needed feeding, or simply holding someone's hand while they were dying. The second was her deep love of children. During the last of her trips to Calcutta, with her health and eyesight failing, she would sit with the children at the orphanage and sing to them, tell them stories, touch them, and remind them that she loved them, as did the Lord. Sister Ella was a small woman, but she made a big impression on the lives of the people she encountered. A group of women from the churches in Perth, Western Australia, wove her life in the "Quilts That Tell Stories" series. "This is the story of a truly remarkable woman who has not sought to acquire riches, fame or status, but who has demonstrated overwhelming qualities of courage, determination, compassion and faith."[26] Sister Ella died in 1998 at the age of eighty-three. She was deeply loved and widely honored.

Conclusion

Let me close this chapter by quoting from Thomas à Kempis' book *The Imitation of Christ*. There he exhorts his readers to imitate the saints who stand in the place of Christ in the world:

> Apostles and Martyrs, Confessors and Virgins, and all of those others who would follow in Christ's footsteps, many and grievous were the trials they went through, caring nothing for life in this world, if life might be theirs in eternity . . . holy people these, true friends in Christ, that could go hungry and thirsty in God's service, cold and ill-clad, worn out with labors and vigils and fasting, with praying and meditating on holy things, along with all the persecutions and insults they suffered . . . and then, the holy Fathers in the desert—how severe that life was, how full of self-renunciation! The long periods of searching trial, the Devil's constant assaults, they prayed to God so frequently and so fervently—with a burning ambition to rise higher in the spiritual life . . . with what clear eyes and true wills they aspired after God!

---

25. Giblet, "Profile: Sister Ella Williams," 19.
26. Whittington, "Women of Compassion," 231–32.

... Strangers in the world? Yes, but close friends, intimate friends of God. How he loved them, how he treasured their love, these men (and women) who thought themselves good for nothing, these people whom the world despised! Kept steady by sincere humility and unquestioning obedience to Jesus—that was how they advanced, day by day, in the spiritual life, and won such graces with God. Why don't we imitate these people, and take up their challenge to go forward, instead of following the unadventurous herd, the slack, growing crowd?[27]

---

27. à Kempis, *Imitation of Christ*, 43–44.

4

The Qualities Embedded in Saintly Lives

"Is there anything so beautiful on earth as the saints?" (Stuart Devenish).

Introduction

IF WE ARE TO take Thomas à Kempis' advice to imitate the lives of those heroes of the faith who have gone before us, we will need to understand what it means to live a holy life. If you and I, living in our small corner of the world, were to feel ourselves called to live the saintly life to which we've been called—where would we start? What would that look like? How might we begin to fold the perfections of the felt presence of God into our patterns of living, evening and morning, work and rest, prayer and worship, service and self-care?

The Qualities Embedded in Saintly Lives

Many people who want to understand what it means to lead a holy life turn to the Apostle Paul's description in Galatians 5:22–24 of the "fruit of the spirit." And they are right to do so. The Apostle Paul's description represents the classical definition of the holy life. The "spiritual fruits" of love, joy, peace, patience, kindness, goodness, faithfulness, gentleness, and self-control are the spiritual energies given by the Holy Spirit to counteract the passions of the sinful nature described in the preceding verses: namely, sexual impurity, idolatry, jealousy, envy, and anger, which characterize the default condition of the human heart in our fallen world. Yet Paul's description of the outworking of the Holy Spirit in the life of the everyday saint—compelling as it is—awaits further explanation as to "how" these qualities are made manifest in real-life situations. What follows in this chapter is an exploration of the qualities that define a saint, as realized in their everyday experiences of applied discipleship. I identify twelve qualities that I believe are characteristic of the lives of ordinary saints. In many ways they are simply re-statements of the "fruits of the spirit" identified by the Apostle Paul, but have a particular emphasis on how these fruits are put into action.

In his 1902 lectures on religion, William James described what he called the "practical fruits" of the spiritual awakening known as conversion in the following way:

> The collective name for the ripe fruits of religion in a [person's] character is Saintliness. The saintly character is the character for which spiritual emotions are the habitual centre of the personal energy; and there is a certain composite photograph of universal saintliness . . . of which the features can be easily traced.[1]

Exploring the practical fruits of saintliness further, James suggested that the practical consequences of saintliness involve the four qualities of self-surrender, strength of soul, moral purity, and charity. He wrote, "The saint loves his [sic] enemies and treats loathsome beggars as his brothers."[2] He also noted, "The best fruits of religious experience are the best things that history has to show."[3] If that is the case, we can say that the qualities of saintliness are worthy of further exploration.

The Apostle Paul found it difficult—if not impossible—to lead a holy life, without the power of the Spirit living in and through him. To transition from an unspiritual existence, (described in Romans 7:24 in terms of being trapped in the "body of death"), to a new life in the Spirit (described in Romans 8 in terms of utter liberation from the body of death) is the chief purpose of becoming a saint. To appreciate what this looks like in our ordinary lives, we must pay attention to the qualities of the saintly life if we are to "work out our salvation with fear and trembling" (Phil 2:12).

The qualities I suggest most clearly characterize the life of an ordinary saint are: (1) love for humanity, (2) overflowing joy, (3) generosity of spirit,

1. James, *Varieties*, 271.
2. Ibid., 274.
3. Ibid., 259.

The Qualities Embedded in Saintly Lives

(4) willingness to suffer, (5) deep humility, (6) essential goodness, (7) profound wisdom, (8) holiness of life, (9) the practice of prayer, (10) an eternal perspective, (11) readiness to resist evil, and (12) forgiving one's enemies. What follows in this chapter is an exploration of these qualities in ways that are consistent with Jesus' teaching, with the lived component of classical Christianity, and that can be adopted into the lives of ordinary believers in their everyday lives.

1. **Love for humanity:** The lives of ordinary saints are characterized by a deep love for humanity. Jesus taught his disciples to "love one another" (John 13:34–35), but it is clear that he expected their *philadelphia* (Greek for "brotherly love") to extend beyond the intimacy of one's inner circle of family and friends, to embrace and include the entire human family. Saints in their millions have felt compelled to reach out to perfect strangers in the name of Christ, putting into action "the love of God shed abroad in our hearts" (Rom 5:5). They have healed the sick, fed the hungry, clothed the naked, cared for the poor and housed the homeless. Such love for the suffering "other" can be seen in the life of Mother Thérèsa of Calcutta, who is probably the most well-known and best-loved modern saint. But we don't necessarily need to move to the slums of Calcutta to be a saint. This same quality of a deep-seated love for humanity is commonplace among every saint who is an authentic follower of Jesus no matter where they live. The saints recognize they are called to love others even as they themselves have been loved—totally, completely, unconditionally. "The measure of love is to love without measure."[4]

2. **Overflowing joy:** The lives of the saints are characterized by overflowing joy. Jesus is described as being "full of the joy of the Holy Spirit" (Luke 10:21), and he was careful to invite his disciples to imitate his joy. The Catholic writer Romano Guardini has suggested that the difference between Christians and non-Christians is that: "The Christian is not permitted ever to despair, ever to be pessimistic even. The Christian does not have the right to say men are bad, society is corrupt, or without hope. He [sic] must simply love the world and remain faithful to it."[5] Joy is the hallmark of the saints. Yet that does not mean they do not suffer hardship, sickness, suffering, and ultimately death. What

---

4. Ellsberg, *All Saints*, 43.
5. Guardini, *Saints in Daily Christian Life*, 105.

it does mean is that "being loved by God" (1 John 4:10) provides the basis for an intimacy and emotional security that is strong enough to know inner peace even in the most difficult of times. The French Jesuit priest and philosopher-palaeontologist Pierre Teilhard de Chardin wrote: "Joy is the most infallible sign of the presence of God."[6] While in his famous *Divine Comedy*, Dante describes how, as he approached heaven, he heard "the laughter of the universe."

3. **Generosity of spirit:** The lives of saints are characterized by an attitude of generosity and open-handedness. They are deeply aware that they follow in the footsteps of Jesus, who washed the feet of his disciples, fed the hungry crowds, and who laid down his life for his friends. Saints have left the comfort of their families and the safety of their homes to cross cultural and language barriers in order to demonstrate the love of Christ for humankind. Many have foregone marriage, wealth, comfort, and the security of home and family in order to risk their very lives for the sake of the love of Christ. They have spent generously out of their own resources to care for the needs of others—often those who are most unlike them in their beliefs, attitudes and way of life. Yet they have displayed a characteristic generosity of spirit by giving until it hurts. Saints believe everyone is loved by God, embraced by him, welcomed at his table and chaperoned into his kingdom. As a result, saints are people who come to their task armed not with bombs, swords, murder, and hatred, but with a deep desire to bless others and to cause them to grow into their full potential as human creatures. All they have to offer in their hands are those gifts they themselves have received, and a generous heart willing to share. They are intent on simply serving others in the name of Christ. In this way, Dorothy Day, the founder of the Catholic Worker Movement, cared for the sick and homeless in New York City for more than forty-five years. "There is always room for one more at our table"—she said.

4. **Willingness to suffer:** Pain is an inescapable part of the human condition. Thomas Hobbes described human life as "solitary, poor, nasty, brutish and short."[7] Pain is universally unwelcome, regardless of whether it is a physical pain, an emotional pain, or spiritual pain. Saints don't choose to suffer. No one in their right mind would make

---

6. de Chardin, *Le Milieu Divine*, 1965.
7. Hobbes, *Leviathan*, 78.

The Qualities Embedded in Saintly Lives

such a choice. The only reason why someone might be willing to suffer on behalf of others is that Christ's voluntary suffering sets the pattern of authentic discipleship. The central event of Christianity is the incarnation, the central "act" that is God's choosing to take on human flesh. God, in Christ, became human—and as a human he chose freely and without coercion to die for the life of the world. Bruce Shelley wrote that "Christianity is the only major religion to have as its central event the humiliation of its God."[8] If Jesus was prepared to experience limitation, humanity, suffering, the cross, sorrow and death, then his followers must also be willing to embrace this way of humiliation. It's not so much that saints *have* to suffer, it is more that they are *willing* to suffer should that be asked of them, and that they are willing to serve others who are suffering.

5. **Deep humility:** Saints' lives are characterized by a deep humility. Saints prize the character qualities found in their Master Jesus who described himself as, "[One] who is gentle and humble in heart . . ." (Matt 11:28–29) and who demonstrated that quality by washing the feet of his disciples. The community of disciples are called to mutual submission, to childlike faith, and to take great pains to "think of others as better than themselves" (Phil 2:3–4). St. Benedict incorporated the "Twelve Steps of Humility" into his Rule. Its purpose was to enable monastic communities to embody in their society a harmonious existence that anticipated the quality of life which will be found in heaven. The twelve steps were designed to invert the image of the powerful warrior, focusing instead on one's capacity to choose absolute mastery of the self and its passions.[9] The Cistercian Abbot Andre Louf noted that humility is "An all-encompassing virtue—the heart of stone shattered and restored to life as the heart of flesh—the virtue from which all other virtues are derived."[10] Such humility is opposed to any deadening habits of heart such as pride, conceit, and arrogance, choosing instead to replace them with the positive virtues of modesty, transparency, and self-control.

6. **Essential goodness:** Ordinary saints possess an immense capacity for goodness. Believing that God is the *summum bonum* (the source of

---

8. Shelley, *Church History in Plain Language*, 15.
9. Holder, *Blackwell Companion to Christian Spirituality*, 111.
10. Louf, *Way of Humility*, 21.

the "highest good"), believers entrust themselves to the providence of God, believing that special grace accompanies their lives from moment to moment. Instead of hungering and thirsting after sin and selfishness they find themselves content with the simple pleasures of quiet evenings, of communal meals with friends, of reading, of music, of prayer, and of conjugal lovemaking as an act of participation in the love of God made manifest in marriage and family. In December, 1867, Dostoevsky wrote to his friend, Maikov: "There is a thought that has haunted me for a long time.... It is to portray a wholly good man. Nothing is more difficult... especially in our time."[11] Dostoevsky's difficulty in depicting an entirely good person in his fiction attests to the difficulty of being an entirely good person in a society that has turned away from God and ultimate value. Saints, however, are besotted with goodness and cannot help but reflect the goodness of God, made known in Christ. "Whatever is noble, whatever is right, whatever is pure, whatever is lovely, whatever is admirable—if anything is excellent or praiseworthy [such as saints]—think about such things" (Phil 4:8).

7. **Profound wisdom:** There is a deep wisdom in the lives of ordinary saints. Although they are often seen as "fools," God botherers, and moral prudes by people who do not understand, Christian saints find themselves in possession of a very deep form of wisdom. That wisdom is centered on Christ, who the Apostle Paul described as the one in whom God had hidden "all the treasures of wisdom and knowledge" (Col 2:2–3). Paul's prayer for the Ephesians was that they "may grasp how wide and long and high and deep is the love of Christ, and to know this love that surpasses knowledge—that [they] may be filled to the measure of the fullness of God" (Eph 3:18–19). From its earliest origins, Christianity developed a *sophos*-Christology that believed Jesus was God's highest wisdom. And therefore those who know Christ have access "to the mind of Christ" (1 Cor 2:16), where the very wisdom of God is to be found. But this divine wisdom is not merely a rational or human intellectual knowledge. Instead, it is an interpersonal and relational wisdom informed by God's own intersubjective love (his trinitarian nature), and his capacity to "reach into" the inner lives of the dispossessed poor, and those who are materially rich yet poor in spirit.

---

11. Wyschogrod, *Saints and Postmodernism*, 1.

The Qualities Embedded in Saintly Lives

8. **Holiness of life:** Holiness is the unique mark of the saints. The prophet Isaiah knew what it was to stand before the utter holiness of God: "Woe is me! For I am a man of unclean lips . . ." (Isa 6:5). The Apostle Paul wrote to the church in Thessalonica, "For God did not call us to be impure, but to live a holy life" (1 Thess 4:9). Although saints often fail in their calling to live a righteous life, they understand, as if "from the inside," that they are nevertheless called to pursue the blessed attributes Jesus spoke of in the Sermon on the Mount. Beauty, purity, contentment, and an abiding grace accompanies those saintly souls whose good habits enable them to draw near to the mystery of God. Through their long obedience and practice of disciplined living, saints understand that it is not by indulging our appetites that the spirit is fed: rather, by starving the body the soul can truly "dine out." The Catholic theologian von Balthasar suggested that we find in the lives of heroic saints "some quality which particularly attracts us so that we penetrate more deeply into the meaning of holiness . . . [in them] the divine quality of *being* . . . harbours boundless interior riches."[12]

9. **Practice of prayer:** Prayer is the habit of holy lives. "Prayer . . . is our response to [the] God who speaks to us in every moment of our existence."[13] Prayer is not a waste of time, in the sense that one says one's prayers for want of something better to do. Rather, saints say their prayers expectantly, lovingly, worshipfully, knowing full well that prayer is their spiritual lifeline to God. The oft-repeated "Our Father" of the Lord's Prayer and the "We believe" of the Creed demonstrate that prayer is the essence of the spiritual life. They also are prayers and confessions that unite believers in a common mode of practice—the practice of prayer. Jesus sweated drops of blood as he prayerfully submitted himself to God in the garden, preparing for the cross. Only one who prays truly belongs to Christ. At times, the Christian spiritual life can certainly feel like a "peak experience," where all ground is holy, where every bush burns, and where God's fingerprints can be seen everywhere. However, there are times when the practice of prayer can seem barren, when the heavens are as brass and God appears to be absent. It is at those times, when prayer seems to be hardest and most pointless, that it is most needful to pray. And when it comes to prayer,

---

12. Von Balthasar, *Thérèsa of Liseaux*, xvi.
13. *Glenstal Book of Daily Prayer*, 7.

Gregory Collins reminds the faithful to "Pray as you can, not as you can't."[14]

10. **An eternal perspective:** Saints look at the world through the lens of a "baptized imagination." Seen from this eternal, "God's-eye" point of view, every human heart is a homing device whose default setting is to seek out God—even if we sometimes choose to rebel against that instinct. When Jesus taught his disciples to pray, "Your kingdom come, your will be done, on earth as it is in heaven," he was inviting them to look at the world from a God's-eye point of view. Cherith Fee Nordling tells the story of the time when, as a girl of fifteen, on her way home from school, she came into her father's office to accompany him home for dinner. Her father was Gordon Fee, Professor of New Testament at Regent College in Vancouver, Canada. On walking into his office, she saw no one behind his desk, but heard movement and went to explore. She found her father lying on the floor, weeping. When she asked him what was wrong, he replied, "Nothing's wrong. I'm just overwhelmed by the love of God for me and for the world!" He had been preparing a Bible study for class the next day, and had been overcome by the awe and wonder of it all.[15]

11. **Readiness to resist evil:** Saints are called to resist evil. Jesus spent a great deal of his ministry confronting evil. Sometimes the evil he opposed was in the form of evil spirits (for example, in Luke 4:33 when he drove out a demon from a man who was possessed), or sometimes it involved putting right the structural sins of society (for example, in John 8:1–11 when forgiving and defending the woman caught in adultery), or sometimes evil in the guise of distorted religious practices (for example, in Matthew 21:12–17 when Jesus overturned the tables of the money changers in the temple, and reclaimed the temple as a house of prayer). The Apostle Paul exhorted his readers in Rome to "not be overcome by evil, but to overcome evil with goodness" (Rom 12:21). Usually, goodness manifests itself in the world through the consecrated lives of holy people who have placed themselves under the protection and guidance of God. Adopting an eternal perspective by seeing things from God's point of view is a powerful reference point when approaching the question of evil. Saints fight evil with

---

14. Collins, *Come and Receive Light*, 45.
15. Nordling, Barry Chant Annual Lecture, Tabor Adelaide, June 24, 2014.

The Qualities Embedded in Saintly Lives

the weapons of righteousness, through their customary acts of justice, mercy, integrity, and purity. By these means evil is "caught out" and confronted. In J. R. R Tolkien's *Lord of the Rings*, the great evil of the power-hungry Lord Sauron is overcome by the most unlikely of heroes—a small band of insignificant hobbits, on account of their humility and down-to-earth, everyday goodness. The biblical principle that "He that is in you is greater that he that is in the world" (1 John 4:4) enables Christians to confront evil in all its forms, wherever it may be found.

12. **Forgiving one's enemies:** Saints are called to forgive their enemies. Jesus' prayer as he was being crucified was, "Father forgive them for they do not know what they are doing" (Luke 23:34). Christians are to forgive one another, to love their enemies, and to "turn the other cheek" (Matt 5:39)—all of which are radical, counterintuitive, and deeply subversive acts. This is why saints are defined as "radical altruists."[16] Although forgiveness comes at inestimable cost, the pardoning of one's enemies (those who have harmed us through violence, theft, murder, rape, or character assassination) emasculates the power of the perpetrator and empowers victims, enabling them to take charge of their lives. The South African Truth and Reconciliation Commission, chaired by Archbishop Desmond Tutu, was set up in the mid-1990s to enable reconciliation between black victims of apartheid and their white oppressors. The Commission was vital in enabling healing for those affected, and was explicitly based on the principle of forgiveness as a pathway towards reconciliation—forgiveness not simply for individuals but for the whole nation of South Africa. This represents an example of the principles of Christian teaching played out at the level of national life, whereby the hard and painful process of reconciliation has been made possible, leading towards a new South Africa whose goal is to provide a "homeland" for all its peoples, regardless of race, religion, political persuasion, and aspirations.

In Praise of Saints

Search as one might, there are few people who have the convictions, moral fortitude, or community will to embody the kinds of qualities we have

---

16. Wyschogrod, *Saints and Post-Modernism*, 58.

outlined above. Yet these twelve qualities are frequently found embedded in the lives of ordinary saints—as both sought-after values, and as real-life qualities which are actualized by way of attitudes, actions, and primary relationships.

Discussing what authentic Christianity looks like, the German theologian Jürgen Moltmann identified two non-negotiable baseline realities. The first is the supremacy and Lordship of Jesus Christ over the church and human history. And the second is the significance of a confessing faith community that "lives out" the implications of their confession in the everyday world. Wherever people confess that Jesus Christ is Lord, there is living faith. Where this is doubted or denied or rejected, there is no true faith. Christianity is alive as long as there are people who confess with the disciples and with the women—with Martha (John 11) and with Peter (Matt 16): "You are the Christ, the Son of the living God."[17]

As I have tried to show in this chapter, there is something absolutely beautiful about saints. The qualities they manifest in their lives relate directly to the beauty of the kingdom of God, because their lives are deeply congruent with the life of Jesus himself, with those who heralded the faith in the earliest periods of Christianity, and the best of Christian faith and practice in the intervening periods of history. There would be no such things as Christianity if there were no saints.

---

17. Lonergan, *Subject*, 3.

The Qualities Embedded in Saintly Lives

In Praise of Saints—by Stuart Devenish

Saints are usually the ones doing the praising
finding words for spirit-matter come down from heaven
and for triune Persons whose origins are glorious
. . . hallelujah, adoration, worship, glory, honor.

But saints are themselves ordinary miracles in whose persons
there has sprung forth amazing forms of life
that are heaven-sent, blood-bought, love-born, mercy-full
. . . that wise onlookers think worthy of praising.

Simple acts of kindness like Jesus taught in his day
regarding the good Samaritan who shocked his onlookers
by his unexpected act of compassion on a fellow traveler
. . . spirit-kindnesses carried in the acts of ordinary persons.

There is in saints' lives a transforming power
goodly of heart, lovely in words, kindly in deeds,
divine qualities enfleshed in a kind of second incarnation
in saints who spend their tears sanctifying the earth
. . . for the love of God and the hope of a better world.

There are times when it is right to wonder
whether saints in all their frailty
are not worthy of the kind of recognition we give to
the heroes of our race whose deeds cause amazement
. . . and praise the saints whose lives reflect paradise in a lesser key.

5

Saints as Persons

living breathing sanctity

"To touch another human soul is to stand on holy ground" (William B. Yates).

Nadia's Face[1]

Faculty and staff were invited to take part in a relationship-building exercise designed to help us see things from the other person's point of view. We were invited to pair up with someone we hadn't connected with during in the previous year. We were to arrange our chairs so that their backs touched one another and, straddling our chairs, were to look our partners directly in the face. At first it sounded simple... but we soon realized how difficult it was to look into another person's eyes for a whole four minutes at point-blank range!

I could tell from the first moment I would remember this encounter for a long time. Nadia and I sat opposite each other. Embarrassment tingled through our bodies. In everyday life we might rub shoulders with strangers on a train or in an elevator—but there is never a time when we are forced to look at such close proximity into the face of another person with whom we are not intimately acquainted. Our discomfort was increased by the fact that we were of the opposite sexes. Our faces were so close we could feel each other's breath and smell each other's body aroma. Uncomfortable

---

1. This event took place at the 2012 annual staff retreat held by Australian College of Ministries, Noonaweena Conference Center, New South Wales. Nadia's name has been changed to protect her identity. Used with permission.

laughter from the other twenty people in the room told us we weren't the only ones feeling embarrassed.

I looked into Nadia's large brown eyes, and quickly fell in. At such close proximity four minutes can seem like an eternity. Without saying so, we realized how vulnerable we both were. Like it or not, nothing we did or said at that moment could help us escape from this group bonding session. Our jobs depended on it! We tried dealing with our awkwardness by talking about the color of each other's eyes. Then we fell strangely silent, but our eyes did their own talking. Nadia's eyes smiled at me. Her gaze conveyed the "I see you" that became the trademark of James Cameron's *Avatar* movie. "I see you, I recognize you, I value you." Seeing myself through her eyes was wonderfully freeing, even energizing. But it was also enormously confronting. What was it about this encounter that deeply humbled me, but at the same time grew me into something larger than I felt myself to be?

Over the long minutes that followed, I felt my consciousness shifting. First, I observed Nadia's outward appearance: her Asian almond eyes, her high cheekbones, her petite nose, full lips, and symmetrical chin. Next, I observed the *real* person behind the appearances. I thought to myself, "Who is this mysterious person? Why haven't I noticed her like this before?" I confess there have been times in my life when I have been completely undone by encounters with other people just like this one. Times like when I have been intimate with my wife, when I saw my children being born, when I watched my father die, when I cradled the crumpled body of my stillborn nephew in my arms, or when a young woman washed my feet. In each of these moments something happened that conveyed the fragility *and* the preciousness of human life. And it happened again in this moment. In the great circle of life, we are inexorably bound to each other in some mysterious way. I came to understand that my own existence takes its significance from such encounters with other people. John Donne was right to say that no man, woman, or child is an island. We belong to each other and take our identities from the relationships that bind us together. It is moments like these that make us human.

By now all sense of time had vanished. My breathing had slowed, and I found myself staring through Nadia's eyes into the mysterious dimensions of her soul. How wonderful and how vulnerable it made me feel to have her look so deeply into my being. I felt she was able to see the *real* me. At that moment it was hard to know whether she was my mother who had given birth to me, or my lover who had touched my inner being. What I saw in this person before me represented the summit of everything that was good about every human person—the dignity, beauty, wisdom, intelligence, and mystery of humanity itself. Surely, the psalmist was right when he said we are "fearfully and wonderfully made" (Ps 139:14). To this day I remain shaken and exhilarated by my encounter with Nadia, whose life and pure existence thrilled me to my core.

Reflecting further on my encounter with Nadia, I discovered that what was most transforming about that moment of uninterrupted engagement was the exquisiteness of meeting another person in their total humanness. We are so used to stereotyping other people we rarely give them a second thought—their due consideration. As such, we don't *see* them as they truly are. We pass over them as if they don't even exist. But when we take the time to truly *see* other people for who and what they are in their truest nature, we discover a wild and passionate beauty in the other person's life that is—dare I say it—*godlike*!

Christianity and Persons

Saint Bede's Anglican Church is located in Semaphore, South Australia. The church was established in 1878 as people settled the strip of land to the north of the burgeoning city of Adelaide (founded in 1836). The beautiful dry-stone church building was erected and the Rev. George H. Farr was installed as the first minister in the parish. A parish school followed soon afterwards, and over the next 140 years, the life of the congregation grew alongside its flourishing host community.

Saint Bede's is named after an early English monk (672–735), also known as the "Venerable Bede." St. Bede is an important figure in Western Christianity. His book *The Ecclesiastical History of the English People* (first published in 731) provides a significant early record of the British Isles. The *History* chronicles the life and times of kings, queens, bishops, priests, saints, and ordinary people. Many churches have been named after Saint Bede, whose example reminds us that the history of Christianity is the history of its people. And this is the point of me telling you the story of St. Bede's Anglican Church. It is more than the story of an institution: rather, it is the story of a community—a community of believing, confessing, sanctified *persons*.

During its 140-year history, the congregation as Saint Bede's has seen something in the order of 6,928 people baptized, 900 confirmed, hosted

2,765 weddings, and many hundreds who have attended its Sunday school, its Mothers' Union, or have been led through its doors into various forms of Christian ministry. Seven people have entered the priesthood or orders from its congregation, and two have become overseas cross-cultural missionaries. Brass plaques on the walls of the sanctuary memorialize the faith of its people. For example, a window depicting St. Augustine, Bishop of Hippo in North Africa (354–430) was installed in memory of William Alexander Swan, rector of the church from 1901–1918; a brass lamp celebrates the life of Major Beresford Campbell of the 12th Bengal Cavalry (d. 1929); the ornately carved pulpit is dedicated to the memory of George Woollcombe Sillifant (d. 1897) and Harriet Sullivan (d. 1930); the John the Baptist window is dedicated to H. C. Roy Martin (1907–1990), mayor of the city of Port Adelaide (1969–1987), bearing the inscription "Devoted husband of Merle'"; the window dedicated to St. Oswald (633–655) is in memory of John Ainsworth Horrocks (1887–1918), who died in France in the Great War; and the Children's Window is in loving memory of Jane Marshall Gibbon (d. 1923), bearing the inscription, "Thy children rise up and call thee blessed" (Prov 31:28, KJV).

The memorial garden outside the church building continues the practice—begun in medieval times—of burying the bodies of the "faithful departed" on sacred ground within the churchyard. In this instance, the bodies have been cremated or buried in nearby community cemeteries, but are nonetheless "memorialized" through nameplates. Just some of those who are remembered are: Edith (Aileen) Salmon (1930–2007) with the words, "In God's loving care"; David Hassold (1925–2013), with the words "Blessed are the pure in heart for they will see God" (Matt 5:8); Elsie Maude Dee Pretty (1919–2001), with the words "With her Lord"; Beatrice Helliwell (1922–2010), with the words "Forever in our hearts"; and Craig Ross Prouse (1948–1994), with the words "Nothing can separate us from the love of God" (Rom 8:39).

Today the incumbent priest at Saint Bede's is Rev. Ken Bechaz, a motorcycle-riding priest and long-term chaplain to people living with the effects of relationship breakdown, mental illness, dementia, and family violence. The ruling archbishop of the Adelaide diocese is Jeffrey Driver. Jeffrey was formerly the director of the St. Mark's National Theological Centre in Canberra, and has served as archbishop of the Anglican diocese of Adelaide since 2005.

This astonishing list of names rehearses the fact that it is saintly people who are indispensable to the continuity of the Christian faith. From its earliest beginning, the history of Christianity has been the story of its saints. It should therefore come as no surprise that the faith community at Saint Bede's can be represented through the names, lives, and testimonies of the various men and women who—in their own times and places—found Christ to be sufficient for their lives.

Christianity is deeply interested in persons. All the great doctrines that form the substance of Christian confession are directly engaged with the dual concerns of the *nature* of persons and the *relationships* between persons. Take, for example, the doctrine of the Trinity. The classical statement concerning the triune nature of God is found in the Nicene Creed, which begins, "We believe in one God, the Father, the Almighty . . . ." It continues, "We believe in one Lord, Jesus Christ, the only Son of God . . . ." And it concludes, "We believe in the Holy Spirit, the Lord, the giver of life . . . ." The doctrine of the Trinity is the professed conviction of the Christian Church that God is three persons in one, as Father, Son, and Spirit. The question of how God can be divided into the three "persons" and yet retain the unity of his Being is not easily understood. But the abiding interest of those who make their confession, "We believe . . ." is the mystery that God graciously makes his intra-trinitarian love that exists between the Father, Son, and Spirit freely available to those persons who make him the object of their affections. For Christians, God is the personal being *par excellence*, who makes his entrance into the world not "as an idea but as a living person."[2] The same God asserts himself "as a personality among all others, and he creates our own selves . . . as truly conscious personalities endowed with self-mastery."[3] The Christian understanding of salvation is that persons form the bedrock of our faith.

Or take as a second example the doctrine of Christology. Readers of the Gospels discover many accounts of the historical human being, Jesus of Nazareth, healing the sick, feeding the hungry, and calling his disciples to follow him. Yet, following his crucifixion, the early Christians made a point of confessing "Jesus Christ is Lord" (Phil 2:11), ascribing the elevated status of divinity to his being. This tension between the human Jesus and the divine Christ invites worshippers to reflect on the dual aspects of the nature of Jesus the Christ. Christology attempts to unpack and help make sense of

2. Bouyer, *Introduction to Spirituality*, 8.
3. Ibid., 9.

this apparent tension. Asserting his humanity, the Nicene Creed declares, "He (Jesus Christ) was incarnate . . . became truly human . . . suffered death and was buried." But it equally asserts his divinity, stating, "(he was) raised on the third day . . . ascended into heaven and is seated at the right hand of the Father. He will come again in glory to judge the living and the dead and his kingdom will have no end." As the Son of God, Jesus is "God from God, Light from Light, and true God from true God . . . of one being with the Father." Thus, allegiance to the person of Jesus, understood as both true God and true human being, was *the* central concern of the fledgling Christian community. It was the Apostle Peter who famously confessed, "You are the Christ, the Son of the living God" (Matt 16:16). And in today's contemporary churches, wherever they may be found around the world, *the* central concern of Christians continues to be this most personal encounter with the one true living God. So it is that Eugene Peterson cautions: "When the church fails to embrace the divinity of Jesus as its own imputed divinity . . . it betrays its core identity as Christ's body. And when the church fails to embrace the humanity of Jesus as its own humanity . . . it betrays its core identity as a dwelling place for God."[4] The Christian understanding of salvation is that faith in Jesus as the Christ forms the bedrock of our faith.

Or take a third example, the doctrine of redemption. The Christian use of the word "redemption" has three specific applications. The first is an *economic* one, where a ransom price is paid in order to pay a debt. In this sense, the end result is the removal of a debt through restitution. And it is Jesus, who through his voluntary embrace of the cross, made restitution by "purchasing men [humankind] for God" (Rev 5:9). The second application of the term is a *relational* one, where persons who previously found themselves in a broken relationship with God, self, and others are now restored into a right relationship with God, self and others. In this sense, the end result of redemption is reconciliation and restoration. The Christian understanding of salvation is that Jesus "loved us and gave himself for us" (Eph 5:2). And the third application is a *positional* one, whereby a sinner's "debt" is "paid up" by another, thus restoring their status or reputation. In this sense, redeemed people are able to return to living complete lives as citizens of the society in which they live, out of the full potential of their humanity. In this instance, the end result is righteousness. The Christian understanding of salvation is that a "righteousness from God comes through faith in Jesus Christ to all those who believe" (Rom 3:21).

4. Peterson, *Practise Resurrection*, 151.

Ordinary Saints

In each case, it is persons—both divine and human—who are the point of focus. The great doctrines that form the basis of Christian confession are directly concerned with the *nature* of persons and *relationships* among persons. This personalist element of Christian teaching is duly acknowledged by those who make their confession: "I believe . . ." (the Apostles' Creed), and "We believe . . ." (the Nicene Creed). Faith that is trustworthy and authentic is always the action of a personal agent who is free, conscious, and willing to act out their belief through the agency of their lives. Many people emphasize doctrines, beliefs, and formulas as the core of the Christian faith. Yet an equal and corresponding emphasis must also be placed on those who confess, believe, and profess their faith, and the significance of their believing in Christ, expressed through their everyday thoughts, words, and deeds.

> Wherever people confess that Jesus is the Christ of God, there is living faith. Where this is doubted or denied or rejected, there is no faith. Christianity is alive as long as there are people who confess with the disciples and the women—with Martha (John 11) and Peter (Matthew 16)—'You are the Christ, the Son of the living God', people who in his discipleship spread and live the Gospel'.[5]

Yet—even after all that—there are still those who want to say with the eighteenth-century Irish writer, James Joyce, "There is no heresy or no philosophy which is so abhorrent to the church as a human being."[6] But we have already seen how central persons are to the Christian faith. Christianity is not interested in denying or repressing the humanity of those who enter into the relationships it offers. In fact the exact opposite is true. Christianity, as a religion that focuses on persons, seeks to enlarge and transform the lives of its adherents, helping them to become more—not less—fully human. If Christ has come to give us "life, and life to the full" (John 10:10), the purpose of faith in Christ is not to erase the true nature of persons, but to restore the redeemed human person to his or her original (creational) image. It is in the lives of saints, as persons, that salvation takes root and grows into something beautiful for God. According to Peter Kreeft, "Saints

---

5. Moltmann, *Way of Jesus Christ*, 39.

6. By which he meant he felt he was not able to express himself fully in the face of the stern demands of his mother, and the moral constraints imposed by the Roman Catholic Church. He determined to leave Ireland for good and live in Paris as a free being able to choose how he lived. See Bloom, ed., *James Joyce*.

are not freaks or exceptions, they are the standard operating model for human beings."[7]

On Being Human Persons

When it comes to the question of how we become fully human, the Judeo-Christian religion adopts a different perspective to that of modern-day thinkers. Anthropologists—for example—describe the development of the human species in terms of a series of historical "ages," including the Neanderthal age, the ice age, the stone age, the bronze age, the copper age, the iron age, and—in our own time—the space age. But in the Judeo-Christian vision of history, there are only three "moments" that matter. First creation, when humanity is *made*. Second the fall, when humanity is put out of relationship with God and so becomes *unmade*. And third redemption, when humanity is *remade* following Jesus' atonement of sin by means of his death on the cross. In each case, what is in view is relationships between persons: divine and divine, divine and human, human and human. And history in the Judaeo-Christian tradition is not so much conceived of as evolutionary (understood as steps of incremental improvement over time amounting to inevitable positive "progress"), but as covenantal (understood as invitation into relationship with God and our fellow human creatures, leading to the fulfilment of our created, i.e., divinely appointed, destiny).

The account of creation—or the *making* of human persons—is located in the Genesis record. "And God said, 'Let us make human beings in our image, in our likeness, so that they may rule . . . . So God created human beings in his own image, in the image of God he created them; male and female he created them'" (Gen 1:26-27 TNIV). In this account of the origins of the human species, humans occupy a unique place in the created order. First they are given authority to rule over the garden, second they are created in God's image (*imago Dei*), and third they are created for the purpose of having a relationship with God. From the moment they are made, human beings have the potential to become more than their biology allows for, because they have the capacity to participate in a relationship with God *and* to become (in some as-yet unspecified way) *like* God. This ability to converse with God and to have a share in his divine life is mysteriously "planted" within redeemed humans as a part of their call to rule the earth as co-regents with God.

7. Kreeft, "What is a Saint?"

The account of the fall—or the *unmaking* of human persons—is recorded in Genesis 3. There, Adam and Eve (the first humans) were given the freedom to eat and enjoy every fruit in the garden, except the fruit of the tree of the knowledge of good and evil. Seduced by the Tempter, they were deceived and so ate of the fruit of the tree of the knowledge of good and evil, in contravention of God's command. There are many moments of human rebellion recounted in the Bible. In every case, it is humanity's wilful rejection of God's gracious invitation into meaningful relationship that brings it undone, a pattern repeated since the time of the fall. At its source, the cause of the fall is a reckless, self-centered, and misconceived human project that attempts to replace God's rightful rule over humankind with a self-sufficient project which seeks to displace God's kingdom with the kingdom of human self-sufficiency. G. K. Chesterton[8] observed that the doctrine of original sin is the only doctrine that is wholly provable—one need simply consult the history books, or examine one's conscience to find proof for this claim. Anger, hatred, murder, rape, violence, destruction, war, addiction, greed, desire, envy, sloth, jealousy, and every other vice—these are what characterize fallen humanity. Likewise, Evelyn Underhill wrote, "We mostly spend (our) lives conjugating three verbs: to *want*, to *have*, and to *do*. Craving, clutching, and fussing, on the material, political, social, emotional and intellectual—even the religious plane—we are kept in perpetual unrest."[9] Wickedness is so widespread and deep-seated in the human heart that it can be observed at will not only in the lives of everyone around us but also in our own lives.

Like the fall, the biblical account of redemption—or the *remaking* of human persons—can be found throughout both Testaments. In the Old Testament, God's commission to Abraham to leave his country, his people, and his father's household, marks the beginning of God's redemptive program in human history (Gen 12). Through Abraham, God promised to call a "great nation" into being—a nation whose life and faith would be instrumental in his provision of blessing to "all the peoples of the earth" (Gen 12:3). In the New Testament, in light of Jesus' death and subsequent resurrection, the Apostle John speaks of Jesus in similar terms: as "purchasing men [humankind] for God from every tribe and language and people and nation. You have made them to be a kingdom of priests to serve our God and they will reign on the earth" (Rev 5:9–10).

8. Chesterton, *Orthodoxy*, 7.
9. Underhill, *Spiritual Life*, 18.

In his epistles, the Apostle Paul explored the characteristics of the "new humanity" that has been redeemed and set free from the law, from sin, death, and the condemnation of guilt. The "old life" was one of slavery to sin where we "used to offer the parts of our bodies in slavery to impurity and ever-increasing wickedness" (Rom 6:19), where humanity was trapped in a downward spiral of captivity to its sinful nature: "Wretched man that I am! Who will rescue me from this body of death?" (Rom 7:24). But, Paul goes on, "If anyone is in Christ, he is a new creation; the old has gone, the new has come" (2 Cor 5:17). Romans 7 describes what we so often are, but Romans 8 describes what Christ has made us to become—controlled not by the sinful nature but by the Spirit to become sons and daughters of God (Rom 8:14). Redeemed humanity belongs to God twice over: firstly by creation, and secondly by redemption. "Redemption brings about a re-creation in order to correct the fall, linking physical and existential wholeness with spiritual, ethical and relational holiness."[10]

Christian spirituality has a unique way of understanding what it means to be human persons in the world, created in the image of God, and then restored, redeemed, and re-created in the image of Jesus Christ the Son of God. We were not designed to be disobedient, corrupted, depraved, degenerate, and reprobate beings. On the contrary, we were created to be in relationship with God and to rise to the level of the full potential of our humanity, which is Christlikeness: "Jesus was man as God intended him to be."[11]

Our discussion of what it means to be human persons, thus far, has laid the groundwork for identifying a series of benchmarks for clarifying what it means to be a human person. I want to suggest that—from the Christian point of view—there are seven key aspects of human personhood. They are: dignity, freedom, beauty, value, necessity, mystery, and reality.

1. Dignity: When the words *human* and *dignity* are joined together, they denote the ultimate value of every human person. From the Christian point of view, because we are made in the image of God (*imago Dei*)—and because God is ultimate in his being—we have a share in his dignity. Regardless of gender, race, religion, [dis]ability, sexual orientation, or social status, every human being is an eternal, sub-sovereign image-bearer of God, who is the ultimate Person or

---

10. Devenish, *Seeing and Believing*, 89.
11. Spader, *Walking as Jesus Walked*, 39.

Being. The United Nations' Universal Declaration of Human Rights presupposes the inherent dignity of each human being as the basis for international peace, built upon an understanding of certain "inalienable rights" belonging to human persons. From the Christian point of view, to infringe the rights and dignity of persons is not only to contravene the law of the land, but is an affront to God himself. "The human being is a kind of second world . . . placed on the earth, another angel, a composite worshipper . . . . Transitory and immortal, visible and intelligible, a mean between greatness and lowliness. He is at once spirit and flesh."[12]

2. Freedom: Freedom is an essential condition of human dignity. Relationships can only be said to be authentic when there is a mutual giving and receiving between the parties that is based upon a freedom that is readily given and completely un-coerced. To that extent, freedom is the precondition of love, and the context in which loving relationships unfold. In the Western world, our consumer economy offers its citizens a form of "radical" freedom that situates free choice in the consumer. The danger however, is that unlimited and unguided freedom—offered without moral restraint—allows us to make choices that have the potential to place our dignity at risk. In everyday life, eating the wrong foods can be hazardous to our health, drinking excessive amounts of alcohol causes us to act in undignified ways, or taking illicit drugs can lead to harm and addiction. In the moral and spiritual arenas, using our God-given freedom to choose against God, represents sin in its worst form. Using the freedom God has given us to choose "against" him betrays the fundamental trust God needed to place in us if we were ever to choose freely for him. Merely making us automatons that are internally wired to "love" God is no kind of love at all. Love is only true love when it is freely given by the lover to the Beloved.

3. Beauty: The philosopher Raimond Gaita—while denying that humanity was created by God—nevertheless describes the human species as "infinitely precious", "sacred", "unique", and "irreplaceable". He identified his moment of "conversion" when he realized the "humanity" of his fellow human beings.[13] My encounter with Nadia, recounted at the

---

12. Harrison, *God's Many-Splendored Image*, 130.
13. Wynn, "Saintliness and the Moral Life," 476.

beginning of this chapter, confronted me with a similar realization of the astonishing and overwhelming beauty of someone "other" than myself. What was most transforming about that moment of uninterrupted being was the exquisiteness of meeting another person in their total humanness. When we take the time to *see* other people for what they are in their truest nature, there is a wild and passionate beauty about another person's life that is—dare I say it—*godlike!* This is especially the case in those touching moments when we notice a baby's innocence, a couple in a loving embrace, or an elderly person's joyful response to life. In his apostolic exhortation *Evangelii Gaudium*, Pope Francis encouraged Christians to foster a renewed "esteem for beauty" because beauty can awaken the human heart to God who is the one in all creation who is most truly beautiful.

4. Value: Joseph Stalin was wrong when he said, "The death of one man is a tragedy. The death of millions is a statistic." And Jean-Paul Sartre, in his play *No Exit*, was wrong to suggest that "Hell is other people." People are infinitely valuable because—in the face of death, meaninglessness, and despair—they are able to love, laugh, and flourish, even as they cling precariously to life on the rim of existence. The Danish philosopher Søren Kierkegaard explored the theme of truth as subjectivity, and living before God through fear and trembling. Only the human person with the capacity for freedom can choose to live a life that is authentic and "proper" to the human condition. Value is another way of expressing the dignity, mystery, and beauty of the human person. Human beings are not only created in the image of God, but we share with him (admittedly in limited ways) something of his eternity and his magnificence. Human persons are of inestimable value, so whenever a curtailment of someone's humanity takes place through imprisonment, torture, disability, and death—the universe is somehow poorer for it. This truth is borne out in a powerful way when exemplary human persons such as saints, mystics, and prophets, risk their lives for others—and pay a high price for doing so.

5. Necessity: Left to ourselves without the consolation of God's loving presence, we are less than what we are created to become. "Where there is no God there is no man. Man without God is no longer man."[14] It is clear that humanity needs God if it is to achieve its God-ordained

---

14. Berdyaev, cited in Baillie, *Our Knowledge of God*, 42.

destiny. And it is also clear that humanity needs exceptional exemplars of authentic humanness in the form of saints and holy persons to set the benchmark for novice humans to strive towards as a measure of moral, spiritual, and vocational development. But in addition, humanity forms an indispensable part of God's purpose and plan in creation. How so? First, because God's desire is to create, and to create in his likeness. Second, because his desire is to love and to embrace to his breast that which he has made. And third, because while God cannot be known as he is, in the mystery of his being, yet nevertheless he can be known indirectly through his works. The highest form and most easily observed of his works is the saint, who is "being transformed into the image [of the glory of the Lord] from one degree of glory to another" (2 Cor 3:18).

6. Mystery: No human person is able to understand themselves completely. We are a deep mystery to ourselves. It was St. Augustine who asked, "What, then, am I, my God? Of what nature am I? A life various, and manifold and exceedingly vast."[15] For Augustine, finding an answer to the question of his own identity meant interrogating his existence. "You, who are you?" [i.e., himself]. And he responded, "A human being."[16] In her lessons on photography, Pat Koehler observed, "We are called to openness, and sin is the closing off of ourselves to mystery. Closing ourselves to mystery is the closing of ourselves to God."[17] An admission of mystery concerning ourselves and the very lives we lead, sends us on a quest to find who it is that speaks to us in the dark—this God who addresses us and calls us by name. "God comes to us disguised as our life."[18] Our own sense of need, wonder, terror, desire, passion, and surprise is what leads us to recognize God's voice, calling in the garden, "Adam and Eve, where are you?" and again, in person, as Jesus invites us to "Come, follow me!"

7. Reality: Humanity is impermanent. Like the grass it "withers and fades" (1 Pet 2:24), and the memory of one generation does not endure to the next. Yet we are moral and spiritual creatures who were created for an eternal relationship with God. As a result, we have a

---

15. Augustine, *Confessions*, 219.
16. Ibid., 207.
17. Zehr, *Little Book of Contemplative Photography*, 35.
18. D'Arcy, in Rohr, *Falling Upward*, 66

share in his eternity. Richard Rohr has observed that the "path of spirituality is an awakening to the reality that we are neither God nor human, but both at the same time."[19] History as a narrative rehearsal of past events is punctuated by the life stories of men and women who have performed their character and faith in the past, in such a way that they shape and influence the present (not to mention the future). History would not exist as we know it today without those cultural, religious, and political heroes who have left their "notch" on the stick of time. To that extent, the present moment springs forth from the heroic imaginings of yesterday's people, who lived their lives not accidentally but intentionally towards making their tomorrow (our present) a better time and place. Human beings always dream of a better world, and imagine themselves as participating in it . . . even if there is no certainty of them doing so. "If man is that being who asks the question of being, he has and has not the being for which he asks."[20] Thus, humans are not transient creatures who are irrelevant to history, rather they are necessary to the making of a real world in the here and now, for the sake of those to come. Persons are "objective entities"[21] on which the social, political, economic, and religious future is built. The irony of all this is that it is the "passing parade" of temporal human beings who lay down footsteps of history which are real, and not merely imagined.

It was C. S. Lewis who penned these foundational words:

> There are no ordinary people. You have never talked to a mere mortal. Nations, cultures, arts, civilizations—these are mortal, and their life is to ours as the life of a gnat. But it is immortals whom we joke with, work with, marry, snub and exploit—immortal horrors or everlasting splendors. This does not mean that we are to be perpetually solemn. We must play. But our merriment must be of that kind (and it is, in fact, the merriest kind) which exists between people who have, from the outset, taken each other seriously—no flippancy, no superiority, no presumption.[22]

---

19. Rohr, *Immortal Diamond*, xiv.
20. Tillich, *Biblical Religion*, 35.
21. Wojtyla, *Love and Responsibility*, 23.
22. Lewis, *Weight of Glory*, 8.

Ordinary Saints

The Testament of Saints

The essence of true Christianity can be seen most clearly in the lives of its *saints*. Outside observers often assume (wrongly) that Christianity is defined by its big-C institutions, its gothic architecture, abstract theological doctrines, conservative moral teachings, or right-wing politics. But those things are only the by-products of faith. The real genius of Christianity lies in its ability to transform people's lives from the inside out and to change the character of the human heart from that of a self-centered sinner to a God-centered saint.

There is a remarkable history of experiential religion that comes to light in Christian history. In the Old Testament Scriptures we find Abraham leaving Ur, Moses carrying stone tablets, Sarah laughing aloud, Job suffering intensely, Esther advocating for her people, Jacob wrestling with the angel, Samuel listening to God, David dancing for joy, Daniel praying in the lion's den, Jeremiah lamenting, and Amos prophesying new things. In the New Testament Scriptures we find Mary marveling at the visitation of the angel Gabriel, James and John leaving their fishing nets, Zacchaeus inviting Jesus to his house, the disciples listening to Jesus' teaching, Peter confessing "You are the Christ," Stephen being stoned for his testimony, scales falling from Paul's eyes, Lydia being baptized, and Timothy leading the first churches of believers.

With the closure of the biblical record we might expect this remarkable history of experiential religion to come to a sudden end, never to be seen again. But it does not. In the subsequent 2,000 years of Christian history this remarkable narration of experiential religion continues unabated. In the earliest history of Christianity we see Perpetua being martyred, Justin defending the early Christian movement, Clement preaching, Antony teaching, Augustine writing his *Confessions,* Irenaeus ruling as a bishop, and Patrick evangelizing Ireland. In the middle history of Christianity we see Anselm renewing the faith of the church, Julian of Norwich searching out the mysteries of God, Teresa of Avila writing her "interior castle" of the spiritual life, Francis of Assisi serving the poor, and St. John of the Cross traversing the dark night of the soul. And in the later period of Christian history we have John Wesley preaching to all of England, Hudson Taylor evangelizing across China, Dorothy Day advocating for the homeless and oppressed, Mother Teresa serving the poor on the streets of Calcutta, Archbishop Oscar Romero being martyred in El Salvador, and C. S. Lewis—the Oxford don and literary doyen—writing children's literature capable of "baptizing the imagination." Whenever Christianity becomes separated from the lived lives of everyday, ordinary people, it loses touch with the very means God intended to make a difference in the world.

But as George Orwell observed, "Many people genuinely do not want to be saints, and it is probable that some who achieve or aspire to sainthood have never felt much temptation to be human beings."[23] Yet for anyone who would turn their face towards God, paying careful attention to their humanity is essential. Such self-knowledge is a vital aspect of what it means to "work out your salvation with fear and trembling" (Phil 2:12). Maurice Friedman stated, "A person cannot approach the divine by reaching beyond the human. To become human, is what the individual person has been created for."[24] And John Stackhouse says it most fittingly when he states:

> The point of being a Christian is not to be a Christian, it is to be a properly functioning human being, and to help other people become properly functioning human beings. The more we can do that, the more we are 'imaging' what the whole point of the gospel is about.[25]

What all this highlights is the centrality of the lives of the saints to the life and witness of the church in our post-modern and post-Christian world. Apart from the inspired narratives of the Scriptures, God's continual providence in the world, and the deep but hidden work of the Holy Spirit in people's lives . . . there is no surer mechanism for transmitting the light of the gospel to the world than through the holy lives of saintly people. Saints' lives are revelatory insofar as they represent in their own persons the substance of their transformative encounter with Christ. As a result, saints' lives become a kind of "living gospel" that radiates through their relationships and dealings with others, and out into the world around them.

In his autobiography *The Seven Storey Mountain*, Thomas Merton recounts how he once told his friend Bob Lax that he wanted to become a good Catholic. "What you should say," said his friend in reply, "is that you must want to be a saint." As he reflected on his friend's reply, Merton wrote:

> A saint? The thought struck me as a little weird. I said: "How do you expect me to become a saint?" "By wanting to," said Lax, simply . . . all that is necessary to be a saint is to want to be one. Don't

---

23. Orwell, in Pai, "Orwell's Reflections on Saint Gandhi," 69.
24. Friedman, *Martin Buber and the Human Sciences*, 97.
25. Stackhouse, "Radical Doubt, Radical Faith."

you believe God will make you what he created you to be, if you consent to let him do it? All you have to do is desire it."[26]

The problem for each of us is essentially the same as that of Merton: *how to become a saint*. And this is where Merton's discussion of the "false self–true self" concept becomes really valuable. First, the "false self" is the person we think we need to present to the world, the person we want others to see—someone who is attractive, confident, and successful. And yet the "false self" is also deeply fearful, deeply aware of its flaws and failings. This ill-formed part of the person believes they have to be someone *else* if they are to be holy. This is the *inauthentic* self who takes the "easy" way out by desiring what others already possess, or arguing that it is impossible for them to become saints because of their excessive passions. But the "true self" is about discovering who we are before God, and accepting ourselves as being totally and utterly "loved by God" for who we are. "For me to be a Saint means to be myself," Merton wrote.[27] "God has made each of us uniquely ourselves, and holiness consists of discovering the true self, the person we are before God, accepting that person, and becoming a saint in the process."[28]

Only persons can be saints, because only persons are truly free to choose to be holy. When Jesus speaks to us, calling as by name to "Come, follow me", that is the moment to embrace him and to be embraced in return. And the way to make our response and to become saints is not to remove or obliterate our humanity, but rather to develop it in such a way that we become more properly human. This will require that our characters, actions, and personalities exemplify the kinds of actions and deeds that are central to the character of Jesus. As understood by a Christian anthropology, fighting against our sinful human nature is likely to be a lost cause because our passions and rebellious wills are set against God. But in light of the redemption won for us in Christ, and with the help of his Holy Spirit, a Christian is compelled (and we are by no means powerless in this) to seek to be "conformed to the image of [God's] Son" (Rom 8:29). By grace, saints choose to "bend" their lives to the will of God and so become living testimonies of the same grace that springs forth in the life of Jesus. Their lives are a form of "lived theology," the truth of which is extruded out through their lives in a glorious mixture of joy and pain, light and shadow, mystery and beauty.

26. Merton, *Seven Storey Mountain*, 238.
27. Ibid., 57.
28. Martin, *Becoming Who You Are*, 58.

Saints' testimonies are offered not simply through words but more powerfully in the form of the persons they become, the way they live their lives, their relationships with other human beings, and the kinds of human beings they themselves are growing into. Saints are a living, breathing sanctity that is more convincing than any other force or power we know.

The Faith of Etty Hillesum

Etty Hillesum (1914–1943) was born into a Dutch Jewish family in the town of Middelburg, in western Holland. She attended the school where her father was headmaster, along with her two younger brothers, Jacob and Michael. Her family was ethnically Jewish, but did not practice their religion. During her university years she studied Slavic languages and Russian in Amsterdam, mixing with left-wing, antifascist sympathizers. So when she turned to Christianity, later in her life, no one was more surprised than she was.

In March 1937, aged twenty-three, Etty became live-in housekeeper to an Amsterdam-based accountant named Hendrik Wegerif. She spent three years there before being transferred to Westerbork, the Nazi transit camp for Jewish detainees on their way from Netherlands to the extermination camps in Germany. It was in Westerbork that she wrote her letters and diaries which we now have in published form.[29]

Under Nazi occupation, the social and economic conditions became very difficult for Jewish families in Holland. Jews were forced to wear the yellow Star of David emblazoned on their tunics. Because of the repressive conditions, buying food, travelling on public transport, or attending social or religious events became impractical. When responsibility for the internment of Jews transitioned from the softer Dutch authorities to the harsher Nazi authorities, conditions became even more difficult. In 1942, Etty applied for a job at the Jewish Council and was appointed to do secretarial work. But she didn't enjoy the work and asked instead to be transferred as a social worker to the department of "Social Welfare for People in Transit" camp at Westerbork.

Life was difficult for Etty, as it was for everyone at that time. In her outer world, everything was chaotic and disordered. In June 1941, she wrote, "More arrests, more terror, concentration camps, the arbitrary dragging off of fathers, sisters, brothers. We seek the meaning of life, wondering

---

29. Smelik, ed., *Etty*.

whether any meaning can be left."³⁰ In her inner world, Etty was struggling to find herself. But possessed of a high-level intelligence and an unusually intense personality, she courageously launched herself into life . . . and love. She met a psychotherapist named Julius Spier, who had studied under Carl Jung. He was a gifted and charismatic figure who practiced chirology, a psychologically informed model of therapy based on palm reading. On meeting Julius Spier, Etty was impressed with his masculinity. She wrote telling him that she was sexually attracted to him, and there followed a passionate affair between them. For the first time she felt understood and accepted by another human being. But she was aware that she still had a lot of growing up to do. She wrote, "I simply need to do a lot of work on myself before I develop into an adult and a complete human being."³¹ Etty began writing a diary sometime in 1941, at the age of twenty-seven and most likely at Spier's encouragement.

From September 1941, as conditions around her grew more difficult, she discovered a contemplative faculty within herself. As she reflected on her experiences she learned to differentiate herself emotionally from Spier and others. She wrote, "My inner landscape consists of great, wide planes, infinitely wide, with hardly a horizon in sight—one plane merging into the next. As I sit huddled in this chair, my head bowed low, I roam across those bare plains."³² At that time, God became a part of her language, and she wrote, "I regained contact with myself, and the deepest and best in me, which I call God."³³ A new integration or *at-one-ness* became a part of her experience, where she sensed a deep connectedness with herself and all human beings. While ethnically a Jew, her religious upbringing had been distant from God, and she felt embarrassed about her early spiritual experiences. But now prayer—which she called "kneeling down"—became important for her. Initially she found herself unwilling to kneel in prayer, but did so increasingly out of a deep sense of her own need. She called herself a "kneeler in training", saying that the act of connecting with God was very intimate for her, "often more intimate even than sex."³⁴

Over the two-and-a-half years that Etty wrote her diary, there is clear evidence of enormous personal and spiritual growth, as she not only grew

---

30. Ibid., 62
31. Ibid., 3.
32. Ibid., 60.
33. Ibid., 83.
34. Ibid., 148.

closer to God as a part of the process of enlargement within her own soul, but as she became deeply aware of her own humanity and that of others around her. She became determined not to waste a single moment of her life. Despite there being many reasons to hate her German captors, she refused to give in to the ugliness of hatred. She tried hard to look into the souls of others, in order to find the deep-seated humanity hidden there. She wanted to "discover the small, naked human being amid the monstrous wreckage" of the senselessness of war.[35] Her attitude to Klaas, who worked for the Jewish Council and who oppressed his Jewish compatriots so cruelly, was not one of hate, but of pity. She wrote, "I should have liked to reach out to that man with all his fears, I should have liked to trace the source of his panic, to drive him ever deeper into himself . . . so as to destroy in himself all that he thinks he ought to destroy in others." She wrote—as if in dialogue with him—offering forgiveness and hope. There is "nothing but Christianity . . . . Yes, Christianity, and why ever not?"[36]

Etty's heart went out to the people of Westerbork. As people confided in her that they were full of fear and going out of their minds, she prayed to God, "Let me be the thinking heart of these barracks,"[37] and, "[I saw] the deadly fear in all those faces . . . . All those faces, my God, those faces! I hope to be a centre of peace in that madhouse."[38] Etty assisted in preparing young mothers and their babies for transport by rail from Westerbork to Auschwitz for extermination. She asked herself, "In what sort of fatal mechanism have we become enmeshed?"[39] And she also faced her own fear as she was confronted by the raw power of the uniformed guards. "My God, those faces! I looked at them, each in turn . . . and I have never been so frightened of anything in my life. I sink to my knees with the words that preside over human life: 'And God made man after His likeness.' That passage spent a difficult morning with me."[40]

What is especially noteworthy about Etty is her deep humanity, and her deep faith in God. Her willingness to embrace suffering and fear and death and dying with courage and conviction are overwhelming. One wonders whether we might have the courage to face it all as she did, and to

---

35. Ibid., 384.
36. Ibid., 528-29.
37. Ibid., 543.
38. Ibid., 496.
39. Ibid., 645.
40. Ibid., 644.

care as deeply for others—even as she stared her own death in the face. "I sometimes imagine that I long for the seclusion of a nunnery. But I know that I must seek You [God] among people, out in the world. And that is what I shall do, despite the weariness and dislike that sometimes overcomes me. I vow to live my life out there to the full."[41] Her deepest desire is to "rest against the naked breast of life"[42]—but she was torn too soon from life, and was sent to Auschwitz along with members of her family. In her diary she rehearsed how she would prepare herself for her last hours before being sent to the death chambers. She wrote of gathering what was left of her strength

> ... from every cranny of [my] body and soul. I would have my hair cut short and throw away my lipstick. I would try to finish reading the Rilke letters before the week was out ... I shall take a Bible along with that slim volume *Letters to a Young Poet*. I'll just take all the faces and familiar gestures I have collected and hang them up along the walls of my inner space so that they will always be with me. And these two hands will go along with me, their expressive fingers like strong young twigs. And these hands will keep protecting me in prayer and will not leave me till the end. And these dark eyes will go with me, and their benign gentle, questing look.[43]

According to Red Cross records, Etty Hillesum died in the gas chambers of Auschwitz on November 30, 1943. Although her friends tried to kidnap her out of Westerbork and away from the barbarity of Nazi imprisonment, Etty would have none of it. For her, remaining in the camp was a matter of solidarity not just with the Jewish community, but with all humankind.

Perhaps the deepest thing she discovered in her spiritual journey was that the secret of her life is interconnectedness. She came to see that she belonged to others, and others belonged to her. She had discovered that she truly only lived insofar as the deepest and best in her was in communion with the deepest and best in others. This is what she had learnt to "hearken to"—expressed in the German word she used, *hineinhorchen*, the meaning of which, when she uses it again towards the end of her diary, extends even further: "The most essential and the deepest in me hearkening unto the most essential and the deepest in the other."[44]

41. Ibid., 154.
42. Ibid., 386.
43. Ibid., 485–86.
44. Ibid., 519.

Saints as Persons

Invitation to Humanity from St. Clements' Church[45]

We extend a special welcome to those who are single, married, divorced, widowed, gay, confused, filthy rich, comfortable, or dirt poor. We extend a special welcome to those who are crying newborns, skinny as a rake or could afford to lose a few pounds. You're welcome if you are Old Leigh, New Leigh, Not Leigh, or just passing by.

We welcome you if you can sing like Pavarotti or can't carry a note in a bucket. You're welcome here if you're 'just browsing,' just woke up or just got out of prison. We don't care if you're more Christian than the Archbishop of Canterbury, or haven't been in church since little Jack's christening.

We extend a special welcome to those who are over 60 but not grown up yet, and to teenagers who are growing up too fast. We welcome keep-fit mums, football dads, starving artists, tree-huggers, latté-sippers, vegetarians and junk-food eaters. We welcome those who are in recovery or still addicted. We welcome you if you're having problems or you're down in the dumps or if you don't like 'organized religion.' We've been there too!

If you blew all your money on the horses, you're welcome here. We offer a welcome to those who think the earth is flat, 'work too hard,' don't work, can't spell, or because grandma is in town and wanted to go to church.

We welcome those who are inked, pierced or both. We offer a special welcome to those who could use a prayer right now, had religion shoved down your throat as a kid or got lost on the London Road and wound up here by mistake. We welcome tourists, seekers and doubters, bleeding hearts . . . and you!

---

45. Sign on the front door of Saint Clements church, Leigh-on-sea, Essex, England, online http://www.stclementschurch.org.uk/.

6

Bodies of Evidence

"Man is a spirit wrapped in flesh"
(Rémi Brague).

Madam Linda Watson

Linda's childhood was an unhappy one. Born into a dysfunctional family and sexually abused at the age of twelve, hers wasn't a good beginning. By the time she reached her upper teenage years she'd had several partners. At age twenty-three, Linda found herself unemployed and living in a flat with three children, with no refrigerator, no beds, no money, and no hope. In an effort to make a life for herself and her children, she found work as a receptionist in a legal firm. A well-dressed female client who Linda described as "looking like Cleopatra" visited the legal firm regularly. One day "Cleopatra" suggested Linda should come and work for her. When asked what that would mean, the lady said she operated a brothel in a nearby suburb. Linda was shocked, but the lady said she would only be asked to provide hand relief for her male clients, and besides, after making $1,000 a month, in a short time she would have enough money to furnish her flat and care for her children. She could leave whenever she wanted to.

So Linda began working in the sex trade. It was easy at first: the money was good and hours were convenient. But soon she was asked to transition from hand relief to "giving her body" to clients. Since she had been "giving herself for free" in her private life, it didn't seem a very big step to take money for pleasure. She was good at her job, so after working in several brothels she was asked by the owner of Perth's leading brothel, Langtrees, to become the madam of that establishment. Linda accepted the promotion and worked in that position for seventeen years. But there is a cost to prostitution. Everyone pays: the customer, the sex workers, their families, their children. Even the madams pay. Linda was making lots of money, living a "fabulous" lifestyle, driving a new BMW, and meeting lots of powerful people—but she was desperately unhappy. She was addicted to Valium and prescription drugs, and her life was filled with violence, abuse, entrapment, and crippling loneliness. She was more existing than *really* living.

Depressed and suicidal, she drove into the country one night, intending to drive her BMW at high speed into a tree to kill herself. But as she aimed the car at the tree, she saw something white out the corner of her eye and braked to a stop. It was some horses running along the fence, close to the road. Distracted by the horses and looking for another way out of her dilemma, Linda cried long and hard there in the darkness on that country back road.

One of her heroes was Princess Diana. "What a life she leads!" Linda thought. "She's got everything going for her. She's beautiful and rich—she'll probably never die!" But just weeks later, the television news blared that Princess Diana had been tragically killed in a car crash. Linda was devastated. She began to fear that God would take *her* life away too. She remembered her mother's prayers for her as a child, attending Sunday School, and the songs she sang such as, "Jesus loves me this I know for the Bible tells me so." She prayed, "God, if you are real, you have to show yourself to me. If you do, I'll never be a sex worker again. Take me away from this life of pain and let me start again." God did speak to Linda in the deep places of her soul. She became a follower of Jesus, the "friend of sinners."

The problem for Linda was who to talk to about this change in her life. A lady named Fran had been making pastoral visits to Langtrees for some time, offering friendship, prayer, and Christian tracts to the girls. Linda spoke to her about her encounter with God, and Fran put her in contact with people like Roslyn and David Phillips[1] and Pastor Dwight Randall. Later, Linda met with the Catholic Archbishop of Perth, Barry Hickey. She was embarrassed, not knowing what to say to an archbishop, but they soon developed a strong friendship. In 1999 a ministry known as Linda's House of Hope was begun, with the Archbishop's help. Its purpose was to rescue young women from prostitution. Although she has encountered much opposition (including death threats) from people in "the industry," criminal

---

1. Phillips, *Courage in a Hostile World*.

elements, and lots of misunderstanding and resistance from conservative groups within the church and its welfare agencies, Linda continues to run a shelter dedicated to rescuing young women from prostitution. With little money to speak of, and battling persistent health problems, Linda remains deeply concerned for the welfare and dignity of young women who work in the sex industry. With particular reference to the well-being of these exploited individuals, she has taken a strong stance in the media and the public eye against the legalization of prostitution, on the grounds that it destroys their humanity, and is toxic for families, the economy, and to society at large. In her fight against the soul-destroying effects of prostitution, Linda has spoken to government and civic groups on the topic both in Australia and in America.[2]

Christianity and "Dubious" Matter

There is a long and inglorious tradition of women who have followed Linda's descent into the oldest profession in the world. But there is an equally long and glorious tradition of women who have discovered Christ and made their escape to freedom. Notable biblical examples include the harlot, Rahab, who assisted the spies Moses sent to infiltrate the city of Jericho (Josh 2). Because of her "righteous" actions, Rahab is included in Jesus' family lineage (Matt 1:5). Then there is Gomer, the promiscuous wife of the prophet Hosea, who nonetheless was appointed by God to play a "supporting role" in her husband's ministry. Her two-timing life mirrored Israel's adulterous affairs with idols. In the time of Jesus, the most famous prostitute (according to tradition) was Mary Magdalene, who—after having had seven demons cast out from her (Luke 8:2–3)—was transformed into a completely different person, and whose life became something truly beautiful for God. Mary became one of Jesus' disciples and a pivotal character in his inner circle. And in subsequent Christian history there has been a long "sisterhood" of women whose lives have been radically redirected away from dishonorable financial gain for sexual services, towards righteous living as an "act" of worship of their Lord, Jesus Christ, who redeemed them and restored them to wholeness. Examples of women who turned from prostitution to Christianity during the early centuries of Christian history include Mary of Egypt, and Pelagia, whose lives form a central part of Western martyrology. In modern times, women like Diana

2. Yancey, *What Good is God?*

Mendiola and Annie Lobert join this exceptional group. Collectively, their lives tell the story of what God can do when a life is handed over to him trustingly and completely. In the same way that the women at Jesus' tomb were the first to bear witness to his resurrection, the lives of these women form a unique chapter in the *Acta Sanctorum* (the acts of the saints), which records the lives of the saints in salvation history.[3]

Throughout Christianity's 2,000-year-long history, there has been a great deal of suspicion shown towards the body as a hotbed of unseemly passions. The consensus of judgment has been that—for better or worse—much of the cause of human sin, rebellion, and disobedience lies at the feet of the carnal body. This tide of opinion has its origins in the language used in the New Testament. For example, Jesus taught, "If your right eye causes you to sin, gouge it out and throw it away.... If your right hand causes you to sin, cut it off and throw it away" (Matt 5:27 and 29). In his letter to the Ephesians, the Apostle Paul warned against "The cravings of the sinful flesh" (Eph 2:3), while John wrote of "The lust of the flesh and the pride of life" (1 John 2:16–17, RSV). Repeatedly, the disciples of the early church were warned to avoid what is "stained by corrupted flesh" (Jude 23). And this jaundiced view of the body is extended in subsequent Christian history, as attitudes intensified and hardened even further. St. Augustine's *Confessions* abound with declarations targeted against the body and its lascivious desires. Augustine refers to "the clanking chains of my mortality," "the concupiscence of the flesh," and he described his body as "boiling over in my fornications."[4] Similarly, St. Basil of Caesarea warned his followers against the passions of the body:

> In a single word, the body in every part should be despised by everyone who does not care to be buried in its pleasures, as it were in slime; or we ought to cleave to it only in so far as we obtain from its service the pursuit of wisdom.[5]

Add to these attitudes early Christianity's adoption of asceticism, whose primary purpose was to repress and contain the "evil" desires of the body, and the adoption of the joyless trio of poverty, chastity, and obedience

---

3. The *Acta Sanctorum* is a 53-volume written history of European saints recorded by the Société des Bollandistes in Antwerp and Brussels, written in Latin and published in its initial form from 1643 to 1794 (see http://acta.chadwyck.co.uk/). Subsequent volumes have been added.

4. Augustine, *Confessions*, 25.

5. Anderson, *On Being Human*, 133.

as the mainstay of monasticism and the Catholic clergy . . . and the case against the body as the source of human wickedness and degeneracy was decided. Without any doubt, the body is to blame for humanity's reprobate state. Gregg Allison puts it this way:

> It is my contention that evangelicals at best express ambivalence toward the human body, and at worst manifest a disregard or contempt for it. Many people, often due to tragic experiences with the body (e.g., physical/sexual abuse), abhor their body, and many Christians, due to either poor or non-existent teaching on human embodiment, consider their body to be, at best, a hindrance to spiritual maturity and, at worst, inherently evil or the ultimate source of sin.[6]

This may be so, but that is not the end of the story. What becomes clear in the telling of Linda's story, and those of her sisters, is that upon leaving prostitution, three things become very apparent. The first is that their life-priorities shifted significantly, to the point where they could no longer in good conscience remain in their former profession. The second is that their change of soul direction compelled them to use their bodies in a very different way from the way they used them previously. And the third is that they felt their bodies belonged to Christ, and that the new values they had come to adopt invited them to "offer their bodies as living sacrifices, holy and pleasing to God" (Rom 12:1). They were not to conform any longer to the patterns of their old lives, but to express their new allegiance to Christ in the most definitive way they were able to, in the way they behaved in their bodies.

Admittedly, stories of the lives of converted prostitutes represent the most "extreme" of cases. But if they manage to showcase the truth that this chapter is attempting to investigate—namely, that the only available mechanism through which the soul's new allegiance can be displayed is the body. Following an encounter with Christ that radically altered the way they frame existence, people like Linda—and the millions of fellow travelers who have discovered a form of unconditional love for Christ that up-sizes their reason for being—have fundamentally changed the way they have lived. Instead of using their bodies to give full vent to their passions and desires through abandoning themselves to unrestrained sensuality, they have chosen a different mode of living. Out of their own free will they have chosen an alternative way of life which is gentler and deeper, and which is

---

6. Allison, "Toward a Theology of Human Embodiment," 5.

more profoundly satisfying than a life of total abandonment to uninhibited pleasure. And at the center of this new life is the use of the body.

One of the most dramatic ways of representing the changes experienced by penitents, worshippers, mystics, and saints is the extrusion of the spiritual realities encountered in their inner lives, outward by "projection" through their physical bodies onto the canvas of the external world. Ultimately, the most compelling evidence of the healing and reintegration of what William James referred to as the "divided self" is a changed life. Ralph Metzner identified a list of ten classical metaphors of transformation of the self in the form of: (a) awakening from sleep, (b) transferring from the illusion to realization, (c) from darkness to enlightenment, (d) from imprisonment to liberation, (e) from fragmentation to wholeness, (f) from separation to oneness, (g) from being on a journey to arrival at one's destination, (h) from being in exile to coming home, (i) movement from seed to flowering tree, and (j) from death to rebirth.[7] In each case, the spiritual transformations these images imply are represented most clearly in the form of concrete changes in our behavior. They do not remain as metaphysical realities alone, but are "performed" through our bodies by way of embodied practice. It may come as a shock to many, but the clearest proof of a life-changing spiritual encounter is how we use our own bodies, and how we treat the bodies of others.

Saints' lives are testimonies in sign language, written in the cursive style of hands clasped in prayer, faces turned upwards in worship, arms reaching out to welcome friends, neighbors, and enemies in hospitable embrace. Despite our tendency to define spirituality as a non-material practice, the physical body continues to press its case. Spirituality that is removed from embodied practice becomes other-worldly, distant, dispassionately removed from the real world. It is a matter of great irony that the Christian spiritual life may well originate in ecstatic third-heaven encounters with God in Christ: but it can never be removed from the living, breathing, moving, feeling person in their embodied state. This makes spirituality a lived experience that is a joint venture between the mind, the body, and the soul of the human being that in its totality is a *homo spiritualitas*—a fundamentally spiritual being.

Donald Williams, in his book *Mere Humanity*, has given us a wonderful description of the human body:

---

7. Metzner, "Ten Classical Metaphors of Self Transformation."

> Intricate engine angels might admire,
>
> material spirit, animated earth,
>
> Crafted casket for celestial fire,
>
> Doomed to die the day it has its birth.
>
> Hands that open, befitting a gracious lord,
>
> able to touch a cheek as soft as mist,
>
> To wield a pen, a brush, a harpsichord,
>
> But just as apt to freeze into a fist.
>
> Godlike image, able to stand erect,
>
> yet by what small and simple things laid low:
>
> A sneeze, a scratch, a germ, and all is wrecked;
>
> A few short years, the time has come to go.
>
> Delicate instrument of love, or lust,
>
> admirably compacted . . . out of dust.[8]

This mysterious body we inhabit houses and supports us throughout our three score years and ten. It contains three enormously powerful *forces* within it. The first force is our natural impulses such as the need for food, sleep, ablutions, sex, and sensory engagement with the world around us. These are normal, necessary, and good impulses, without which we are unlikely to survive long in the ordinary, everyday, workaday world. The second force is comprised of the tensions that exist between the forces of good and evil at work in the world, and which seek to co-opt our bodies to their cause. Generally speaking it is in our bodies and the appetites that operate there, where evil most powerfully expresses itself. And the third force is the power of the human will to make choices between the competing demands of the body, its impulses, and the "causes" one chooses to serve in the world. We put our bodies to use, "employing" them in the service of good or evil, light or darkness, others or self. These three forces are on "permanent duty" in our bodies. There is a very real sense in which we need to come to grips with these power dynamics within the human person engaged in the spiritual life, if we are to properly understand the role of

---

8. Williams, *Mere Humanity*, xi. With permission.

the body not merely as the place where evil dwells, but as a vital partner in putting our body to use as a part of our vocation of righteousness. In other words, the body is our partner in being and becoming a saint. For saints, it is through the human body that the beauty, simplicity, and unconditional love that are the key components of earth-bound holiness, are most fully and wonderfully expressed.

God and Flesh

There is a clear yet often overlooked connection between spirit and flesh recorded in the biblical record. The level of physicality is surprising in its extent. In the Old Testament, God creates human beings "in his own image" out the *humus* (from which the word *human* is derived) of the earth. And everywhere there is the corporeal stuff of bones and bodies, ribs and flesh, muscle and blood, bellies and breasts, semen and babies. The covenants or relational contracts between God and Israel are accompanied by the physical signs of circumcision, the ark of the covenant, and blood sacrifice—first on rough-hewn altars and then in Temple worship. In the frequent recorded encounters between God and his people, God is nothing if not interested in everything material and physical in the "real" world he created.

And that level of interest is expressed most clearly in the fact that God himself participates in the human story. He does not do so from outer space at a safe distance from humanity. No. What we note about the great "moments" in salvation history is that they are the occasions when God "comes down" and gets up-close and personal with members of his human family, in order to reveal himself in his person, his will, his purposes, and his works.

> We may say that God wrote his own autobiography . . . . It is unique, because the author appears, personally and without disguise, as a character in his own story; but it is still a story that he is writing, and he is obliged to handle his own character as a character throughout the succession of events . . . . The whole story is contained within the mind of the maker, but the mind of the maker is also imprisoned within the story [and] cannot escape it.[9]

---

9. Sayers, *Mind of the Maker*, 87–88.

As much as it might surprise us, God is not afraid of getting his hands dirty. He himself takes on flesh. Stephen Webb—citing the theologian Karl Barth—states:

> Indeed, "We must keep in mind that the Holy Scripture not only speaks of God's wrath, mercy, etc., but also—to the even greater confusion of all who want to spiritualize the text (adjusted for sense)—his nose, his back, his arm, his right hand, his finger, his feet." These descriptions of God, Barth says, should be taken at least as seriously as concepts derived from an immaterialist metaphysics. Indeed, the more we try to imagine God as immaterial, the more we become trapped in materialism, since we end up thinking of God as "chemically distilled absolute spirit." The essence of God is "one great anthropomorphism", the way of God is "also corporeality." . . . Jesus Christ is the eternal place of God.[10]

In a poetic way that only she could write, the poet Anne Sexton wrote of "God's incarnational desire to inhabit a body . . . . He envies the bodies, He who has no body."[11] For God, the solution to the problem of evil was not withdraw from materiality into the realm of unconnected spirit, but to take on flesh in the form of the incarnation of his Son Jesus and to wrestle with evil in the form of hand-to-hand combat.

In my book *Seeing and Believing*, I wrote:

> As a metaphysical artist, God's best work is done in nature's fabric. Emonet has written, 'To know God, one must begin by regarding the things God has made, and what God has given them of perfection in the roots of their very being.' Nature and this earthly life are never to be mistaken for enemies or strangers by the God-faring pilgrim, but as the stage on which the drama is set or the workshop where the offering is prepared. While redemption was conceived and commanded in heaven, it must be played out here on earth. During our mortal lives, the only address that redemption has is here on earth![12]

What then of the earthly life of Jesus? In the Gospels, Jesus' ministry is characterized by his miracles, in the form of feeding the hungry, healing the sick, giving sight to the blind and raising the dead. At the transfiguration, when Jesus "showed" himself in his glory to his disciples, his self-revelation

---

10. Webb, *Jesus Christ, Eternal God*, 291.
11. Sexton, "Earth," 431–32.
12. Devenish, *Seeing and Believing*, 6.

was accompanied by accompanying manifestations such as the physical presence of Moses and Elijah. At the crucifixion, we make much of the relational adjustments between the just God and the suffering son to pay for the penalty of human sin ... but the fact is that was only possible because it was enacted through Jesus' physical body. There is visceral physicality to be found everywhere in the form of Jesus' naked body, blood, the wood of the cross, spears, hammers, nails, sweat, pain, and trauma. At the resurrection, there was yet more visceral physicality in the form of Jesus' resurrected body. It was John Updike who stated that, "Make no mistake: if he [Jesus] rose at all it was as his body."[13] And this physicality sets the scene for all that follows, first in the parallel resurrections of "holy people who had died" and their "appearance" to many people in resurrected form (Matt 27:52-3), and second there was Jesus eating fish and breaking bread and thus demonstrating that he was not a ghostly apparition.

At Pentecost—the occasion of the sending of the Holy Spirit that we might expect would be the most ephemeral and ghostly occasion—there is an intense eruption of physical manifestations in the form of noise, wind, speaking in tongues, and the "utter amazement" (Acts 2:7) of the onlookers. No ghostly apparition, but heavenly flesh. The narratives of redemption unfold in such a way that they demonstrate the lengths to which God will go to reach out to his human creatures—taking upon himself human form in Christ's incarnation, in order to learn our language, embody our nature, pay the penalty for our sin, and invite us into a quality of relationship that is intrinsic to the trinitarian relationship. This makes us not simply a lower order of creature—as might belong to servants in a household—but rather singles us out as "heirs and joint-heirs" in God's heavenly family (Rom 8:17). Even if we cannot claim to share in hypostatic union with God—as the Son does with the Father—nevertheless Athanasius could write in the fourth century, "He became human that we might become God; and he revealed himself through a body that we might inherit incorruption."[14] And according to the Christian tradition, God prepared a body for Jesus, "A body you prepared for me" (Heb 10:5)—and it was by means of that body that he worked the miracle of salvation for human beings who were trapped in sin. "This is my body, given for you" (Luke 22:19).

What is even more amazing, however, is that the culmination of the salvation event was Jesus' ascension to the Father in heaven, in the form of

---

13. O'Connell, *Updike and the Patriarchal Dilemma*, 29.
14. Christensen, *Partakers of the Divine Nature*, 34.

his resurrected human body. Despite all this talk of the body as the source of human corruption and the precinct of all that is wicked and evil within humanity, Jesus returns to heaven following his resurrection carrying the "trophy" of salvation into his Father's presence, in the form of the sanctified human body. His entry into heaven wearing the garment of flesh, is a kind of preannouncement of the arrival of all those who will follow in the decades, centuries, and millennia that were to come. If we discovered previously that the spiritual life is an embodied practice ... what we discover here in this section is that Jesus' high-priestly ministry had as its centerpiece the offering of his body as a means of reconciling the totality of the lives of his People back to God ... in their bodies, their souls, and their beings.

Saints as Christ's Agents

One of the most noticeable features of the Old and New Testaments is the amazing array of people who take part in the unfolding drama of God's redemptive history. Out from the pages of the Bible there marches a vast procession of people who found themselves—willingly or otherwise—to be "actors" in God's redemptive drama. Anyone who has grown up in the Christian tradition is familiar with their stories. They have shaped our lives in more ways than we can know. We cannot see their faces, but their names and selected scenes from their lives have come down to us through the chronicles of time as messengers from God. Representatives from the Hebrew Bible include the obedient Abraham, the beautiful Rebecca, the leader Moses, the kingly David, the weeping Jeremiah, and the questioning Habakkuk. And representatives from the Christian New Testament include the diminutive Zacchaeus, the candid Nathanael, the blind Bartimaeus, the betrayer Judas, the doubting Thomas, the passionate Mary Magdalene, the thunderbolt Paul, the merchant Lydia, the intellectual Apollos, and the husband and wife ministry team Priscilla and Aquila, whose partnership in the gospel the Apostle Paul so deeply appreciated.

Christians have traditionally understood that only written canonical texts such as the Scriptures are in any way *revelatory*. But the fact that human persons under divine inspiration were both the writers of the Scriptures, and were themselves "actors" within the unfolding redemptive story, demonstrates that the lives of saints—ancient and modern—are themselves also revelatory. Many would argue that the rightful center of theology is the study of God in his glory and sovereignty. But Jesus' appointing of the apostles to carry on his ministry shows that Christian theology cannot ignore humans as the agents of the kingdom of God on earth. It is upon the testimony and the lives of the apostles that historic Christianity builds its house. The fact that saints' lives reveal God's purposes and manifest his kingdom is borne out by the inclusion of biographical chapters such as Romans 16, Philippians 4, and Hebrews 11, in the canon of the New Testament.

The biblical narratives show that God intentionally adopts the risky strategy of placing the fate of his redemptive agenda in the hands of a small group of untested, unready, and unlikely people. In his address to the 2013 World Youth Day in Rio de Janeiro, Brazil, Pope Francis told his three-million strong audience, "Jesus is calling you to be a disciple with a mission. . . . Jesus Christ is counting on you! The Church is counting on you! . . . 'Go and make disciples of all nations.'"[15] The pontiff's words recall the fact that God is committed to a divine-human partnership. Despite its unequal nature—God being the greater partner and humans being the lesser—nevertheless this divine-human partnership appears to be a central part of God's self-limiting yet mission-expanding strategy in the world. God could have redeemed humanity by means of divine *fiat*: "Let them be saved!" in much the same way that he brought creation into being: "Let there be light" . . . etc. But instead, he chose to include his fallen creatures as key players within his redemptive drama, and as his foremost strategy for spreading the gospel of his son, Jesus Christ, throughout the world. We might describe this divine-human partnership as God's "strategy of skin"—where he chooses to work with saints and sanctified persons who become his appointed servants, and his "fellow workers" (in the language of the Apostle Paul in 1 Cor 3:9 and elsewhere).

When describing how the Lindisfarne Gospels[16] might have come into being, the American poet, Melissa Range, wrote:

> Before the stepwork and the fretwork,
>
> before the first wet spiral leaves the brush,
>
> before the plucking of the geese's quills,
>
> before the breaking of a thousand leads;

---

15. Pope Francis, "World Youth Day Address," 2013.

16. The Lindisfarne Gospels represent the high point of Anglo-Celtic devotion and creativity. They were written ca. 715 by St. Eadfrith in honor of St. Cuthbert. For color, beauty, and distinction they can be compared to the Book of Kells.

before the curving limbs and wings of hounds,

cats and cormorants knot into letters,

before the letters knot into the Word,

Eadfrith ventures from his cell.[17]

What Range brings to awareness in these lyrical stanzas is that the Lindisfarne Gospels did not draft themselves. They were dependent on Eadfrith "venturing" forth to do what he believed was God's work. The bottom line is: no Eadfrith means no Lindisfarne Gospels, and no Lindisfarne Gospels means a diminishment of the presence of God in the world. In a parallel manner, no human agent means no effective witness to Christ and his kingdom. But Eadfrith's "venturing" forth to do God's work is not an isolated incident. It repeats God's habitual practice of calling holy people to do his holy work through the agency of their holy lives.

Would Judaism exist if Abraham had not obeyed God and ventured forth to discover new lands? And would Christianity exist if the apostles had remained on their fishing boats and at their tax collector's booths? God's spirit-work is done by embodied and redeemed human persons. This is the principle that repeats itself time and again throughout history. Saints are central to the work of God, through Christ, in history.

And so, before the spread of the church across Asia Minor, the Apostle Paul readied himself in Damascus. Before pagan Ireland could be evangelized, St. Brendan set off in his coracle. Before the gospel could enter the Moravian Empire (today's Czech Republic), Saints Cyril and Methodius made their journey east. And before the remarkable growth of the Christian church in China, Hudson Taylor undertook medical training in order to be of some use in that great land to which he had been called to serve. "I used to ask God to help me; then I asked if I might help him. I ended up asking him to do his work through me"—he wrote in his journal.

It appears to be an intentional strategy on God's part to choose a people for his own purposes, into whose personal and communal lives he invests his own trinitarian life and the values of his kingdom, so they may be living witness to his gospel. God chose Israel as his agent of salvation. Jesus chooses the saints—departed and living—to be his agents in the church and in the world. Like Jesus, saints are the messengers, the message, and the working 'model' of Christ's redemptive good news. In other words, alongside the textual "witnesses" which are commonly accepted as revelatory of

---

17. Range, "Scriptorium," 172. With permission.

the divine purposes, we find that the biographies of individual men and women are also *revelatory*. Human subjects, therefore, can be described as God's "agents" and appointed "representatives" of his work on earth.

This notion of agency is discussed at length by Barclay and Gathercole in their work entitled *Divine and Human Agency in Paul and his Cultural Environment*.[18] There, the authors describe the origins of agency in the cultural context of first-century Palestine, in the teaching of the Pauline writings. For the purposes of this chapter, I have chosen Barclay and Gathercole's definition of "agency" as closest to my own, when they write:

> God and humanity are . . . within the same spectrum of being, and the agency of one is shared with the other, rather than standing in competition against it. Human agency is bound up with that of God, because the two are essentially identical when properly aligned . . . Humanity is most itself not when it is 'self-sufficient' vis-a-vis God, but when it acts in dependence on God, and wills what God has willed. For human beings participate in the nature of God, and might even be described as 'fragments' of God: what makes them most effective as human agents is what they share with God.[19]

If the Apostle Paul can use phrases such as, "God's fellow workers" and "ambassadors," to describe himself and his missionary band, it is surely not out of place for us to think of our own calling in terms of becoming "partners with God," and as being involved in his sanctifying work on the earth, through the agency of our own lives.

In summary, then, any talk of the spiritual life is incomplete until we ground the spiritual in the life of the corporeal human person (and the faith communities to which they belong), since the spiritual life is necessarily lived in our everyday existence through the materiality of our bodies. Biblically speaking, it is not possible to think of the spiritual life without thinking of the great actors in redemptive history, such as Abraham, Moses, Sarah, David, St. Paul, Lydia, Stephen, or some other concrete individual. It is human persons—embodied persons—who express their redeemed state and their new allegiance to God in Christ by means of their risky, temporal and daily lived obedience. If we can say that God decrees redemption from his throne in heaven, we must also say that it is flesh-and-blood human persons who cooperate with the divine agenda, by intentionally embodying

---

18. Barclay and Gathercole, *Divine and Human Agency*.
19. Ibid., 6–7.

the new reality in their own lives in a form of bonded but free "agency." Heaven comes to earth in the lives of everyday human beings who have been remade and re-minted into the image and likeness of God in Christ.

Performing Saints' Bodies

One of the best-known statements concerning the role of the body in the spiritual life is provided by the fourth-century theologian, Tertullian. He declared: "The body is the hinge of salvation."[20] In other words, it is through saints' bodies that the spiritual life is brought into contact with the material world of things—with everything that is associated with human life and materiality. And equally—from the earthly and material side of things—it is through the loving actions of embodied saints that ordinary people become most keenly aware that God is at work in the world. One could even say that—in Celtic terms—saints represent "thin" places. Here "thin" does not refer to the girth of saintly midriffs, but refers instead to the narrow distance between the sacred and the profane in the lives of holy people. Saints' bodies are blessed things. They become the meeting point where the creases of self, spirit, soul and soft tissue meet. As Nancey Murphy writes:

> If souls are saved *out of* this world, then nothing here matters ultimately. If it is our bodily selves that are saved and transformed, then bodies and all that go with them matter—families, history, and all of nature.[21]

I have in my hands a book written by Tony Cupit, entitled *Stars Lighting up the Sky: Stories of Contemporary Christian Heroes*.[22] Tony has been a pastor, missionary, leader and denominational executive for the Baptist World Alliance in Australia. He spent the first years of his ministry in Papua New Guinea with his wife Margaret, translating the New Testament into the language of Kyaka Enga people. Tony has recorded the life stories of fourteen people who are living examples of the changed life that has resulted from their transforming encounter with Christ. He describes them as being "innocent and pure as God's perfect children, who live in a world of corrupt and sinful people. [Who] . . . shine among them *like stars lighting up the sky*" (Phil 2:15, GNB). It is a lesson in pure grace to read the stories. Each

---

20. Tertullian, in West, *Theology of the Body Explained*, 6.
21. Murphy, *Bodies and Souls, or Spirited Bodies?*, 28–29.
22. Cupit, *Stars Lighting up the Sky*.

in their turn offer fresh insights into the saintly life. I will select just a few for the purposes of illustration. There is the story of Sare in Azerbaijan, a one-time drug addict who encountered Christ and became a witness to the gospel in a majority Muslim nation. Sare's ministry has led to the establishment of a large and vibrant Christian community. Then there is the story of Leena in Andhra Pradesh, India, who Cupit describes as a "Baptist Mother Teresa," pouring out her life to serve the hungry, homeless, and helpless people of India. Or Pastor Olayee, in Liberia, northern Africa. During the tumultuous years of 1997–2003, Olayee was the senior minister at the Providence Baptist Church in Monrovia, Liberia, located on the southern rim of Africa's northwest coast. Bordering countries like Sierra Leone and Nigeria, and surrounded by political, military, and religious upheaval, the church grew under Olayee's leadership. He became chaplain to President Charles Taylor, and—despite the tensions—was able to speak into the life of his city, his nation, and his region.

Through these and other biographical narratives I have included throughout this book, I invite you to notice how the faith of these people was not left on the shelf, locked between the covers of their Bibles, or retained safely within the four walls of their homes or church buildings. Instead, their faith was lived out, or we might say "performed" through their lives. While their acts of kindness, wisdom, leadership, and courage worked for the benefit of their fellow human beings, they were performed at very great risk to themselves and their families. Because they lived in and were surrounded by poverty, violence, sickness, and overwhelming human suffering, they could have been struck down at any time by violence, illness, financial ruin, or political upheaval. Yet in the midst of such terrible personal risk, they put their faith in Christ into action.

What do I mean by "performance"? As is often the case, dictionary definitions offer multiple possibilities. One definition of performance relates to playing one's part as an actor in a scripted play or theatre piece. This first definition of performance relates to role-play. A second definition relates to artistic performance, in which a musician or artist or dancer performs their craft in the form of artistic expression in order to respond to the creative impulse within themselves, as well as to entertain others. A third definition of performance pertains to what is basic to one's identity in terms of gender, ethnicity, language, culture, and such. So, for example, an indigenous person lives out their identity as a mode of cultural performance in a predominantly white, Anglo setting. Or a female "performs" her gendered identity in the traditionally male-dominated settings of business or politics of the academy. And a fourth definition of performance—closely linked to the third definition—highlights the importance of "testimony," where a person, group, or community "lives out" the faith that lies at the core of their convictions and defines the truthfulness of their lives—even if that testimony is not recognized as valid by the dominant culture. This last definition of performance is the one I want to develop further here, in order to clarify what I mean by the title of this section-heading "performing saints' bodies."

Christianity is a religion of *witnesses*. Biblical references to "witness" begin with the early disciples being witnesses to Jesus' resurrection (Luke 24:48), to the good news of salvation found in the gospel of Christ (Acts 1:8), to the glory of Christ as "eyewitnesses to his majesty" (2 Pet 1:16), and to the real and touchable Jesus whom the Apostle John described as someone the disciples were "touching with our hands and seeing with our eyes" (1 John 1:1). The task of the witness is to bear testimony to what they have seen and experienced. And inevitably bearing witness means putting one's body to work as a living sign of the reality and power of the spiritual realities the witness wishes to display or signify.

Bearing witness and giving testimony is the responsibility of every saint. Giving testimony is a performative act in at least four important ways. First, it is usually a *subversive* act by a minority people who point to a reality that is usually not recognized by the majority population. Second it is always a *truthful* act in that it points toward something that is essential to the nature of human life but is not commonly sanctioned. And third it is *invitational* in the sense that it invites observers who have not yet experienced conversion to try to understand the gospel transformation being identified as necessary for themselves. And fourth, it is *performed* as an act of witness. This is where verbal testimony is augmented by a kind of lived testimonial—a form of embodied witness that carries particular weight and substance in a world where people take note of what we do as much as what we say.

This notion of embodied performance comes into special focus when we speak of the martyrs. Walter Wink describes martyrs in this way:

> Martyrs are not victims, overtaken by evil, but hunters who stalk evil into the open by offering as bait their own bodies. Those who are willing to sacrifice nothing or very little, offer nothing or very

little to history. It must be said that they offer little or nothing to their own souls.[23]

Obviously, people engaged in acts of subversive, truthful, invitational, and performative witness put their reputations at risk. In extreme situations, such performances of testimony can end up putting their lives at risk. "It is the actions of the Christian community that exegete the Christian message. To say that Christians believe in God is true but uninteresting until the community takes a certain shape to reveal the character of the Christian God."[24] It is in saints' bodies that the spiritual life is performed—otherwise, the spiritual life remains abstract and disconnected from everything that is earthly, material, and in need of salvation. As Dallas Willard was wont to say, "Our bodies become the showplace of his greatness."[25]

With regard to the sanctified life, only through the body can we properly participate in worship, community, brotherly or sisterly love, obedience, repentance, and the like. And only through the body can we go on pilgrimage, perform the spiritual disciplines, receive the sacraments, or "announce" our faith through personal testimony—or in its ultimate expression in the form of martyrdom. Whether we like it or not, the flesh is the place where our spiritual life lives itself outwards into the world in a kind of tragicomic performance of our faithful witness to the spiritual life which certainly is grander than our human physicality, but inevitably performs itself outward through our physical beings. With wit and humor, Thomas Oden writes:

> We students of God, look at us: God's own image scratching our eczema; irritated by hemorrhoids, yet capable of refracting the divine goodness; biped animals who dream of eternity; playing God yet being bums, clowns, and louts—yet bums who can say from the heart, "God bless"; clowns who mime the posture of Superman; louts who can conceive of the idea of perfect being. We are curious about divine judgment, but a little less so than about the brakes on our car; recipients of rationality who cannot balance our bank accounts; living souls puzzled by death. Such a creature it is who takes up pen and ink and scribbles vague sentences about God; who breathes polluted air and speaks of Spirit; who uses the name of God mostly to intensify cursing, yet who call God the Adorner of creation. It is because humanity is a paradox that the

23. Wink, *Engaging the Powers*, 161.
24. Oudshoorn, "Speaking Christianly as a Missional Activity," 5.
25. Willard, *Renovation of the Heart*, 137.

human study of God is and remains a paradox, strewn with blood and flowers, with passing wind and singing hymns.[26]

Geoff and Di Hall Go to China

China wasn't where they thought they would end up living and working. But once they got there they just knew they'd made the right decision! Outwardly, Geoff and Di Hall have a certain zest about them. With their energy and passion for life, they could probably have succeeded at anything they turned their hands to. Geoff was born in Essex in the UK in 1951, the third child in a family of ten. His father was an accountant, and as a family they attended Leigh Road Baptist Church. Despite having ten children of their own to feed, parent, and educate, the Hall family made it a practice not only to donate money themselves, but also to raise money for Dr. Barnardo's Home for Children by knocking on people's doors in the district. But in 1969, Geoff's parents saw fresh opportunity for their children in Australia, so the family migrated as "£10 Poms." Once settled in Perth, Geoff's mother commenced fostering needy children. And so a sense of obligation to care for others in need became an important hallmark of the Hall family's life.

Di was born in Perth in 1953, to her parents John and Joy Finkelstein. Tragically, her father died when she was very young, and her mother raised her and her three siblings as a single mum. Despite them having less than adequate resources to meet their own needs, Di's mum took in needy Aboriginal girls, offering up their home as a safe haven. Di recalls one occasion sitting down to dinner and her mother saying grace without there being any food on the table. Just then there was a knock at the door. The visitor turned out to be the driver of a vegetable delivery truck that had broken down outside their house. The driver wanted to know if he could "dump" food with the family so it didn't have to go to waste.

Geoff and Di married in 1973. Over time, they had two children of their own, and adopted a third child (a boy) from South Korea. Today the family has grown up and produced seven grandchildren. Professionally, Geoff and Di worked together in television production, where Geoff had a twenty-five-year-long career as a film editor in television and drama productions. They created their own film and media company and contracted to the large television stations in Australia and beyond.

26. Oden, *Systematic Theology*, 496.

Alongside their media activities, Geoff and Di also developed a deep concern for children with special needs. It began with children experiencing developmental disorders such as autism, and extended to the children of refugees from Bosnia, Somalia, and Vietnam. Di, in particular, set up a support group to provide assistance in finding housing, schools, writing, language learning, and the resources that recently arrived refugee families need to adjust to the culture of their new home country. In 1994 Geoff realized the power of media to promote the needs of children around the world, and travelled to over fifty countries making low-budget videos of the plight of needy people—especially children—using the films to promote their charity work. Along the way they discovered the International China Concern organization. In 2012, Geoff and Di began working full time in a care facility for mentally and physically disabled teenage boys in Henyang (a city of three million people in Hunan Province in south central China).

While China's economy is booming and the living standards of its people are rapidly rising, the level of care provided to abandoned and disabled children and youth remains at low levels. As a result, International China Concern—a Christian charity—was established in 1993 to help create full and meaningful lives for China's needy children. In an interview with ICC workers, it was reported that, "Some children are left at the gate, some at the hospital, and one boy was found floating down the river in a bucket."[27] There are many similar stories: just one belongs to Gong Gong, who was born with Down syndrome and abandoned by his family on his eighth birthday. The result of a long-term lack of care was that Gong Gong could offer little more than a distant, blank stare at people. Yet after building a relationship with him over time, Geoff had Gong Gong running, laughing, and jumping into his arms. Another story relates to the discovery of two teenage girls, Tao Tao and Ju Ju, living in dirty and cramped conditions in another "care" facility. Unclean, poorly fed, and living with severe autism, the girls were visited daily by Di and other ICC staff who gained their trust. Eventually they were transferred into the care of ICC. They joined a relationship circle of other girls their own age, who similarly had experienced rejection and abandonment. Now several years later, both girls are living changed lives, who are now developing into whole people in a community that loves and welcomes them. There are great needs among children and the disabled in China, just as there are everywhere else in the world. In China, however,

---

27. Szabo, "China's Forgotten Children," 98.

the need is particularly noticeable and urgent owing to the sheer numbers of children involved.

As far as Geoff and Di are concerned, God is a God who "raises the poor from the dust and lifts the needy from the ash heap, he sits them with princes and has them inherit a throne of honor" (Ps 113:7–8a). They began their work with International China Concern with a specific focus on abandoned babies, many born prematurely and some diagnosed as HIV positive. Within a short time, Di was introduced to the needs of a small group of teenage boys who she felt lacked opportunity to discover their skills and abilities. As a result, she introduced them to simple arts and crafts activities. The program proved a great success and by the time to Di and Geoff left China three-and-a-half years later, the art group had grown to more than forty young people and is now managed by local staff.

During that time, ICC had been able to move their operations to a five-story purpose-built building where they can now provide a family-style live-in community to those in need, with access to health, education, and exercise facilities. As followers of Jesus, who is a friend of sinners, one who heals the sick, who cares for the poor and raises the dead, these two ordinary saints left their home, their comforts, their security, their family, and a stable source of employment, to travel across the world to rescue unwanted children in China. They did this in order to restore the humanity of the children, to offer hope, and to offer these needy children the love of God who loves them "beyond measure." Geoff and Di did all this in the name of Jesus Christ.

Saints' Bodies—by Stuart Devenish

Saints' bodies are weak and sometimes broken,
still, their bending and bowing are indices of grace
as they make room for the Holy Spirit in their human spirits.
All pensive and poised, they perform heaven
on earth long before trumpets announce
the coming of a new day to a passing age.

Saints' faces are often anguished by tears,
but are also frequently lit by a shining exuberance,
as the *real presence* of something exquisite

Bodies of Evidence

projects itself outwards through their eyes.
Their faces, canvases of exemplary goodness,
personify the tactile embrace of God.

Saints' hands are serving hands,
wrinkled by humanity and scored by time.
Through busying themselves with the care of others,
giving a cup of grace and a loaf of hope,
eternity writ large in the small features
of their hands which—some say—are God's hands.

Saints' lives are notable by the fact
that they are directed intently towards
performing the values of another world
where love, mercy, and righteousness change hands
as the currency which is asked and given
from charitable hearts, debtors no more.

So we honor the saints
whose lives, bodies, faces and hands hallow the world,
benedictions of self forgetfulness,
as they give away their lives, unmindful of their state,
descending the *via dolorosa*
that makes the righteous blessed—happy saints!

7

Holy Wounds

"Our wounds are our glory"
(Julian of Norwich).

Suffering Humanity

Every person who has ever lived knows what it means to suffer. Some people suffer more than others, but the truth is that all our lives are characterized by affliction of some sort. Somewhere between birth and death, love and hate, hope and abandonment . . . the dark shadow of pain and sadness rests upon us all. From headache, to toothache, to heartache, to living in fear of the dark or our own approaching death . . . the shadow comes to each of us. It comes unannounced and always finds us unprepared for the visitation of a most unwelcome guest. On a grand scale, human history presents itself to us as one long scream, filled with war, plague, famine, poverty, injustice, violence, and oppression. And on a smaller scale, our own personal lives—although we would wish it otherwise—are no different. Everyone who has ever lived knows what it means to suffer.

As pastor and "soul friend" I have travelled alongside many people as they have journeyed through the "valley of the shadow of death" (Ps 23:4). For each person, the "shadow" of suffering visited them in different forms: stillbirth, sexual abuse, thoughts of suicide, domestic violence, betrayal, illness and impending death, grief, tragic loss, fear and neurosis, deep loneliness and gnawing despair. As a consequence, I have learned over time to be careful what I say about suffering. One ought not to say too much about suffering, because every person's experience of the "shadow" of suffering is different and unique to them. I do not "own" their experience, nor do I understand it fully. Therefore to pontificate about the causes and cures of suffering—like Job's accusers offering trite commentary from the sidelines—does not relieve suffering but only increases it. But I have also learned that my own affliction and mortality acts as a bridge that enables me to connect compassionately with others in their suffering. And since suffering and pain are present everywhere, one should not make the opposite error of saying too little about it. During seasons of "darkness" when death and despair knock on our door like the proverbial Grim Reaper, everyone needs to hear words of comfort, encouragement, and guidance. The spiritual life frequently comes to us through the unwanted "gift" of suffering. Our human sufferings and struggles lead us—often out of our deepest sense of need—to places where healing and comfort can be found. The entry point into the spiritual life is usually via one of two doorways, both old and both well-trodden. The first door is love, and the second door is suffering. Wise ones learn to speak of both, often.

The Fellowship of His Sufferings

At the heart of Jesus' invitation to become his disciples is his summons to enter into the fellowship of his sufferings. Jesus himself went through many ordeals in the lead up to his crucifixion. In this world he found "no place to lay his head" (Luke 9:58). He felt keenly his estrangement from the Jewish religious tradition (because he both superseded and transformed it). And at times he experienced deep frustration at his disciples' failure to understand his teachings regarding the kingdom of God. When Jesus called his audience to become his disciples, they were to "Repent and believe the good news" (Mark 1:15), to "Come, follow me" (Mark 1:16), and to "Deny themselves and take up [their] cross daily" (Luke 9:23). The decision to follow Jesus as both Lord and Christ brought with it the probability that suffering would follow as an inevitable consequence. If the world rejected Jesus the Son of God, then it would also reject his followers (John 15:18). It can be taken as a given that "people will insult you, persecute you and falsely say all kinds of evil against you because of me" (Matt 5:11). Such is the level of misunderstanding and hatred towards those who follow Christ that, "You will be handed over to be persecuted and put to death and hated by all nations because of me" (Matt 24:9).

Ordinary Saints

In the early period of Christian history, it was the Apostle Paul whose life most vividly exemplified the suffering that lies at the core of the Christian life. He was falsely arrested, imprisoned, whipped, shipwrecked, left hungry and naked, and was stoned and set upon by mobs and endangered on all sides (2 Cor 11:25–29). Yet even in the midst of being persecuted for his faith, the apostle desired to "have a share in the fellowship of his [Christ's] sufferings" (Phil 3:10). It was in the midst of pressure and persecution that Paul learned to transcend his sufferings.

> We also rejoice in our sufferings, because we know that suffering produces perseverance; perseverance, character, and character hope. And hope does not disappoint us because God has poured his love into our hearts by the Holy Spirit, whom he has given us (Rom 5:5).

It was out of Paul's "weakness" that he learned how to be strong (2 Cor 12:9). "For Christ's sake I delight in weaknesses, in insults, in hardships, in persecutions, in difficulties. For when I am weak, then I am strong" (2 Cor 12:10). Paul found a way to draw near to Jesus through prayer, worship, the reading of Scripture, and a life lived in obedience to the gospel. As a result, he was transformed into a person who was "persecuted, but not abandoned, struck down, but not destroyed" (2 Cor 4:10). For Paul, "our present sufferings are not worth comparing with the glory that is to be revealed" (Rom 8:18). The suffering he experienced was what marked the "difference" between the triviality of the old life lived in search of the dumb pleasures of the animalistic self, and the heights to which the converted, transformed, and re-minted disciple/saint is capable of attaining. Paul learned to live out of his "transformed" self, in order to live his earthly life out of the resources of the heavenly life that burned within him.

From its earliest beginnings, the life experience of Christian saints has been marked by suffering. The Bible itself has been called a "text in travail,"[1] that tells the story of holy people who refused to live ordinary, unremarkable lives. Instead, they determined to live heroically for Christ. The list of people named in the "faith" chapter of Hebrews 11, closes with a description of how they were mistreated. They were persecuted and mistreated, they wandered in deserts and lived in caves in the ground. The text informs us that "the world was not worthy of them" (Heb 11:38).

---

1. Rohr, *Job and the Mystery of Suffering*, 90.

Holy Wounds

The early church in Asia Minor (as described in Peter's epistles) suffered at the hands of the state-sponsored persecution against Christians for their supposed "disloyalty" against the ruling regime of the day. The Apostle Peter wrote to encourage the early believers to be faithful to their calling as followers of Christ, and not to be discouraged by the senseless abuses arrayed against them. They were to "participate in the sufferings of Christ" (1 Pet 4:13) and to bear the insults their oppressors hurled at them, as if they were an affront to Christ himself. Instead of being "shaken," they were to prove their faith genuine by serving as soldiers of Christ. Jesus' gentle encouragement to such suffering communities is to remind his "little flock" to not be afraid, because "your Father in heaven has chosen gladly to give you the kingdom" (Luke 12:32).

Holy Sadness

But not all suffering experienced by saints implies physical persecution from sources exterior to their lives. Instead, saints may experience other forms of sorrow, in the ordinary run-of-the-mill circumstances of life. I call this kind of sorrow experienced by saints in their inward lives a form of "holy sadness." It is "holy" because it springs from a righteous desire for a better world: "Your kingdom come, your will be done." And it is "sadness" because it is not yet despair . . . what the psychologists call clinical depression. Instead, it is a form of religiously generated melancholy that belongs uniquely to saints. Holy sadness is a lingering, uncomfortable disquiet that rests upon the soul of redeemed people like the kind of nostalgia for home and hearth, felt by expatriates and travelers who have been away from home too long.

At its roots, holy sadness is a by-product of the deep-level transformation that follows after a life-changing encounter with Jesus Christ. This kind of radical transformation was spoken of by the Russian novelist Leo Tolstoy:

> It happened to me as it happens to a man who goes out on some business and on the way suddenly decides that the business is unnecessary and returns home. All that was on his right is now on his left, and all that was on his left is now on his right; his former wish to get as far as possible from home has changed into a wish to

be as near as possible to it. The direction of my life and my desires became different and good and evil changed places.[2]

Such a radical conversion resets the compass of travelers on the earth, meaning they now travel by a new "north star." Believing souls are delivered into a new place, a new world, which has a new horizon as its primary reference point, with a new set of alternate reference points that causes saints and holy people to travel as pilgrims rather than as mere tourists. Tourists never get off the bus. Pilgrims immerse themselves deeply in the life God has given them. Tolstoy again provides us with the necessary insight by writing:

> I remember that I only lived at those times when I believed in God. As it was before, so it is now. I need only to be aware of God to live; I need only to forget him or to believe in him, and I died... I live, really live, only when I feel him and seek him. "What more do you seek?" exclaimed a voice within me. "This is he. He is that without which one cannot live. To know God and to live is one and the same thing!"[3]

The holy sadness that dispirits saints arises from the realization that something is fundamentally wrong with the world. The world they see around them is socially, morally, and spiritually "broken." The world reported on the six o'clock news—a world of bombs and murder, hatred and greed, violence and despair—is not the world that God intends for his created order. Instead, those touched by holy sadness can see another world that is very different, a world that is ordered by God's righteous decree which demands right relationships, right living, and right ordering of our desires. In such a world, justice, truth, and righteousness are the expected outcomes. Christians understand that in the world as originally intended by God, and in the fully redeemed world to come, no baby ought to die at birth, no person ought to fall sick, no child should be sexually molested, no woman should be murdered by her partner, no one ought to be hungry, poor, homeless, or oppressed. There ought not to be any such thing as greed, war, poverty, injustice, terrorism, and ecological disaster. The biblical narratives picture redemption as the "restoration" of all things. The prophet Isaiah described this ideal state as the "wolf living with the lamb, and the leopard lying down with the goat, the calf and the yearling together" (Isa 11:6–7). And the

---

2. Tolstoy, *A Confession*, 307.
3. Ibid., 64–65.

Apostle John, in the book of Revelation, foresaw "a new heaven and a new earth," and the "dwelling of God being with men" as a result of him "making everything new" (Rev 21:1–5).

The reason saints experience holy sadness is because of the "gap" between the everyday world they inhabit in their bodily selves, and the sanctified world they inhabit in their spiritual selves. Rightly or wrongly, saints apply the values and virtues of one "country" (heaven) which they take to be the "real world," to the values and circumstances of another "country" (their earthly existence), which is passing away. They are homesick for heaven. They long for the "ultimate good" that they have discovered in their Father's house, to be available to their friends and colleagues, neighbors and family members. And it is clear that their imaginations are not wrong or misguided. They have read correctly the text of redemptive history as if it were the proper one, where wrongs are put right, where those who have suffered injustice are recompensed, the dead are raised, those who have rebelled against God are judged, and a "right order" is restored. Saints long for the day when "The kingdom of this world has become the kingdom of our Lord and of his Christ, and he will reign forever and ever" (Rev 11:15). That day will be the final day, when their race is run, when the kingdom has come, and when history will have achieved its fulfillment. But it is not yet.

Because of the pervasive nature of "holy sadness," saints need to be careful not to fall victim to the slough of despond identified by John Bunyan in his legendary pilgrim tale *Pilgrim's Progress*. Instead, they must learn to become wise as serpents and harmless as doves, even as Jesus sends them out into the world like sheep amongst wolves (Matt 10:16). With Søren Kierkegaard, we are to realize that "life must be understood backward but lived forward."[4] Saints orient themselves in the world by looking backwards to the biblical text as the "defining" text for their lives. And they live intentionally in a forward-moving direction by always looking towards the Lord's return to institute his kingdom. As the German social theorist Jurgen Habermas has written, "Christianity and nothing else, is the ultimate foundation of liberty, conscience, human rights, and democracy . . . . We continue to nourish ourselves from this source. Everything else is postmodern chatter."[5]

---

4. Bottum, "Judgment of Memory," 49.
5. McClay, "Our Buried Sentiments," 167.

The Pattern of Ministry

As a theological educator, my task is to train Christian leaders for ministry in the church and in the world. In addition to exposing them to the great teachings of the historic Christian faith, it is of great importance for them to understand the pattern of ministry experienced by Jesus, their Master. The pattern of ministry that Jesus himself experienced is likely to be the template which those who follow him as his appointed "agents" in the world will also experience. Although my work is focused on helping pastors and priests to understand the scope and nature of their ministries, I am strongly of the opinion that much of what goes on in the theological classroom is also directly applicable to ordinary Christians, or saints. Sometimes this requires some adjustment of language to ensure that nonprofessional readers of theology who do not have the background training to easily read and understand knotty texts, are able to grasp the significance of what is being discussed. But there is also a case to be made that ordinary saints need to be open to learning new language, concepts, and ideas. In what follows, I will discuss a fourfold pattern of ministry offered by Michael Gorman, which is based on Jesus' own example.[6] I believe it is essential for every Christian to know and understand this pattern of ministry, on the basis that if it was true for Jesus—our great "model" in ministry and service—then it is also likely that we, as his disciples and servants, will also experience the same pattern of experience.

Downward Movement through Kenosis

Kenosis (meaning "self-emptying") is the Greek word taken from the christological hymn in Philippians 2:5–7, that describes the downward descent of Jesus from his previous position of power and privilege at God's right hand. *Kenosis* refers to Jesus' voluntary self-emptying of his right to divine privilege. Jesus, the second person of the triune God, chose voluntarily to submit himself to the will of God and—as a consequence—suffered a cruel death on the cross. What we learn from the principle of *kenosis* is that ministry always involves a downwards step into humility. Jesus' willingness to be humbled is what lays the foundation for him being elevated by God following his resurrection, to "the highest place" (Phil 2:9), with the result that "every knee should bow in heaven and on earth and under the earth,

---

6. Gorman, *Inhabiting the Cruciform God*.

and every tongue confess that Jesus Christ is Lord" (Phil 2:10–11). And God himself is also implicated: the historian Bruce Shelley has observed that "Christianity is the only major religion to have as its central event the humiliation of its God."[7] Although God's willingness to suffer in Christ is unexpected and counterintuitive, nevertheless it is his willingness to suffer and to weep with us that discloses his divine compassion for us.

Death by Crucis

Crucis (Latin, referring to "crucifixion") involves a movement towards the cross as the necessary precondition for effective ministry. According to Gorman, all of Paul's theology is *cruciform*, i.e., if Christ's purpose was to "come into the world to save sinners" (1 Tim 1:15), his means of salvation was through the cross, which he chose as his intentional strategy, rather than as a sign of weakness or victimization. Because he was the "lamb of God slain before the foundation of the world" (Rev 13:8), Jesus' crucifixion was a deliberate redemptive "move" which—although on the surface it looks like defeat—actually becomes the means to his victory over evil and death.

Restoration via Anastasis

Anastasis (Greek, meaning "resurrection") is the first step in restoring Jesus back to fullness of life. Jesus' resurrection leads to his elevation and glorification at God's right hand. It is in the resurrection that God's power is most dramatically seen to be at work. Typical of God's way of working, *kenosis* is the costly first step that prepares Jesus for his cruciform ministry that was intended to benefit others. His resurrection "seals" his victory, and announces that all those who believe in him by faith can also participate in the kingdom of which he is now the absolute Ruler and Lord. *Anastasis* is *the* central fact of Christian ministry. Hence the title of Eugene Peterson's book, *Practise Resurrection*,[8] that invites ministry leaders to make resurrection, joy, and spending out of God's spiritual resources the central theme of their ministries.

---

7. Shelley, *Church History in Plain Language*, 3.
8. Peterson, *Practise Resurrection*.

Elevation via Theosis

Finally, Gorman identifies *theosis* as the completion of all Christian ministry. Looking at Jesus' ministry, it is only after he has been through the process of *kenosis, crucis,* and *anastasis* that he can show himself to be the divine Son, and to live out of the divine nature given to him by the Father. Hearing Christ's call to, "Come, follow me . . . and I will make you fishers of men . . . . Feed my sheep . . . I have given you the keys of the kingdom," Christian disciples are invited to participate in the divine nature (2 Pet 1:4) as their spiritual birthright. The notion of *theosis* is controversial in some circles, because it appears to overly elevate redeemed persons into the divine godhead. But it deserves to be reflected upon more carefully, because it is a biblical concept, which—although it has fallen out of use in many circles—is much discussed by Patristic (and Eastern Orthodox) commentators, and offers us an important "key" to understanding the nature of post-transformational, redeemed human persons who have been restored to the fullness of life God has given them. The truth is, we are closer to God than we know!

The Thorn in the Flesh

Inevitably, saints bring to their callings the weaknesses that arise from their humanity. Nowhere is this more evident than in the life of the Apostle Paul. He confided to the church in Corinth that he was given a "thorn in the flesh" to prevent him from developing the sin of pride after he had been caught up "to the third heaven" (2 Cor 12:2). After his elevation where he had met Christ in an ecstatic encounter, he was brought low by suffering. There is uncertainty as to the exact nature of Paul's "thorn in the flesh." But it is widely thought to be a disease of the eyes, because Paul used an *amanuensis* (the stenographer of the first-century world), and because he signed his name with "such big letters" (Gal 6:11). We can infer, but not presume, that his eyesight was weak and that he had trouble seeing. If that was the case, it is all the more noteworthy that the person who wrote more than half the canon of the New Testament was all but blind!

Whatever the nature of his affliction, Paul asked the Lord to spare him from it on three separate occasions. But the Lord did not grant his request. Instead he used the thorn in the flesh to teach Paul that ministry is not something we can do out of our "fleshly" abilities and powers, but something that God in Christ does through us as a work of his Spirit. Thorns in the flesh remind saints that their work in the world "is not by might, nor by power, but by my Spirit says the Lord" (Zech 4:6).

Physical ailments of any kind are deeply distracting to our primary tasks of prayer, worship, service, study, and the mission of the gospel to serve others in the world in the name of Christ. If the saint does not already feel inadequate to the task of "being their brother's keeper" (Gen 4:9), of "bearing one another's burdens" (Gal 6:2), of "the daily pressure of our concern for the church" [with Paul] (2 Cor 11:28), the fact that they must also "bear in our bodies the marks of Jesus" [again with Paul] (Gal 6:17) brings home the fact of their human insufficiency. Pain is the great teacher, the gift nobody wants. Its lessons are the hardest and deepest to learn. But there are lessons in the "painful moment" that the saint who is a true disciple of Jesus Christ, the "suffering Messiah," must learn.

Somehow it is in the crucible of our own suffering that we develop a sympathy with God's heart for the lost, the lonely, the hurting, and the abandoned. Because of their calling to minister to the great hurt of the world, saints come to know a great deal about suffering. Their knowledge of the subject is not a kind of "book learning" that one reads in a story and then carries out at a distance from suffering humanity. Instead, it is an experiential kind of learning, that is held in the deep chambers of the person's being. It is a form of knowledge that is held not simply in the body, but also in the heart. "All real saints are fashioned in the crucible of God. To be all they became, they were broken, crushed between mortar and pestle. Gradually their soft nothingness was changed to that of granite from which God fashions monuments to his own glory."[9]

Like anyone else, saints and holy people want to avoid pain and suffering and to push it away. No one in their right mind (at least no one I have ever met) wants to suffer. "On our part," St. Ignatius wrote, "We want health rather than sickness, riches rather than poverty, long rather than short life, and so in all the rest; desiring and choosing only that which is most conducive for us to the end for which we were created."[10] This is our natural human inclination. But Jesus gives his saints, disciples, and ministers the "gift" of suffering, in order to teach us the extent of his love for all humankind. Hence the thorn in the flesh is the background condition that establishes without any doubt the universal need for broken humanity

---

9. Wangerin, *Mourning into Dancing*, 33-34.
10. Martin, *My Life with the Saints*, 85.

to be healed, for lost people to be "found," and for suffering souls to be offered solace. This is why saints are not immune to pain and suffering. In fact, we can say that they are especially sensitive to suffering. There is something universal about suffering that—regardless of our age, race, culture, language, gender, and social status—is recognizable by others. I am not at this moment languishing in prison, hungry, sick, or alone . . . but I can intuit something of the wretchedness of being in those circumstances. I am not at this moment lost at sea, as many asylum seekers and refugees are, travelling in leaky boats to seek a new life of freedom and possibility: but I can sympathetically re-experience the risky nature of their journey. And I am not at this moment coping with the diagnosis of terminal cancer, forced to confront my own mortality in this way . . . but because of my capacity as a thinking and feeling human being, I can identify with the person who must make the awful adjustment to a life cut short too soon.

Heroic holiness does not, as a rule, arise by itself out of nowhere. Instead, it arises in the face of an evil so horrendous, so terrible, and so vast that it can no longer remain silent. The holy hero must speak out and act on the injustices he or she sees, even if that person knows responding to evil in that way will threaten their very own existence. It was C. S. Lewis who stated that, "God whispers to us in our pleasures, speaks to us in our conscience, but shouts in our pains; it is his megaphone to rouse a deaf world."[11]

The Dark Night of the Soul

According to Bonnie Miller-McLemore, all pastoral theology has its starting point in human suffering.[12] One of the best-known images of human suffering arising out of the Christian spiritual tradition is the "dark night of the soul." St. John of the Cross (1542–1591) was born to a poor family in Fontiveros, Spain. In order to pay for his education John studied with the Jesuits then entered a Carmelite monastic order. Ordained at the age of twenty-five, he moved to a Discalced (barefoot) Carmelite monastery as its confessor, then to a farmhouse where he established the first monastery for (male) Carmelites. However, a group of committed traditional (shoed) Carmelites banned the Discalced (shoeless) variety, and took John as a prisoner to Toledo. When he refused to recant he was imprisoned in

11. Lewis, *Problem of Pain*, 81.
12. Hummel, *Clothed in Nothingness*, vii.

a windowless cell. He was given bread and water three times a week, after which he was whipped for his obstinacy. He wrote some noteworthy poetry during this time (*The Spiritual Canticle*), before escaping and finding refuge with some nearby nuns. He and Teresa of Avila were effectively the co-founders of the Discalced Carmelite order. He became rector of colleges in Baeza and Segovia.

John's writings include several significant poems and essays, entitled *The Dark Night of the Soul*, the *Spiritual Canticle*, and *the Living Flame of Love*. During his middle years John became familiar with mysticism and spoke in his writings of the elevation of the soul toward union with God. Like Teresa, he learned much through his own experiences of suffering and marginalization, and learned to grasp hold of the powerful resources he found in God and in the interior life. Sadly, John was distrusted by his superiors and was eventually removed from the Friary at la Peneula to Úbeda, where he died as a result of the inhumane treatment he received. He was canonized in 1726 and made a Doctor of the Church in 1926. John's spirituality can be described as being characterized by deep mystical discernment, that pays attention to the journey of the soul toward its completion in Christ.

Often the experience of the dark night of the soul is understood as abandonment, despair, and unspeakable anguish. But that is not how John understood it. Using the accepted spiritual formula of the soul's natural ascent towards God, John voiced his stance from the point of view of a mature contemplative reflecting on his experience of "the Beloved." True contemplatives speak from a "state of perfection," which is essentially a form of union with Christ/God. They have already passed through the early stages of those novices in the spiritual life with their struggle to focus on God as their first priority. Instead, they have gone on to better things by learning to focus more specifically through the use of the spiritual exercises on the nearness of God. If God wished to abandon them, then so be it. Still, John rests his faith on his beloved (doesn't every true disciple?). In this state of passive waiting, all worldly strivings cease (cf. Ps 131), and the soul "abandons itself" to God who alone has freedom to either wound, reward, or give ecstasy as he wills. The dark night is not primarily an experience of darkness, torment, humiliation, emptying, or abandonment by God, but a place of preparation and "waiting" for delight, rest, arousal, and spiritual ecstasy, arising precisely because of the soul's proximity to God.

Voluntary Vulnerability

With the rise of the "positive psychology" movement founded by Martin Seligman, there is at the present time much popular concern for human well-being and flourishing.[13] The principles of the positive psychology movement are spelled out in the PERMA mnemonic as a process of (1) Positive emotion and satisfaction with one's life, (2) Engagement with the world via curiosity, (3) Relationships with others to maintain social balance, (4) Meaning as something which is life-affirming and filled with purpose, and (5) Accomplishment as mastery over one's life circumstances. As positive psychology understands things, the person who is happy, strong, performing at their peak, achieving their goals, and "in sync" with the world is the PERMA person who is (in terms of the values of this world) happy, flourishing, and has achieved a state of human well-being.

But the classical Christian spiritual tradition understands things somewhat differently. Following the Christian principle of giving up your life in order to regain it (Matt 10:39), Christianity offers an alternative pathway to human well-being and even flourishing. Contrary to the "taking control of your life" approach recommended by positive psychology and other human potential movements, Christian saints represent a "special case" within the Christian spiritual tradition. This special case is marked by a principle I call "voluntary vulnerability."[14] Voluntary vulnerability is when a person who is whole, healthy, happy, and right with God through faith in Christ, nevertheless chooses to give up their "right" to ensure their own needs are met. Instead, they relinquish any claims to their own comfort and well-being, in order to act in the best interests of others, not themselves. It is the classic case of the "strong caring for the weak" (Rom 15:1), which represents the "signature" of St. Paul's apostleship to the Gentiles (Rom 15:14–22). Importantly, this approach is adopted not merely by human initiative, but because voluntary vulnerability is God's preferred way of doing things.

It begins with God himself. Theologians generally agree that because God, in his divinity, is all powerful and everlasting, he is not susceptible to change. In him there is "no shadow of turning" (James 1:17, KJV). Because he is not susceptible to change, he does not suffer as we do. But because God is also a community of persons (Father, Son, and Holy Spirit), in

---

13. Seligman, *Flourish*.

14. Devenish, "The Contribution of Spirituality to our Understanding of Human Flourishing," 49–64.

whose likeness the human family is made—*imago Dei*—he is free, and in his freedom (and love) he chooses to limit himself to the human condition. It is most uniquely in the person of Jesus of Nazareth, that God can be seen to suffer. During his earthly life Jesus wept, experienced hunger, was oppressed by his enemies, and ultimately died a human death. And in Jesus, God also chose to suffer. So, theologians such as Jürgen Moltmann can speak of him as the "crucified God,"[15] while Jeff Pool sees "God's wounds" as something God voluntarily allows into his intra-trinitarian life.[16]

In the section in this chapter relating to the Christian pattern of ministry, we discovered that all Christian ministry takes its lead from Jesus' willingness to lay down his life in order to save fallen humanity from sin and disorder. The pattern of kenosis, crucis, anastasis, and theosis is evident in Jesus' own ministry. This is what voluntary vulnerability looks like. Jesus, who is well, whole, strong, and righteous, puts to one side his heavenly and earthly well-being, in order to care for the weak and the dying, the sinner and the victim of injustice. And this is the pattern of ministry that also applies to saints. In chapter four we explored the qualities embedded in the lives of ordinary saints, including their love for humanity, overflowing joy, generosity of spirit, willingness to suffer, deep humility, and so on. This does not mean that saints are "sick souls" without backbone and who meekly allow the strong to walk over them. On the contrary, only those who are strong (in faith) are able to choose voluntarily to live in a way which is deeply Christlike, to put aside their own interests in order to fulfill their calling as disciples of Christ. Although neither comfortable to the flesh nor decorous in the eyes of the watching world, this is the principle of voluntary vulnerability that lies at the heart of Christian discipleship.

> Even though I am free of the demands and expectations of everyone, I have voluntarily become a servant to any and all in order to reach a wide range of people: religious, non-religious, meticulous moralists, loose-living immoralists, the defeated, the demoralized—whoever. I didn't take on their way of life. I kept my bearings in Christ—but I entered their world and tried to experience things from their point of view. I become just about every sort of servant there is my attempts to lead those I meet into a God-saved life. I did all this because of the Message. I didn't just want to talk about it; I wanted to be *in* on it! (1 Cor 9:19–22, The Message).

15. Moltmann, *Crucified God*.
16. Pool, *God's Wounds*.

Saints and the Averted Face

I want now to pay attention to one of the most painful aspects in the life of any saint—when they turn their back on God and "backslide." At some time in every believer's life, there comes a moment when—even if they don't deny God completely—they are at least tempted to revert to their old life. This is a time when the once lovesick heart is tempted to reverse its original decision for Christ, by "taking back" their earthly lives and to run away from God. That was true of the people of Israel when they longed to return to the "leeks and onions" of Egypt (Num 11:5). This was the experience of Jonah, who resented God for having mercy on the hated Ninevites, whom he despised. And it is also the journey of Judas, who "sold out" for what he thought was a better offer. Backsliding is that "season" of faith when the believer who could previously not get enough of God, chooses to avert his or her face and to look away from God. Choosing to avoid God altogether, they prefer a form of self-imposed exile rather than to live any longer in his presence. What follows is the season of spiritual "midnight."

The initial move of the converted heart was towards God in what, for all intents and purposes, was a complete abandonment of the self, in order to become what God asked it to become. The movement was the first step in a passionate journey of self-abandonment whose goal was to embrace God. This step was made voluntarily, of course: remember that love can only be love when it is given freely. But it is also a journey of transformation from death to life, from darkness to light, from cocoon to moth, and from agony to ecstasy. Now, a counter-movement of regression takes place, from a season of pure sunshine, love, and personal embrace to a season of disappointment with God, of resentment and antipathy. Whether through some kind of "buyer's remorse," or the retention of some bitter seed of the willful self, or simply the unanticipated cost of discipleship . . . the bond of love is broken. What follows is a season of bitterness of spirit. So soon after the wedding bands were exchanged, a divorce is called for.

What comes into awareness is a certain "putting into reverse" of the spiritual life, of falling out of love, of recidivism. In Jesus' teaching in the parable of the Two Sons (Matt 21:28–31), the backslider is the person who at first says yes, but when confronted with the cost of discipleship and the distractions of everyday life, forgets their first love and effectively says no. Two proverbs of folly describe most vividly what's going on: "A dog returns to its vomit," and "A sow that is washed goes back to her wallowing in the mud" (2 Pet 2:22). The Apostle Peter's diagnosis is correct. The source of the about-face results from secretly carrying a treacherous "slavery to depravity" as its driving mechanism (2:18–19). Such people would have been better off not to have known the way of righteousness (2:21).

At its core, the root cause of unfaithfulness lies not with God, but in the human heart itself. But we try and blame him nonetheless, as if God were at fault. It is so easy to blame God for all of life's disappointments, like a rebellious child who, despite being given the best of food, clothing, education, toys, and distractions, still accuses its parents of bad parenting because they have withheld some small plaything it desires. But it is not the parents who are rude, arrogant, and willful. Rather it is the headstrong child who obstinately insists—against all advice to the contrary—that cotton candy and caramel apples are the basis of a good diet. In a similar fashion, neither do bad friends, destructive habits, or immoral behavior provide the necessary foundation for a holy life that is pleasing to God. But try telling that to the rebellious teenager! And try telling rebellious saints after they have averted their faces from God, that he still loves them. After seeking out their manifold "altars for sinning" (Hos 8:11), they blame God for not taking better care of them! The intentions of the heart (what St. Augustine called the *ordo amoris*, the "order of the heart," or the knowing and willing center of the self) are all too susceptible to such flights of fancy and egotistical distempers. How do I know this? Because, regrettably, I have been in those places many times myself.

There is a French word that well describes this reluctance to continue in the spiritual path. The word is *ressentiment*. The philosopher Max Scheler says there are two elements to *ressentiment*.[17] The first is a re-experiencing of an emotion that was initially positive, but that has become negative. An example might be a good friend who through a series of circumstances has become your worst enemy. In this case, *ressentiment* becomes not friendship but hostility. The second element of *ressentiment* is its tendency to sit below the surface of the emotions as a memory of rancor and hatred. A hostility has established itself "under your skin," so to speak, such that what was once tenderness has become rage. Like the more familiar English word "resentment," the notion of *ressentiment* highlights a deep-level accusation and grievance that sits in the soul and festers. If left unattended, it becomes unhealthy and fatally threatens our physical, mental, and spiritual well-being.

---

17. Scheler, *Ressentiment*, 2.

There are only two options open to the rebellious saint turned sinner, following a bad case of the "averted face." The first option is to abandon all connections with Christianity altogether, and to willfully regress deeper into one's old life, as is the case with the great mass of people who have turned away from the Christian faith since the 1970s. As the driving ideology of Western culture, consumerism reinforces the "rights" of the consumer to freely choose what products they will or won't purchase ... a mind-set that is easily applied to the spiritual life. In short, the ethos of consumerism is deeply acidic to the spiritual life. Assuming (falsely) that one can take back one's old life, and abandon the "ties that bind"—the sad sack saint turns away to live a life of remorse, emptiness, confusion, and regret.

But there is a second option open to those who have adopted—for whatever reason—the posture of the averted face and the recalcitrant disciple. Like the prodigal son, it involves "coming home" to the "Father's house," having realized that one's life was much richer, fuller, and better off there. It involves a process of "right remembering," in order to call to mind the reason why they turned to God in the first place. Right remembering requires a process of deep-level repentance—or *metanoia* (Greek for "having another mind")—that clears the air and offers a way of restoration to new beginnings. It is to hand one's life over again in a form of penitential rededication to the work of God in one's true life, and to start again—remembering that discipleship is rarely an easy path strewn with roses, but rather is often a pathway marked by tears, brokenness, and of constant new beginnings as God continually "welcomes" his wayward sons and daughters home. True saints need to find this highway of restoration many times in their spiritual journeys.

Saints and Suffering

As we draw this chapter towards its conclusion, I want to call the reader's attention to six simple lessons to do with suffering. Simple, I say ... but not easy. Simple ... but of great pastoral importance. Simple in the sense that they lie at the heart of the saintly life, but because they are so basic, they can easily be overlooked.

The first lesson is that our own suffering acts as a bridge of compassion to the sufferings of others. Let me tell a story. Geoff Wild was my first-year church history teacher at the Baptist College of Western Australia in Perth, Western Australia (now Vose Seminary). It was 1981, and

I was a young trainee pastor. What was significant about Geoff was that he identified so closely with the early Christian martyrs, with Perpetua and Felicity, Polycarp of Smyrna, and Justin Martyr in particular. It was as if he somehow understood them and their willingness to "give up" their lives. It took me some time to realize that Geoff spoke about these men and women as if they were long lost friends, because he himself was dying of cancer. His own humanity and his own suffering were the "bridge" by which he came to understand the faith of these men and women who had "risked" everything for Christ. He himself was staking his life on Christ, saintly man that he was. The lesson I want to draw to your attention is that our suffering frequently acts as a "bridge" to the suffering of others, enabling us to do more than exercise "cold" sympathy from a distance, but instead to offer a "warm" compassion from alongside them.

The second lesson concerns the centrality of "holy tears" to the saintly life. Living with the "bread of tears" (Ps 80:5) is part of our human condition. The psalmist describes God as one who collects our human "tears in a bottle" (Ps 56:8)—indicating that God "feels" with our human pain and sympathizes with us as we bear our cross. Saints are often "experts in the art of dying."[18] Sometimes this is the result of persecution, such as when Christians fled their Muslim oppressors in Turkey over the period 1915–20, when 1.5 million of Turkey's Armenian Christians were killed or forcibly deported in a systemic campaign of ethnic and religious cleansing, or in a similar extermination of Christians in the Middle East at the present time. And sometimes simply bearing the weight of the world and the presence of evil is enough to send us into a frenzy of holy tears. In his difficult reflection entitled, *Tears and Saints*, E. M. Cioran observes that "Agony is Christianity's normal climate. Everybody dies in this religion, even God, as if there were not enough corpses already and time weren't the slaughterhouse of the universe!"[19] He goes on to suggest, "The whole of Christianity is mankind's fit of crying, of which only salty and bitter traces are now left to us."[20] But there is a time coming when our tears will be dried, our weeping will be no more, and our crying will turn to laughter. It is the anticipation of a restored future filled with hope, holiness and a humanity under the reign of God . . . that drives saints to press through the pain barrier towards a better world where Christ reigns as Lord and King over a new and redeemed creation.

18. "Experts in the Art of Dying," 10.
19. Cioran, *Tears and Saints*, 115.
20. Ibid., 30.

The third lesson—as difficult as it may be for us to understand—is that "Our wounding is not a barrier to the grace of God, but rather a means to becoming agents of reconciliation and peace for others."[21] God disciplines those whom he loves (Heb 12:6), and if we find ourselves in the grip of a "painful grace," then we—*if* we are able—are to bear it with grace and dignity. God is aware when sparrows fall from the sky, when melancholic seasons rest on the souls of his saints, and when great men and great women pass from this world. "Precious in the sight of the Lord is the death of his saints" (Ps 116:15). Yet the wounding that comes our way is not the result of a malicious and vindictive God whose purpose is to judge and to destroy our memory from the earth. On the contrary, redemption is a reframing of death, in which our lives are not seen simply as a dramatic personal tragedy, but rather a part of a larger good-versus-evil drama played out on the big stage of history . . . and the small stage of our personal lives. With this in mind, the wounding that may weigh painfully upon us can be seen as bound up with the "faithful wounds" (Prov 27:6) God himself has suffered on our behalf. God does not cause them, but rather allows such wounds to redirect our attention to him and what he has done for us in Christ. The mercy is that God has himself in Christ been through our struggles with us and understands "from the inside"—so to speak—our pains, and works within us to soften them and help us to see that there is a greater purpose beyond our own small lives.

The fourth lesson is that suffering exerts a shaping power upon saints in formation—one that ensures that we give priority to those things which are of ultimate (rather than trivial) value. In the late 1980s, I was a member of OMF International, a mission agency whose priority is to reach the unreached in East Asia. One of my duties was to ferry the (then) well-known J. O. Sanders to his preaching appointments on those occasions when he visited from New Zealand. J. O.—as he was affectionately known—had a close association with the Overseas Missionary Fellowship/China Inland Mission, serving variously as its General Director, and its "Minister at Large." During one of his many sermons, he told a story against himself. He had preached on suffering and holiness. He felt it was a great sermon: he had put everything he had into the preaching of it. But afterwards, over a cup of tea, he heard two elderly ladies talking about the sermon. One said to the other, "He'll make a great preacher someday . . . after he has suffered a bit!" Whether we like it or not, suffering exerts a deep-level shaping

---

21. Herrick and Mann, *Jesus Wept*, 91.

influence upon us. "Every struggle in the soul's training, whether physical or mental, that is not accompanied by suffering, that does not require the utmost effort, will bear no fruit."[22] Suffering clears the fog from our spiritual lives, and enables us to see what is real and what is not. It is the unwelcome teacher know one wishes to listen to, the painful lesson no one wants to learn . . . but which everyone must encounter at some time in their lives.

The fifth lesson concerning the spiritual life is that we struggle most when dealing with the suffering of innocents, such as women, children, and those victimized by evil. Saints and servants who must deal with the reality of sin and suffering on a regular basis—particularly when it is these who suffer—have a great deal to bear. Karen Smith tells the story of a pastoral letter written by Bishop John V. Taylor. The Bishop had been asked to pay a pastoral visit to a family whose infant child had died of crib death. The question posed repeatedly by the family was, "Why? . . . Why this beautiful child?" In response, Taylor could not honesty tell them that it was all part of God's providence and that one day they would understand. Rather, he said to them that:

> Their child's death was a tragic accident, an unforeseeable failure in the functioning of the little body, that so far from being willed or planned by God, it was to him a disaster and frustration of his will for life and fulfillment, just as it was for them, that God shared their pain and loss and was with them in it. I went on to say that God is not a potentate ordering this or that to happen, but that the world is full of chance and accident and that God has let it be so because that is the only sort of world in which freedom, development, responsibility, and love could come into being, but that God was committed to this kind of world in love and to each person in it, and was with them in the tragedy, giving himself to them in fortitude and healing and faith to help them through. And the child was held in that same caring, suffering love.[23]

Lastly, the sixth lesson I want to highlight is that while God in Christ has promised a future of eternal peace and rest, nevertheless he taught his disciples that, "In this world you will have trouble" (John 16:33). Saints are not to hoard their spiritual energies, or to hide inside a cocoon of safety. Instead, saints are to live lives out there in the real world. But they will be lives of truth, and testimony, and advocating for the needs of others.

---

22. Job and Shawchuck, *Guide to Prayer for Ministers*, 113.
23. Smith, in Taylor, *Christian Spirituality*, 106–7.

And therefore our lives will often be ones where struggle, hardship, and a deep encounter with the pains of the world will be at work. We are not to pay attention to our own safety but to spend and be spent for the sake of a cause bigger than ourselves, and to depend upon the Spirit of God to energize and resource us on the road for the sake of the kingdom and for the cause of Christ and his gospel. Faith is an adventure—sometimes a costly one—as was the experience of the Apostle Paul, Perpetua and Felicity, St. Ignatius and all the martyrs of the Christian faith of whatever denomination, affiliation, or theological predilection. Our lives do not belong to us but to Christ, who "loved us and gave himself for us" (Eph 5:2). He did this to "redeem us from all wickedness and to purify for himself a people that are his very own, eager to do what is good" (Titus 2:14). We are, as Henri Nouwen wrote, "wounded healers" who achieve victory in the spiritual life not out of our knowledge of Christ through mere doctrines and dogmas, but out of a burning and passionate desire to follow him in the world, no matter what the cost. Saints know a great deal about suffering. But they also know a lot about happiness . . . deep, love-saturated, pure, beautiful, and holy happiness. The kind of happiness that cannot be found anywhere else.

I want to finish with a quotation from Frederick Buechner, one of my favorite writers. He is able to convey something germane to human experience that I believe is central to the lives of every saint, and so I include it here as a way of writing a benediction over the doorway of saintly suffering:

> The world floods in on all of us. The world can be kind, and it can be cruel. It can be beautiful, and it can be appalling. It can give us good reason to hope and good reason to give up all hope. It can strengthen our faith in a loving God, and it can decimate our faith. In our lives in the world, the temptation is always to go where the world takes us, to drift with whatever current happens to be running strongest. When good things happen, we rise to heaven; when bad things happen, we descend to hell. When the world strikes out at us, we strike back, and when one way or another the world blesses us, our spirits soar. I know this to be true of no one else as well as I know it to be true of myself. I know how just the weather can affect my whole state of mind for good or ill, and just getting stuck in a traffic jam can ruin an afternoon that in every other way is so beautiful that it dazzles the heart. We are in constant danger of being not actors in the drama of our own lives but reactors. The fragmentary nature of our experience shatters us into fragments. Instead of being whole, most of the time we are

in pieces, and we see the world in pieces, full of darkness at one moment and full of light the next.[24]

Enough! Enough now of suffering and unhappy saints whose faces are turned away from love, and even life itself! It is time to start living again, and such living begins with a continual conversion of the heart. So, dear saint, it is time to return to your prayers, and to your new discoveries of the mystery, wonder, and the overwhelming embrace of the love of Christ for you.

---

24. Buechner, *Longing for Home*, 109.

8

(Extra)ordinary Saints on Parade

"ALL THE WORLD'S A STAGE, AND ALL THE
MEN AND WOMEN MERELY PLAYERS..."
(WILLIAM SHAKESPEARE).

Introduction

FROM THE VERY FIRST moment I began to write this book, I knew that any attempt to speak about saints from a purely theoretical perspective would be a dismal failure. Ultimately, saints are best known by their embodied actions in the world. Sooner or later we need to see their faces, text the texture of their lives as they live them in the real world. Here in this chapter, I want to tell the stories of eight people or groups of people, whose life stories are—I believe—powerfully representative of ordinary saints in the everyday world.

Mommy Olga: Prison Chaplain

Olga Robertson is one of the most courageous women I have ever met. For fifty years she has been the chaplain in Bilibid Prison in Muntinlupa, Manila, Philippines. Bilibid is a sprawling complex of dilapidated low-rise buildings surrounded by razor wire fences and security guards. The word *bilibid* means "tethered" in the Tagalog language, and there is no mistaking that this prison, with its sullen grey walls and stench of too many people crammed into too small a place, is a place of captivity. There are about 16,000 male inmates incarcerated in the prison. Bilibid houses the

Philippines' most hardened criminals. Olga (known as "Mommy Olga" by everyone who knows her) has run a church in the high-security section of the prison for an incredible fifty years. She came to the Philippines in the 1940s with her father, who served in the Portuguese diplomatic service. As a young woman she met and married a US soldier after World War II, but when she gave birth to twin daughters he abandoned the family, leaving her to raise the girls alone. Olga came to faith in Christ, and began searching for something useful to do with her life. With the support and encouragement of Dr. Bob Pierce, the founder of World Vision, Olga began a ministry among prisoners on death row in Bilibid prison. Surrounded by hatred, violence, and distrust, Mommy Olga's life of faith has become a beacon of love and generosity.

I met Olga in 1985 during a brief period of missionary service in the Philippines. I visited the Bilibid Prison at the invitation of World Vision, to observe some of the ministries they were supporting at the time. What shocked me was that a place like this—with the extent of its hunger, violence, and terror—could even exist. What I saw in the faces of the inmates was desperation and oppression, surrounded on all sides by a kind of hopeless despair. But what I saw in Olga's face was a gentleness that wasn't afraid of the violence, but that instead brought perspective and dignity to the suffering the prison represented. I remember being told the story of a riot having taken place sometime before my visit, in the maximum security section of the prison. Armed prison guards had refused to enter the prison to quell the riot, for fear of their lives. Instead, they sent Mommy Olga in to pacify the rioters and to negotiate a resolution to the prisoners' complaints. "She has prayed with rapists and murderers as they passed from this life to the next in the electric chair and has even been effective in getting at least one prisoner's death sentence commuted."[1] For fifty years Mommy Olga lived in the midst of pain, suffering, and indignity, yet managed to ennoble people by treating them as individuals—as persons—and so help them to find hope, faith, and their forgotten humanity in the midst of it all.

Doug Croot: Tribal Missionary

Australian missionaries Doug and Bev Croot joined New Tribes Mission in 1967 and went to serve among the Owininga people in the Sepik River basin in the north of Papua New Guinea. The first years were given over

---

1. Scheller, "Olga Robertson."

to language learning, Bible translation, and bearing and raising their five daughters. As a city girl, Bev found the outdoor life of camping and rivers and forests and gardens a struggle—but the Owininga people were a delight and the work for God was fulfilling. Doug—on the other hand—was a farm boy who thrived in the outdoor life and the tropical heat. In the late 1970s, a lesion developed on the bridge of Doug's nose. After surgery it disappeared . . . only to reappear in the mid-1980s. After medical tests, the biopsy returned with news that the growth was cancerous. Although Doug always wore a hat and sunscreen, the sunlight reflecting off the water during their frequent river travel had caused great damage to Doug's skin over time. Despite Doug's diagnosis, the Croot family continued their missionary service, translating Genesis 1–12, Mark's gospel, Acts, Romans, Ephesians, 1 Thessalonians, 1 Corinthians, and Titus into the local language, and establishing a church in the village. Across the span of their thirty-three years of missionary service, the Owininga tribe has grown from 240 people to about 500 people. Improved healthcare, having their own language in written form, education, and improved farming practices have greatly benefited them. But it came at great personal cost to Doug and Bev. As the cancer spread on Doug's face, his nose had to be removed. Then it spread upwards through his sinus into his eye. His left eye needed to be removed, then his cheek, then the upper palate in his mouth, then his gums and teeth, and finally he became blind in his right eye. Despite the serious facial disfigurement he suffered, Doug continued to be cheerful during his twenty-one years of illness, radiation therapy, and many surgical procedures (including twelve major operations in the final twelve months of his life). Whenever he was asked if he'd do it all again, Doug never hesitated in his answer. Yes—he would do it all over again, and so would Bev and the children.

As his eyesight decreased, someone gave Doug an audio bible. He had many favorite Bible verses, one being the "thorn in the flesh" passage, where Christ reassured the Apostle Paul, "My grace is sufficient for you, for my power is made perfect in weakness" (2 Cor 12:7). Another favorite verse was God's provision of "manna in the wilderness" to the people of Israel journeying in the desert, providing each day enough for that day's journey (Deut 8:16). Another was the man on the side of the road who was blind from birth. When the disciples asked Jesus, "Who sinned, this man or his parents?" Jesus replied, "Neither this man nor his parents sinned, but this happened so that the work of God may be displayed in his life" (John

9:2–3). Doug and Bev's courage in the face of their own deep suffering, yet also the needs of others, is truly remarkable.

Stephen Goldit: Warrior Priest[2]

Stephen Odok Ajawino Goldit was from the Shiluk province of South Sudan near the Nile River. In appearance, Stephen was a large man with black skin and scarifications around his temples and forehead. He had a quick mind and a lively sense of humor, never missing an opportunity to learn or to share a joke. Though he never married, he had a caring and sensitive pastoral heart. As a young boy, he was conscripted as a freedom fighter to resist the Islamic National Army that was invading from the north. On one occasion, when he was caught in a crossfire, Stephen knelt down and asked God to rescue he and his fellow boy soldiers. The boys were miraculously kept safe. In 1965 the Islamic militia from the north invaded his village and murdered 187 people, including his father. As a result, Stephen's Christian faith intensified and his prayer life deepened. He joined the armed revolt against the Islamic government, and fought for the liberation of the Sudan in a bloody civil war. He knew God was working in his life, and went to Khartoum to study for the ministry. He was ordained as a priest in the Episcopal Church of Sudan in 1980, and served as priest at All Saints Cathedral in the capital, Juba, and also as a religious education teacher at the Juba Girls' Secondary School. Concerned to increase his education, Stephen applied for and was granted permission by the Archbishop to study at the Near East School of Theology in Beirut, Lebanon. When it came time for him to return home to the Sudan, war had broken out, yet again, and so Stephen remained in Beirut, ministering to refugees. He applied to the UNHCR to migrate to Australia. He was granted a visa and arrived in Melbourne in May 2004.

He served the Sudanese congregation at St. James Anglican Church in Dandenong, while continuing his studies at the Melbourne School of Theology. Stephen ministered to migrant communities in the ethnically diverse Dandenong area who were far from home and forced to make a new life for themselves. Although deeply affected by cultural isolation and the loss of his family in the Sudanese civil war, he remained positive and optimistic about the future. "God is at work in his world, and we must be willing to work with him in his mission," was his advice. His positive spirit

2. Stephen's story is told in Nichols, ed., *From Every Nation*, 1–10.

and pastoral heart encouraged many. I met Stephen when he enrolled in a class I taught on cultural anthropology, during which time we developed a friendship. The irony was, I had a postgraduate degree and could teach the subject, but he spoke four different languages and had crossed more borders and cultures than I could imagine. At sixty-four years of age, Stephen was keen to return to Sudan to visit what remained of his family, and to set up a memorial plaque in memory of his mother and father and brothers who had been killed in the bloodshed of the Sudanese civil war. He bought his air tickets and laid his plans. But tragically, on the plane on the way home Stephen suffered a heart attack and died. He never saw his beloved Sudan one last time. Because of the compelling nature of his life story, and his love for those exiled from their homeland, I have included his story here. This is my memorial plaque to Stephen Goldit, the Christian warrior priest.

Cathy Woods: Indigenous Children's Nurse

Cathy grew up in Zambia, in Southern Africa, as one of three daughters born to Australian Baptist missionary parents, Ted and Jenny Woods. Owing to her upbringing, she grew up with a deep sense of call to serve the poor and marginalized. After returning to Australia Cathy commenced nursing training in 2000, at Deakin University in Melbourne. She undertook several short-term mission trips to Townsville and Bangladesh, to "test" her missionary call. A year's graduate medical study in Sydney marked a turning point in Cathy's life. She returned to Melbourne where she served in the Emergency ward in an inner-city hospital. As a nurse, Cathy obtained skills in critical emergency care and drug and alcohol interventions. She met numerous indigenous patients and developed a special bond with them, being invited to speak at several family funerals. It was while she was preparing to go to Africa for a further short-term mission trip that she learned that a pediatric nursing position was available in a remote Aboriginal community in the far north of Australia's Arnhem Land. She applied for the position, spending the next seven years of her life there.

The community has a shifting population of 3,000 residents, almost half of whom are children. Cathy worked with two Aboriginal healthcare professionals, to care for people suffering from acute and chronic illnesses, as well as providing emergency out of hours healthcare. In her early years, she treated many acutely sick infants suffering dehydration secondary to diarrhea. Cathy asked God to help her know how to care for these people.

She was involved in two significant preventative health programs: the first was a vaccination program for 600 children that included a vaccine to prevent a bad strain of diarrhoeal illness. The second program was aimed at preventing anemia and failure to thrive in 0–4 year olds. The second program was co-sponsored by the Red Cross. Both programs saw a significant increase in the health and well-being of infants and young children. One particular crisis arose when Cathy needed to fit an intra-osseous drip into the leg bone of a dying infant. Although trained, she had not applied the method previously and prayed for guidance. The procedure went well and the child lived.

There was much sadness in the community in the wake of a series of suicides that deeply affected the community. Cathy was also deeply impacted by the loss, and sought to care for the grieving families. During her time there, Cathy cared for many in the community, opening her home and feeding the hungry, healing the sick and giving spiritual care to those in need. Finally, in 2014, weary and in need of rest, Cathy resigned her position and returned to Melbourne to reconnect with her family once again. Cathy continues to acquire new nursing skills in order to care for the sick and needy in Christ's name. Though she is still a young woman, Cathy has "given away" her life to serve her neighbors in Christ's name. And in so doing she has used her freedom (Gal 5:13) to "Love her neighbor as herself."

Don Byrne: Industrial Chaplain

Don and Valda Byrne are the brightest and happiest of people—yet they and their family have journeyed through seasons of great darkness together. In the early 1970s they served as missionaries in the Philippines. During that time, several of their children attended a boarding school where they were abused by a house parent. Only later in life, as adults, were their children able to acknowledge that they had been molested. This has been the cause of very real pain in their lives. Later, on returning to Australia, Don did extensive counseling training at Royal North Shore Hospital in Sydney. Soon after, he was appointed by the BHP Company to serve as chaplain at Newman and Port Hedland in the rugged northwest of Western Australia, where the workforce of 5,000-plus people (mostly men) experienced significant challenges as a result of extreme isolation. During that time Don acquired further skills in helping people recover from post-traumatic stress disorder. The workforce was gripped by severe alcohol and drug abuse and addiction, marriage and relationship breakdown, sometimes resulting in suicide. Don clocked more than 13,000 hours of counseling in the eight years he was chaplain, much of that assisting workers, foremen, and shift teams—as well as families—in dealing with isolation, physical stress, and emotional burnout. Don encountered numerous tragic deaths in the form of suicides, road accidents, and industrial accidents, such as an eighty-ton haulpack rollover where the ore load crushed the driver to death, one worker who became trapped in a conveyor belt, another who was electrocuted, and another who had his head crushed in a machine. Don oversaw periods of intense caregiving, and ran debrief sessions for the workforce. Don was also "on call" for the local hospital and high school. People trusted him and felt free to unburden themselves to him. As a result, Don himself burned out twice—despite having the best of support.

In 1996, the last year of his role as BHP chaplain, he dealt with fifteen mine-related deaths. It took him six years to recover from the emotional stress after he left. Don's sense of humor, deep faith, and stable inner life enabled him to be the best that he could be for others. He told others that tears are a constructive way of coping with pain and suffering, and with regard to human imperfections, Don maintained, if the glass is not cracked then God's light can't shine through. Don was awarded an Order of Australia medal in 2000 for his services to the community.

Will Voung: Social Worker

Will is the eldest of two sons born to a Chinese-Vietnamese family, living in Australia. His mother and father had migrated to Australia independently of each other, as "boat people" in the late 1970s. Along with a tide of other migrant families, they were full of hope and expectation. Will grew up with the weight of his parents' expectations resting on his shoulders. When his academic performance failed to measure up, he began to resent his parents. He began to struggle with the meaning of life. After dropping out of his engineering course at university, Will's life took a right turn as a result of an encounter with God in his late teens. He felt a call to become a social worker and to share God's love with people in need. Having completed a social work degree in 2010, Will now provides intensive rehabilitation to men and women with spinal cord injuries. Causes of spinal cord injury include motor vehicle accident, cancer tumors, degenerative diseases such as Guillain-Barré syndrome, as well as the misuse of illicit drugs. As a result, most patients are paraplegic or quadriplegic, and face deep emotional and physical challenges imposed by their disability on a daily basis. Many patients become angry, depressed, fearful, and carry a sense of shame.

As a Christian, Will believes God has called him to address the needs of the "whole person" in their physical, mental, emotional, and spiritual needs. In the context of a large public specialist hospital, this is not easy. Many health professionals define "health" in one-dimensional terms as something limited to the proper functioning of the body. But many of Will's patients cannot feed themselves, toilet themselves, or live normal lives, so they need a form of care that is extensive and holistic. Will's approach is to work with each person on a relational basis, in a way that acknowledges their dignity and right to be cared for. He believes himself to be an agent for change and transformation. Although he cannot "fix" people or remove their pain or sorrow, he can nevertheless create a space where people can find hope, purpose, and meaning in their lives. Reflecting on his life and work, he wrote, "I have encountered the mercy of God in the midst of my own pain . . . through that, God has enabled me to sit with pain and suffering rather than to run away from it or to project it onto other people. This means I can choose to let go of my tendency to control, manipulate and hide instead of choosing to trust that he will transform and heal me and others in the midst of pain and suffering."

Annemarie, Frances, and Puleng: Teachers of Spiritual Direction

In South Africa in 1998—just as apartheid was ending—two young white women in their early twenties approached the Jesuits (Society of Jesus) in South Africa with a vision for spreading Ignatian spirituality in the community. Their names were Annemarie Paulin-Campbell, and Frances Correia. With the support of the Jesuits they began the work of teaching people new ways of praying in parishes. They soon met a young black woman named Puleng Matsaneng, who also felt called to this work. As they began to work in both black and white communities, they discovered that many people were severely traumatized by the experience of apartheid. In particular, they discovered the years of apartheid had left a profoundly negative impact on the images of God and self among those who had endured discrimination and repression. The team began by offering prayer weeks in churches and communities, designed to help people learn how to pray, and to encourage them to share their experiences with God and with one another. They soon realized that many people found sharing their stories with others a powerful way of processing the pain they had been carrying for extended periods of time. One woman whose husband had committed suicide and whose son had died of HIV/AIDS found the experience of a safe place to share her story deeply healing. An elderly black woman whose son had been killed by the security police told her white guide, at the end of a week of prayer in her township parish, that she had not wanted to speak with a white woman because her experience of whites was so painful. At the end of the week of prayer, during which she had been able to share the pain of losing her son, she reported a profound sense of healing.

At times, the stories people told were deeply distressing ... like the story of the woman whose tiny baby had been brutally raped. Over and over people said that the experience of learning to pray with the Scriptures, engaging the imagination and being really listened to for the first time, offered healing and a genuinely therapeutic experience. Over time the three ministry leaders trained some of the women and men in suburban and township contexts to become facilitators of retreats for others in need of prayer and healing. Now, as part of the Jesuit Institute in Johannesburg, these three young women offer intensive training programs at different levels, to equip those with the necessary gifts and callings to become retreat facilitators, prayer guides, and spiritual directors. Spiritual directors have to work with people while remaining acutely sensitive both to the trauma many still carry from apartheid, and to the diverse cultural backgrounds of the people who come wanting to deepen their relationship with God. Twenty years after apartheid, teaching people to pray with Scripture and to reflect on and share their stories is proving to be a powerful instrument for healing and reconciliation.

The Vocation of Holiness

I am privileged to have met all the people whose stories I have told in this chapter. Each person has a certain quality of essential goodness about their lives, the first of which is that none of them would want to be called anything other than *ordinary*. They don't want to be called saints. Several were at first deeply embarrassed about having their stories included in the book alongside such eminent persons as Saint Damien of Molokai and Etty Hillesum. I had to coax their stories out of them in order to share them with a wider readership. But their stories are worthy of being told because individually and corporately they demonstrate the qualities I have been trying

(Extra)ordinary Saints on Parade

to bring to the surface throughout this book, namely that saints do not live for themselves but for God, and so develop that happy knack of "giving away" their lives as a result of their vocation of holiness, to benefit others.

So what have I observed in these peoples' lives that represents the essential features of the vocation of holiness?

1. God-ward aspect: The new birth of conversion marks the beginning of a person's spiritual journey. Sanctification is everything that follows, through an unfolding process of what Joel Green calls a "conversionary journey" that is God-ward in its deepest orientation.[3] After the initial transformation of God-ward change, believers—a.k.a *saints*—make a point of taking as their starting point the divine model of God's self-giving as the decisive model they adopt for their own lives. In my doctoral work on the repositioning of saints' values during conversion, I discovered that conversion and sanctification are dual processes that have a self-authenticating logic. In both cases believers now have a new starting point and new values, a new identity, a new heart, a new language, and a new way of being in the world that profoundly alters their previous idea of life. They now have a new operating principle. This results in them coming to embrace God's call to a vocation of holiness that is a movement towards becoming *like* God, in a world where holiness is desperately needed.

2. Self-ward aspect: When we speak of people apprehending a religious vision for life, it is not so much that saints grasp a hold of God—rather it is that they feel themselves to be grasped by God so completely that their reason for being takes a 180-degree turn. Lawrence Cunningham observed that, "A saint is a person so grasped by a religious vision that it becomes central to his or her life in a way that radically changes the person and leads others to glimpse the value of that vision."[4] This deep-level change means that the new person who is born out of religious encounter with God in Christ can be completely happy in their new way of life, even when they bear the greatest of burdens. A radical ground-figure shift has taken place: as described by C. S. Lewis, "I believe in Christianity as I believe that the Sun has risen: not only because I see it, but because by it I see everything else."[5]

---

3. Green, *Conversion in Luke-Acts*, 79f.
4. Cunningham, *Meaning of Saints*, 65.
5. Lewis, *They Asked Me for a Paper*, 165.

3. World-ward aspect: In our consumer-oriented world, the first impulse is to *grasp* wealth, power, and beauty out of a desire to satisfy our passions. But in opposition to this self-focused approach, saints share a "family resemblance" insofar as they strive to give away their lives. Jesus' teaching shapes this new awareness: "If anyone would come after me, he must deny himself and take up his cross daily and follow me. For whoever wants to save his life will lose it, but whoever loses his life for me will save it" (Luke 9:23–24). This reversal of values is the reason why saints can adopt a vocation of holiness that takes pleasure in giving their lives to others, even if it comes at significant cost to themselves.

4. Other-ward aspect: Many people have identified a certain "displacement of self" in the saintly life, and mistaken this tendency as a death wish or guilt instinct belonging to weak and troubled souls. But the reverse is true: only the strong can choose to spend their lives for the world, for others, and for the sake of goodness itself. Only those who are secure in their vocation of holiness can take it as a godly value worth fighting for . . . and sometimes even dying for. Saints consistently spend out of their own resources in order to benefit others. In each of the biographies I have discussed in this chapter, this kind of generous self-giving can be seen. When attempting to define saints as moral agents, Andrew Flescher defined saints variously as extraordinarily virtuous, as feeling a sense of responsibility for others, as performing altruistic actions, and even finding self-fullfilment in the service of others.[6]

It is in these ways that we can speak of the vocation of holiness as something central to the lives of ordinary saints . . . a vocation that sets them apart among all the groups of people in the world, as something unique, precious, beautiful, as being "champions" of the human race, or to borrow Aristotle's phrase, as "great souls" who reconfigure the worst aspects of human suffering, violence, and greed, and turn it into something beautiful for God. In essence, the character of saintly lives is a form of godliness that is "projected" outwards onto the social and human landscape of every place, situation, and circumstance encountered by saints in the course of their vocations of holiness.

---

6. Flescher, *Heroes, Saints and Ordinary Morality*, 219–20.

9

The Laughter of Saints

"Our mouths were filled with laughter and our tongues with songs of joy" (Ps 126:2).

Introduction

A ROMAN CATHOLIC PRIEST, a rabbi, and a Baptist pastor walk into a bar ... religious humor is just as funny—perhaps more so—as any other kind of humor, be it dark, screwball, slapstick, farcical, or ironic. Part of the appeal of religious humor is the deep irony that God in heaven chooses to unfold his life here on earth among us mere mortals. In his book entitled *Comedy*, Wylie Sypher cites Franz Kafka's observation that "The comical is present in every stage of life, for wherever there is life there is contradiction, and wherever there is contradiction the comical is present."[1] Sypher extended his discussion of the comical in the religious realm with Kierkegaard's observation that, "Existence itself, the act of existing, is a striving, and is both pathetic and comic in the same degree."[2] Thus faith contains a deep sense of contradiction and brings with it a honed sensitivity to the comical that rests somewhere between the absurd, the impossible, and the feasible. There is a long-standing exploration of this theme in Christian literature, in such works as Dante's *Divine Comedy* and Erasmus's *In Praise of Folly*. Although not in any way as wise or as entertaining as those wondrous classics, our exploration of the laughter of saints in this chapter brings together these

---

1. Sypher, *Comedy*, 196.
2. Ibid.

themes of the divine and the human, life and death, the unexpected and the mundane, as both comedy and tragedy.

People Who Laugh at Saints

In 2010, the *Sydney Morning Herald* ran a story entitled "Dawkins derides sainthood as Pythonesque."[3] The story arose out of comments made by the eminent atheist, Richard Dawkins, in his address to the Global Atheist Convention held in Melbourne in October 2010. Dawkins's remark references the well-known British comedy group Monty Python, and constitutes an approving nod to their ability to take the mickey out of everything—including faith and religion. You may remember that Monty Python was a group of British comedians, the best-known of whom were John Cleese and Michael Palin. Monty Python produced numerous hilarious sketches beginning with the *Flying Circus* in 1969, and concluding with *The Meaning of Life* in 1983, which enjoyed a number of reprises. The group's religious explorations were focused in the controversial film *The Life of Brian*—a spoof on the life of Jesus. The satire was targeted not so much towards Jesus himself, but rather towards his followers, who mistakenly ascribed Messianic attributes to Brian (the film's hapless Jesus substitute), when in fact Brian had no interest in or capacity for such a role.

Dawkins continued the satire began by Monty Python by observing how funny it is in a scientific age the lengths to which the Roman Catholic Church has gone to authenticate the credibility of claims concerning the holiness of people who have been nominated (usually posthumously) for canonization as saints. This includes accounts of miracles attributed to so-called saints. According to Dawkins, such arguments are deeply amusing to people who have been educated in the rationalist logic of scientific Western education, on the grounds that making saints seems both preposterous and superfluous. Dawkins was surprised by the level of support which many in the Australian community—including the prime minister at the time, Kevin Rudd—gave to the canonization of Sister Mary McKillop as Australia's first official saint. This persistence of the religious consciousness in the minds of a supposedly secular Australian public astounded Dawkins, whose job it is to promote the value of atheism based on scientific rationalism, as the only credible worldview for a modern secular society.

3. Maley, "Dawkins derides sainthood as Pythonesque."

The Laughter of Saints

Poking fun at holy people is a pastime as old as time itself. Saints—with their naive expectation that goodness and righteousness ought to be the default setting for living in the world—are easily made a laughing stock. Whether standing up against the schoolyard bully in defense of a new kid at school, or appealing to moral conscience in a world were immorality has clearly become the new social norm . . . acting on one's calling as a saint is a risky business. Depending on the situation, one may win the day—or lose one's life! According to the Jewish writer Abraham Heschel, "The prophet's duty is to speak to the people, 'Whether they hear or refuse to hear.' A grave responsibility rests upon [them]."[4] Everyone knows the behavior of prophets is on occasion very strange—e.g., Isaiah's walking around naked (Isa 20), Jeremiah carrying a ox yoke on his shoulders (Jer 27–28), and Hosea's marriage to a prostitute (Hos 1). As a spokesperson for the divine purpose, whose task it is to speak an unpopular message to a resistant culture—of "speaking truth to power"—saints (like prophets) are prepared to ruin their reputations and become "holy fools," people who are radically out of step with the *status quo* ethos of society. Perhaps it's not surprising then that the only way most people in the Western world have of coping with the audacity of God's spokesmen and women is to laugh at them, because invariably what they have to say does not "fit" with the contemporary secular version of right-mindedness. But those who laugh at saints may well be able to hear the echoes of their own conscience, or the voice of God resounding within. There may come a time when they realize the joke's on them. We must never forget that people laughed at Jesus because the things he did and said shocked and surprised them. When Jesus told the mourning crowd that the little girl was not dead but merely asleep, they "laughed at him, knowing that she was dead" (Luke 8:53). Their laughter soon turned to wonder, however, when he led her by the hand into their midst. And in the world of first-century Palestine, when Rome's brutality and military might were on display for everyone to see, it seemed completely incongruous to say, "Blessed are the meek, for they will inherit the earth" (Matt 5:5), and "Blessed are the merciful for they will be shown mercy" (Matt 5:7). In God's kingdom, these qualities—along with the other beatitudes listed in the Sermon on the Mount—are the only valid currency, and thus supersede all other claims to power, whether of Caesar and the Roman Empire, or of the modern secular state and its marketing arm—the media.

4. Heschel, *Prophets*, 19.

If people laughed at Jesus for the things he did and said, can we expect them not to laugh just as hard at his followers? But "Wisdom is proved right by her children" (Luke 7:35). The laughter of derision may yet prove the first awkward step of a long journey towards conversion, as the Apostle Paul discovered on his own journey towards faith in Christ.

God and Holy Joy

Everyone has a theology that informs their understanding of the "big-ticket items" in life such as life and death, meaning and value, good and evil, God and self. And in these post-Christian days, many people's innate theology—including that of many poorly taught Christian half-saints, unfortunately—is derived more from media and popular cultural sources, than it is from the Bible or from direct encounters with God himself. This leaves us open to a variety of misunderstandings about such issues. Perhaps the biggest blunder we make in the "God Department" is our willingness to accept uncritically a Simpsons-style caricature of God as a grumpy, negative, moralizing Grandpa in the sky, whose task it is to keep a tally of our misdemeanors and sins. And when it comes to the populist understanding of religion—things are no different. For many people, religion is little more than a long list of prohibitions framed in the negative, i.e., things one *must not* think, do, or say. But what if we've got it all wrong, and religion—or the Christian version of it—is a charter for the "good life," giving permission for what we *can* or *should* be doing, as redeemed children of a loving and personal God? One of the primary tasks of theology (defined as "God talk") is to bring together our faithful understandings of Scripture, from which we obtain a fuller understanding of the "good news" in the gospel of Jesus Christ, and what we believe God is saying to us in our contemporary cultural context. It may just be that we need to correct our mistaken views of God, and to rediscover him as revealed most fully in Jesus, as a loving Father, a welcoming Householder, a restoring Healer, and as the true source of everlasting and heavenly joy.

I happen to believe that God has a sense of humor! You only have to remember the story of God speaking through Balaam's ass to have a laugh at Balaam's expense (Num 22:21ff.). And you only have to read the book of Jonah to discover that Jonah's petty and selfish affection for his shade plant is nothing compared with God's magnanimous love affair with the rebellious city of Nineveh (Jon 4:6–11). God has a tremendous sense of humor—the proof lies in his creation of the Australian kookaburra, the

New Zealand kiwi, the African meerkat, the South American aardvark, the North American beaver, the Mexican axolotl salamander, the Scottish capercaillie, or the European blind mole.

Indeed, in the biblical narrative God laughs often. There are many references to laughter and joy: "The joy of the Lord is your strength" (Neh 8:10), "In your presence there is fullness of joy, and at your right hand are pleasures forevermore" (Ps 16:11), "There is a time to weep and a time to laugh, a time to mourn and a time to dance" (Eccl 3:4). We are told that God who is "enthroned in heaven" laughs at his enemies (Ps 2:4), and that he "laughs at the wicked, for he knows their day is coming" (Ps 37:13). God's laughter does not equate to the vengeful, insane laughter we might associate with comic book megalomaniacs. Instead it is the laughter of God's heavenly perspective: our human effort to outwit God through some self-deceiving Faustian attempt to provide for ourselves and make secure our own destiny, are nothing if not laughable. Can you imagine anything more ridiculous? The literary critic and social commentator Terry Eagleton wrote:

> The God of Christianity is friend, lover and fellow accused, not judge, patriarch and superego. He is counsel for the defense, not for the prosecution.... For Christian faith, the death of God is not a question of his disappearance. On the contrary, it is one of the places where he is most fully present... [Jesus] is a sign that God is incarnate in human frailty and futility. Only by living this reality to the full, experiencing one's death to the very end, can there be a path beyond the tragic.[5]

Only if we take evil, the tragic, and despair seriously, can we begin to imagine the counter-possibility that God is "counsel for the defense, not for the prosecution"—as Eagleton tells us. The God of the Bible is a God who laughs, and the God who invites us to laugh with him.

I also happen to believe that Jesus had a good sense of humor. Many in the church have tried to pooh-pooh the importance of laughter, replacing it with a dour and legalistic form of religious life and practice. But that kind of religion is completely foreign to the Way of Jesus. The early church asked the question, "Did Jesus ever laugh?" and arrived at the answer, "No, he only wept" (John 11:35). But that is like saying that Jesus felt hungry but never ate anything, he felt tired but never slept, he felt sad but never sought the remedy of joy, laughter, celebration, or sharing a joke with his

---

5. Eagleton, *Culture and the Death of God*, 160.

disciples. Concerned to maintain the dignity and probity of their version of Jesus, some early disciples tried to repress any hint of laughter on Jesus' face. One important fourth century example is St. John Chrysostom (c. 349–407, Archbishop of Constantinople), who warned Christians against the levity and lewdness of the circus and theatres of his day. His advice was to "suppress all laughter" on the grounds that neither Jesus, nor Paul, nor the apostles nor any of the saints ever laughed . . . but instead attended to the serious matter of keeping their own souls.[6] Yet contemporary scholars have come to realize that such warnings were intended to sound a warning against Christian believers laughing in an improper manner, in witless, silly, and frivolous hilarity that lead to sinful impropriety. There is an appropriate balance between a proper "sober, grave and temperate" Christian character (Titus 2:2), and the "inexpressible and glorious joy" that belongs to the saints as they anticipate receiving the salvation of their souls (1 Pet 1:8–9).

Jesus' parables included stories of lost sheep, lost sons, and lost coins. But in each case, those lost things were "found." And whenever a "finding" took place, there was great "rejoicing in heaven." Rejoicing, then, becomes the central theme of the kingdom of God and one of the "rules of the household" (so to speak) for citizens of the kingdom of God. The fact that Americans, the English, and the Australians all laugh at different things, tells us that humor is culturally conditioned. And as for the Irish sense of humor, it is quite likely that anything said with an Irish accent "sounds" funny. Yet holy joy is the domain of the people of God, regardless of their earthly culture or background.

James Martin asked his colleague Amy-Jill Levine about humor in the New Testament. She pointed out that many of the stories told by Jesus in his preaching and teaching—although often out of reach to our own twenty-first-century understandings—were either very funny, very raw, or very offensive. Jesus knew how to really "connect" with his first century audience.

> The parables were amusing in their exaggeration or hyperbole . . .
> the idea that a mustard seed would have sprouted into a big bush
> that birds would build a nest in would have been humorous.[7]

We can surmise then that parts of the parables were not simply clever, but actually funny to a first-century audience.

6. Chrysostom, "Sermon 6 on Matthew."
7. Levine, "Most Infallible Sign."

The Laughter of Saints

Sarah Laughed

The very first instance of laughter in the Old Testament has to do with the subject of sex for those over sixty. The story focuses on a woman named Sarah, and contains the most infamous laugh in all of Scripture. Abraham and Sarah had been asking God their whole married lives for a child, but they had remained barren. Seventy-plus years of asking lay behind them. In the narrative (Gen 18), three angelic visitors came calling at Abraham's tent beneath the great oaks of Mamre. While Abraham is engaged in preparing a meal for his guests, as was the custom of Middle Eastern hospitality both then and now, the three visitors prophesy that Abraham's wife, Sarah, will have a son in the coming year. Listening at the entrance to the tent, Sarah laughed to herself. She knew full-well that at 90 years of age she is "past the age of childbearing" and that at 100 years of age, Abraham would struggle to rise to the task of sexual intercourse. She asks, "After I am worn out and my husband is old, will I now have this pleasure?" (Gen 18:12). Sarah's laughter captures three main tensions. The first concerns why on earth it took God so long to get around to answering her prayers for a child anyway. The second is the irony of experiencing sexual pleasure at their ripe old age—an irony mirrored in our own time as the elderly are urged to remain full of life, and sexually active. And the third tension is the sheer relief of the glimmer of hope that God's promise that Abraham would become a "great nation" might finally be fulfilled (Gen 12:2–3).

There is irony, there is tragicomedy, there is embarrassment when Abraham and Sarah's friends discovered they have been having "relations"—and at their age! And there is enormous relief in the story. In response to Sarah's laughter, and Abraham's equal skepticism, the three visitors counter by asking, "Is anything too hard for the Lord?" (Gen 18:14). Up to this point, the human answer would have been, "Yes." But that was about to change. Twelve months later, as promised, Sarah gave birth to a son they call Isaac, whose name in Hebrew means "laughter" (Gen 21:3). As Sarah then declared, "God has brought me laughter, and everyone who hears about this will laugh with me" (Gen 21:6). Everyone, that is, except Hager and Ishmael—who, we are told, were "sent away," presumably in tears.

While the outworking of God's will in human history is no laughing matter, there is a great deal of humor contained in many of the biblical stories. It is also true in our own lives which contain enough tensions, complexities, and impossibilities to give us cause for much frustration and amazement . . . and also (I suspect) tickle God's funny bone.

Ordinary Saints

A Litany of Holy Laughter

Here is a selection of gathered humor that will put a smile on your saintly face.

'Dangerous Recreations in the Monastery'—by Ivan Head[8]

(For St Mary McKillop).
As an occupational health and safety matter
they installed a nun-slip floor
in the Monastery.

It became habit forming
and abbot forming.
It also encouraged monkey business.

St Linoleum was able to glide across it by will power alone.
St Thomas said, 'Nature abhors a vacuum' and took his name off
the cleaning roster.
Mother Superior's red sandals were a scandal.

but she said, 'No action without traction
and no reaction without attraction'.
Sr Wilhemina the Methodist was a back-slider.

St Simon Stylites always scored a 10 when crossing the floor
by opting for high degrees of difficulty
3.5 with a half-pike
he stole from the Refectory Fridge and used to bribe the judges.

Professor Franz Bibfeldt

The American theology professor Martin Marty is known for his sense of humor, and his propensity to take himself and his fellow academics lightly. While studying at Concordia Seminary in Missouri (1949–1952), he concocted a fictional scholar named Professor Franz Bibfeldt. Through Marty's creative efforts, Bibfeldt developed an academic profile that would be the envy of any international scholar. He has a current Facebook page, a Twitter

---

8. Used with permission.

account, and has published a book entitled *The Unrelieved Paradox: Studies in the Theology of Franz Bibfeldt*, now in its second edition.[9] His works have been cited by luminaries around the world. He received a mention in the *University of Chicago Magazine* in February 1995, and his works have been quoted—even pilloried—by noteworthy theologians. The esteemed French philosopher, Jean-Luc Marion, even wrote a piece in the *Criterion* journal entitled 'This is Not Funny! From the Quest for the Historical Bibfeldt to Bibfeldt with/without Being."[10]

St. Teresa's Hair Shirt

St. Teresa of Avila corresponded regularly with her family. On one occasion she wrote to her brother Lorenzo with the words, "I send you a hair shirt . . . . You may wear it on any part of the body so long as it feels uncomfortable . . . . I laugh as I write, for you send me sweets, presents and money, and I repay you with a hair shirt."[11] In the same letter, she gave spiritual advice on prayer, the presence of Jesus, and the nature of her mystical writings—along with references to sardines, sweets, money, repairs to one's house, health remedies, and the benefits of hand warmers in the cold of winter.

Jewish Humor[12]

> A Jewish father was very troubled by the way his son turned out and went to see his rabbi about it. "Rabbi, I brought him up in the faith, gave him a very expensive Bar Mitzvah and it cost me a fortune to educate him. Then he tells me last week, he's decided to be a Christian. Rabbi, where did I go wrong?"
>
> The rabbi stroked his beard and says, "Funny you should come to me. I too, brought up my son as a boy of faith, sent him to university and it cost me a fortune and then one day he comes to me and tells me he wants to be a Christian."
>
> "What did you do?" asked the man of the rabbi.
>
> "I turned to God for the answer," replied the rabbi.
>
> "What did he say?" asked the man.

9. Marty and Brauer, eds., *Unrelieved Paradox*.
10. Marion, "This is not Funny!"
11. St. Teresa, *Letters of St. Teresa*, 219.
12. Rifkin, "5 Best Jewish Jokes Ever."

"He said, 'Funny you should come to me...'"

God as an Irish Pyromaniac[13]

An Auslan sign language specialist translated sermons for deaf and hearing-impaired churchgoers in a large church. When she went on holiday, a "temp" was brought in to do the translation. When the regular translator returned several weeks later, she asked one of the people in her deaf congregation named Barry (name changed) how things were going for him at church. Barry attended church only infrequently, mostly to socialize with other people, not because he had a faith of his own. It seemed things hadn't been going all that well. Lacking experience, the "temp" translator often guessed the best hand signal to convey the meaning of the preacher's message. On one occasion the preacher was telling the congregation how compassionate God is. The word for compassion involves a hand signal that begins by pointing to the heart and then gesticulating away, as if to indicate generous self-giving. But the part-time translator didn't know the word for compassion, so ad libbed with something she felt would convey God's expansive generosity. But what Barry received in the communication was that God was an Irishman! Whereas the lesson given was, "God is compassionate, and his followers should also be compassionate," what Barry understood was "Since God is an Irishman, he wants us to be Irish too!" Things became worse, however, when the preacher began to tell the congregation how God sent flames of fire at Pentecost. Barry had not heard about Pentecost before, and was quite surprised to hear that God was an Irish pyromaniac who insisted on us joining him in his activities of lighting fires. Barry wasn't sure he wanted anything to do with a God who was, he had been assured, an Irish pyromaniac.

Insuring Churches against "Acts of God"

I was visiting a church as a guest speaker some years ago. After the service, over a cup of tea, I spoke to a man in the congregation. I asked him what he did for a living. He was an insurance agent. He spent his days selling insurance policies to small businesses and families, making sure they had adequate insurance to cover them for accidental loss, theft, fire, and storm

---

13. This is a real story told to me in person by the Auslan interpreter.

damage. But his specialization was in selling insurance to churches to ensure them against "acts of God." The insurance industry describes acts of God as "events which are outside human control," by which they mean such things as floods, earthquakes, and tornadoes. It seemed hilarious to me that while many churches could do with a bit of "shaking up" as a result of a fresh encounter with the divine, here was an insurance agent doing his best to insure the church against acts of God! Don't tell me God isn't laughing!

Groucho Marx

James Martin described the following scene. Groucho Marx—the great American comedian—was once in a hotel lobby when a priest, in his clerical collar, rushed over to see the great film comedian. "Thank you, Groucho, for bringing so much joy and laughter into peoples' lives!" He said. "Thank you," Groucho replied, "for taking so much joy and laughter out of them."[14]

The Laughter of Saints

The Apostle Paul's mention of the "obedience of faith" (Rom 1:5) has a parallel component to it, in the form of the "optimism of faith." If there is any substance to the biblical teaching that God prepares a table for us in the midst of our enemies and our cup runs over in the wilderness (Ps 23:5) . . . and that all things will be placed under Jesus' feet when he returns as Lord and King (Eph 1:22)—then it is the duty of every saint to live out of the optimism of faith as the leading edge of their discipleship. We are to rise above the "holy sadness" that periodically grips our souls, and embrace instead a lifestyle where joy, peace, and a deep expectancy that God is in his heaven and all is well on the earth exudes from the Christian community like water from the sea.

Richard Dawkins is wrong to think that saints are unaware of how silly they look in the world, or how zany Christianity looks when viewed "through the eyes" of the everyday person. One of the greatest causes of hilarity among saints is themselves. In the course of my pastoral duties over the years—alongside the tragedies and the disasters—there has been raucous laughter at the crazy things saints do. The truth is that saints often laugh at themselves. And Dawkins had better get in line if he wants

---

14. Martin, *Between Heaven and Mirth*, 144.

to laugh at saints. Because standing in front of him will be the saints who know how ridiculous they look in the eyes of their "worldly" onlookers. Some of the most ardent fans of *The Life of Brian* are not atheists, naysayers, and unbelievers, but believers themselves. Like the prophets and their Lord before them, saints are "voices crying in the wilderness" (John 1:23). As such they frequently serve as the moral conscience of the community, and the litmus test of their culture for the depth dimensions of morality, virtue and righteousness. Perhaps it is this very serious side of saints, mystics, and martyrs that is so easy to distort by way of caricature and misrepresentation... much of it humorous. As such, if you want to truly understand the perspective of the religious consciousness, it is much more profitable to laugh *with* saints than to laugh *at* saints.

Holy laughter has special significance for the people of Toronto, Canada. The "Toronto Blessing" began in 1994 in what became known as Catch the Fire, a Vineyard church located adjacent to the Toronto International Airport. One Sunday in 1994, the Spirit of God fell on those gathered in worship, and manifested itself in people laughing, shaking, falling over, and appearing to be "drunk on the Holy Spirit," like some modern-day Pentecost. The moment was marked by joy, repentance, first-time conversions, and re-dedications of those who had been on the spiritual journey for some time but who had lost the joy of the Lord. The small fellowship became Toronto's premier tourist destination, as upwards of 50,000 people (including significant numbers of international tourists and pilgrims) found their way to their doors. As a global religious phenomenon, the Toronto Blessing received more than its fair share of criticism on the grounds that it was too subjective, too experiential, not focused on Christ enough, not biblical enough, not evangelistic enough, and so on. Yet today, over twenty years later, the Toronto Blessing stands as the longest-running and most noteworthy movement of the Holy Spirit in recent history.

The well-known British writer J. R. R. Tolkien, in his essay "On Fairy Stories," coined the word *eucatastrophe* (a construct of two Greek words: *eu*, meaning well, and *catastrophe*, meaning to overthrow, destroy, or turn away). With this newly coined word Tolkien intended to convey the sense of being overwhelmed by a surprise ending, or an unexpected turn of events. We find these things in the gospel, where God snatches an unlikely victory from the jaws of defeat, and subsequently alters the course of history—despite not everyone knowing or understanding this. Eucatastophe is a quirk of history that enables saints to see a sinful, fractured, and dying world caught up in the "catastrophe" of the present moment—and to see the possibility that Christ will remake the world as he intends it to be, in the very next moment.

Elie Wiesel, the famous Auschwitz survivor turned author, wrote a number of award-winning books. One of those was a novel entitled *Night*.[15] Here is an extract relating to saints:

> "Shimon Yanai thinks you're a Saint," Kathleen said.
> My answer was a loud, unrestrained laugh.
> "Shimon Yanai says that you suffered a lot. Only saints suffer a lot."
> I couldn't stop laughing. I turned towards Kathleen, toward her eyes, not made for seeing, nor for crying, but for speaking and perhaps for making people laugh. She was hiding her chin in the neck of her sweater, concealing her lips, which were trembling.
> "Me, a Saint? What a joke..."
> "Why are you laughing?"
> "I'm laughing," I answered, still shaking, "I'm laughing because I'm not a saint. Saints don't laugh. Saints are dead. My grandmother was a Saint: she's dead. My teacher was a Saint: he's dead. But me, look at me, I'm alive. And I'm laughing. I'm alive and I'm laughing because I'm not a saint..."

Yet there were many "living saints" who emerged out of the horrors of Auschwitz and the death camps of Germany during the Second World War. And—like Kathleen in Wiesel's story—there are many "living saints" past and present, who have felt deeply uncomfortable about being called "saints." For example, Dorothy Day resisted been called a saint. "Don't call me a saint," she often used to say. "I don't want to be dismissed that easily." Evidently, if you want someone to laugh, to squirm, or feel embarrassed or out of place, just call them a saint! Yet the Catholic theologian Karl Rahner urged all believers to:

> Laugh. For this laughter is an acknowledgement that you are a human being, an acknowledgement that is itself the beginning of an acknowledgement of God. For how else is a person to acknowledge God except through admitting in his life and by means of his life that he himself is not God but a creature that has his times—a time to weep and a time to laugh and the one is not the other. A praising of God is what laughter is, because it lets a human being be human.[16]

---

15. Wiesel, *Night*, 76.
16. Rahner, in Martin, *Between Heaven and Mirth*, 200.

10

The Evocation of Saints

> "It is a goodly life that you lead, friend, no doubt the best in the world, if only you are strong enough to lead it!"
> (Kenneth Grahame).

The Chapel of the Insurrection

On September 16, 2015 Anthony Fisher, the Catholic Archbishop of Sydney, opened a beautiful new chapel opposite Sydney University. The St John Paul the Great Chapel was named after Pope John Paul II (1920–2005). Present at the ceremony were dignitaries and members of the community. It was a time of great celebration.

But in the years that preceded the opening of this new chapel, it was a different story. The old chapel (then called the "Chapel of the Resurrection") had long been closed. The Chapel of the Resurrection stood on the grounds of St Michael's Roman Catholic Residential College, directly across the road from Sydney University. As a place dedicated to the worship of God, the chapel had been an important hub for (Catholic) Christian chaplaincy on the campus of Sydney University, providing a focal point for students in their academic, religious, and social lives. It was a place where hope and care were offered to the young, the disconsolate, and the distressed of heart and mind.

But over time, the chapel had become derelict. Services of worship were no longer offered, the choir no longer sang the *kyrie eleison* ("Lord have mercy"), the smell of food and the sounds of laughter that contribute to community life had disappeared. The chapel doors and windows were boarded up and graffiti covered its walls. The chapel was inhabited by litter, vagrants, and the ghosts of fading memories. At the time the abandoned site was a symbol of the decline of the once dominant Christian religion in the Western world, now forsaken by the very children whom the church had once baptized and given succor to.

When I visited in 2012, someone—probably a university student fresh from a politics class—thought it amusing to replace the first two letters of the word "resurrection" inscribed over the doorway of the chapel, with the letters "in." The Chapel of the Resurrection, where students once celebrated the resurrection of Jesus Christ, now wore the unlikely title of the Chapel of the *Insurrection*. An insurrection—so the dictionary tells us—is an act of uprising, an open revolt against an established authority. The established authority might be the state, the church, or some long-standing authority that exerts a powerful force over its culture and its people. An insurrection is carried out by insurgents who seek to change the established order by means of uprising and revolution—always passionate and sometimes violent—and to replace it with a new status quo.

There is a powerful narrative is to be found in the Chapel of the *Resurrection-become-Insurrection* for twenty-first-century saints. Christianity has always been a social renewal movement, based on the life of Jesus, who came teaching about the kingdom of God, who healed the sick, fed the hungry, raised the dead and gave hope to the poor. Jesus offered the world a kind of insurrection that replaced the old status quo, and in its place established a new "normal." And following his ascension, early Christianity posed a radial form of "insurrection" against the selfish, greedy, and godless forces at work in its time. The community that demonstrated it belonged to Jesus, managed to subvert history by their love for one another and their having something life-giving to offer the society in which they lived. And in our own day, authentic Christianity represents a deep-seated challenge to self-centered consumer culture. The need of the hour is for Christians to "resurrect" the genius of the Christian faith as an insurrection against the tired, established order of consumer culture, greedy big business, and selfish citizens. A new "normal" is being called for, made evident in the lives of the saints who are able to make manifest the life, love, power, and presence of Jesus Christ in the world. It is saints, not religious institutions, that properly "realize" God in the world. Christianity's trophies are not its church buildings, its organizational structures, or its theological confessions... but the exceptional lives of the saintly people it produces.

The Evocation of Saints

Several periods in the history of Christianity have been referred to as an "age of saints." One such time was the era of monastic Christianity, whose best-known saints were Anthony (the founder of monasticism), along with Pachomius, Basil, Benedict, Augustine, Jerome, Athanasius, and others. Another age of saints was the era of Celtic Christianity, whose best-known saints were Patrick, Brigit, Brendan, Ninian, Columba, David, and Aidan.[1]

Out of these ages of saints there also arose a *cult* of the saints, which sadly came to focus on the preservation of supposedly holy relics and the questionable veneration of men and women to whom were ascribed a divine power of their own. For example, St. Jerome referred to early saints such as St. Peter and St. Paul as "altars of Christ."[2] But the early cult of the saints may have been more a remnant of paganism than of the godly practices for faithful believers. Despite the popularity of the saints and the reputed "wonder-working" powers of certain relics, these things were subject to widespread abuse. Keickhefer noted the prestige that a church or monastery could boast, on the basis of the number of holy relics they had in their possession:

> Reading Abbey... possessed 242 items altogether, including bones from Sts Aethelmod and Branwelator; a rib and another bone from St David;... bits of the Blessed Virgin's hair, her bed, and her belts; the hand of St James; the head of St Philip, and the head, jawbone, investments, one rib, and some hair from St Brigid.[3]

The Protestant Reformation, in particular, posed a challenge to the cult of the saints. Martin Luther's criticisms were particularly withering. His frequent objections to the veneration of the saints included what he saw as its tendency towards blatant idolatry, the impossibility, on theological grounds, of saints acting as "mediators" between heaven and earth, the belief that saints possessed no more virtue or dignity than any other Christian,

---

1. Bradley, *Colonies of Heaven*, 160–61.
2. Sweeney, *Lure of Saints*, 27.
3. Keickhefer, *Sainthood*, 5.

The Evocation of Saints

and possible contamination of the legends of the saints through historical accretion and poetic embellishment.

At that time, it was commonplace to appeal to the saints in heaven through the practice of "invocation," asking them to intercede on behalf of earthly supplicants. This practice continues today where Mary, the Mother of God is implored to "pray for us." The help and intercession of patron saints is also invoked by supplicants who find themselves in circumstances of special need. They make their request that patron saints pray on their behalf, in the belief that they possess special virtue and uninterrupted access to God's divine ear.

I am not suggesting that we return to the practice of "invocation" or the cult of the saints. I do, however, affirm with the Nicene Creed the significance of the "communion of saints"—past and present—and the importance of reverencing the martyrs and the "blessed departed." Instead, I want to invite the reader to consider an exchange: that we exchange invocation for evocation. According to the dictionary, the word *evocation* means "to call forth" or "to summon." Instead of the practice of "invocation," I believe the times in which we live require us to "call forth" the lives of saintly people. Invocation asks us to pray to holy people in heaven. Evocation asks holy people on earth to live the heavenly life in the strength of Jesus their Lord. Evocation is a call to today's saints to holy action as an antidote to the evil of the current age. Holiness, which is the peculiar quality and characteristic of the saints, is not essentially an idea, a moral creed, or a set of practices, but an ingredient in saints' lives that points to its source in God. "Be perfect as your heavenly Father is perfect" (Matt 5:48).

My call, then, is for holy people, in these post-Christian times, to "stand up and be counted." Rabbi Abraham Heshel once observed that "What we need more than anything else today is not textbooks, but text people. It is the personality of the teacher which is the text that the pupils read; the text they will never forget."[4] Similarly, living saints, real persons and actions, are the best proof of the credibility and authenticity of Christianity's truth claims. If the "proof is in the pudding"—as the old saying goes—then the credibility of the gospel is best demonstrated by the authentic lives of those saints who confess, live by, and promote the good news to their family, friends, and neighbors. The lives of living saints are the manifesto of a reality that exists beyond the present status quo.

---

4. Heschel, "Spirit of Jewish Education," 19.

Ordinary Saints

A World in Need of Saints

If ever there was a time when saints were needed in the world, it is today. For all our technology, material wealth, and possessions, our houses, cars, supposed "freedoms" to live our lives any way we choose, we citizens of the twenty-first century are in real trouble. Most of us are knee deep in a slush pit of financial debt, broken relationships, clinical depression, addictive behaviors, guilt about the past, and anxiety about the future, unable to wrestle our willful emotions under control. The American sociologist of religion Robert Wuthnow has observed that we live in perilous times, when the war against terror, weapons of mass destruction, panics and pandemics, and the environmental catastrophes that our "smart" technologies have produced, are causing more pain than we know.[5] If we were to stop long enough to take stock of our situation, we would discover that the self-centered lifestyles, the greed of the consumerism that feeds us, and the competitive "system" that lies at the heart of our economic, political, and social structures are killing us. And if we were to look "within" for the answers to the problems that confront us, we would be confronted by a shocking truth—like Old Mother Hubbard when she went to the cupboard—we would discover that our emotional and spiritual reserves are running on empty. There is nothing there! Sue Monk Kidd has observed, "We have lost the ability to probe the soul, to know and refine its experiences."[6]

I suggest therefore that saints have something unique to give the world. Although the faith that burns within them and generates the compassion they embody is not well understood, it may just be that such "true believers" point the way to our earthly and spiritual survival. They have something the world really needs. Something basic to what it means to be a human being in harmonious community, living our lives before God and a watching world. Although far from perfect, and subject to the tremors and traumas of mortality, they have nevertheless discovered how to live holy and wholesome lives. It is by way of a relationship with the creator God who invites us to become his sons and daughters, members of his "new humanity" able to live at the "peak" of our human potential because we have been put right with God, right with our neighbor, and right with ourselves.

You may like to cast your mind back to the early pages of this book, where I offered a working definition of what it means to be a saint in three

---

5. Wuthnow, *Be Very Afraid*.
6. Monk Kidd, *Firstlight*, 17.

parts. The first defining attribute I listed was *submission*. Saints are people who have heard Jesus' call to "Come, follow me" and who have made the deep, all-encompassing, life-changing decision to submit their lives to Christ and to follow him no matter what the cost. The second attribute was *gratefulness*. Saints are people who recognize that Jesus' voluntary death on the cross destroyed the power of sin, removed the burden of guilt, and replaced it with a new way of living in the world. They know themselves to be loved by God generously and without condition or reserve. That is why they worship Christ as their Lord, their brother and their friend. And the third attribute was *generosity*. Having received God's generous and overwhelming love in Jesus, saints find their greatest pleasure in performing their calling as citizens of God's kingdom, by "selling all" (Mark 10:21) and giving away their lives and their worldly goods to the poor and the needy. Saints have a deep-level conviction that only when they "give up" their lives will they truly find them, and when they spend their lives in service of others in the name of Christ, in return they are given the treasures of heaven. On the last day, when judgment comes, these people can expect to hear Jesus' welcoming salutation, "Well done, good and faithful servant. Come and share your master's happiness!" (Matt 25:21 and 23).

Why Saints Have Currency Today

In bringing this book to a close I want to propose four reasons why the lives of saints have special currency today for contemporary Christianity. The *first* is that the lives of saints represent an extension of Christ's own life. The incarnation—Christ's taking on flesh and "becoming human"—is what sets Christianity apart from all other religions. Saints as redeemed human persons are also "the standard operating model" for human persons.[7]

The *second* is that saints' lives are revelatory. As von Balthasar observes, saints' lives are the best apologetic for the gospel:

> It is not dry manuals (full as these may be of unquestionable truths) that plausibly express to the world the truth of Christ's gospel, but the existence of the saints, who have been grasped by Christ's Holy Spirit. And Christ himself foresaw no other kind of apologetics.[8]

---

7. Kreeft, "What is a Saint?"
8. Von Balthasar, *Glory of the Lord*, 494.

It may just be that in a context that demands "proofs" of the validity of any truth claims made, that saints' lives represent the most convincing "hermeneutic of the gospel"[9] available to the watching world in our times.

The *third* reason is that the history of Christianity is the history of its saints. Christianity's trophies are not ultimately its denominational structures, church buildings or theological formulations, but the quality of the people it produces. Jürgen Moltmann wrote somewhere that the "church that ignores its saints is sure to fall into disrepair." And by the same token, the church that gives priority to its saints, that nurtures the spiritual life, and that frees them to live faithfully and courageously in the contemporary world, has begun to "remember" the genius of its mission strategy over these long years.

And the *fourth* reason saints have special currency today is that the making of saints is the church's first priority. According to Eugene Peterson, "Our primary work is to make saints. We're in the saint-making business."[10] And according to Peterson, being in the "saint-making business" requires that churches and ministry leaders must give priority to the spiritual life. The spiritual formation component of Christian ministry needs to move from an afterthought to the first priority. Being saints, making saints, restoring saints, and informing people maturing in their spiritual lives now becomes a matter of deep urgency for Christian congregations throughout the Western world. Making saints, being disciples, and training up the net generation of believers is where the urgency lies.

You Will Be My Witnesses

Christian saints in the twenty-first century are called to engage with the real world and the real people who live in it, in ways that are credible, authentic, and genuine. We are not to hide ourselves away like "lights under a bushel" (Matt 5:15), but instead are to "let our light shine before men [sic] that they may see your good works and praise your Father in heaven" (Matt 5:16). Christianity has always relied upon its apostles, preachers, pastors, priests, prophets, seers, mystics, and holy men and women to represent the genius of the gospel. As Richard Beck has pointed out, "Before there was a Bible or creeds or orthodoxy or an authoritative teaching

---

9. Newbigin, *Gospel in a Pluralist Society*, 227.
10. Peterson, "Business of Making Saints," 22.

The Evocation of Saints

tradition there were the martyrs and the saints."[11] And as Dietrich Bonhoeffer wrote, "The primary confession of the Christian before the world is the deed which interprets itself."[12] In just the same way that Jesus was the messenger, the message and the model of the kingdom of God, so the life of the saint—the activated disciple of Jesus in the world—is to be all three things simultaneously. We are to be the messengers, the message, and the working model of the kingdom of God.

Saints march into a world full of danger and uncertainty, with no resources other than their faith, their sanctified lives, and their awareness of the presence of Christ in the form of the Spirit working in and through them. The only weapons they have at their disposal are the force of their moral lives and the slender apparatus of prayer, righteousness, compassion, and mercy. They are to overcome evil by living out of a countercultural reality that posits the goodness of God as the source and destiny of all existence. To that end, they bend their bodies, minds, wills, and resources to establishing what William Willimon called "colonies" of heaven on earth. By the way they live, through their example of justice, mercy, and truthfulness among themselves and with their neighbors, they not only announce the kingdom of God but they "inaugurate" that kingdom through the efficacy of their persons and the communities of faith in which they live. Goodness, mercy and love are a saint's "stock in trade." The power they wield is nothing more (and nothing less) than the power of a transformed life. And the laughter with which they announce the alternate reality of the redeemed life that they regard as ultimate, demonstrates clearly that the joy of God is the source of their strength (Neh 8:10).

What do you do when you have found the reason for the world's existence? When everything that is wrong with your personal world has been put right? When all your wounds have been healed? When all your questions have been answered? When the dark and irreconcilable past has been put right and all that was previously broken has now been restored—what comes next? There are only two possible answers. The first is to live out of the richness of the experience of being loved by God . . . to love the world in return and seek to heal it with every fiber of your existence. Saints choose to give their lives away out of the sheer exhilaration of the joy of self-giving, only to receive it back, "pressed down, shaken together and running over" (Luke 6:38). And the second is to try (so far as it is possible) to understand

---

11. Beck, "Witness of the Saints."
12. Bonhoeffer, in Hauerwas, "Dietrich Bonhoeffer's Political Theology," 19.

the mystery and the grace of the new life that has been given to them without cost, without condition, and without limit. No wonder the Apostle Paul asked for his scrolls and parchments. He wasn't trying to find his way to God. He was trying to understand why it was that God had reached out to him in Christ, and where he "fitted" in the divine plan and purpose.

Saints are witnesses to the "new thing" (Isa 43:19) God is doing in the world. God is calling men and women, families and communities, schools and workplaces, towns and businesses, cities and nations to be attentive to the hope, peace, joy, love, mercy, compassion, and truthfulness that belongs to the human family, whose "first son," hero, and chief representative is Jesus Christ. As Jean-Piere de Caussade wrote:

> We are in an age of faith; the Holy Spirit no longer writes Gospels, except in our hearts; saintly souls are the pages, suffering and action the ink. The Holy Spirit is writing a living gospel with the pen of action, which we will only be able to read on the day of glory when, fresh from the presses of life, it will be published. Oh what a beautiful story! What a beautiful book the Holy Spirit is now writing! It is in press; not a day passes when the type is not being set, the ink not applied, the page is not being printed.[13]

If ever there was a time when saints need to manifest through their lives the life of God, and the faith of Jesus his Son, it is now. We are to "go and do likewise" (Luke 10:37), and to bear witness to the things that we have seen. As disciples who are "at large" in the world, saints are great-hearted people whose lives are a "heritage of humanity", and living treasures of the human race. If Christianity is ever again to recover its voice and its reputation as a meaningful contributor to society and culture, a third age of saints will be required to broker the presence of God in our time.

Saints as Radical Christians

There is much talk about "radicalization" in our world—tragically much of it negative. The kind of harm that radicalized militants and movements are causing through their hateful bombings, murder, beheading, and other despicable activities . . . represents the worst forms of brutalization and destruction of humanity. Such people have nothing useful to "bring to the table" in the building of a new world and a new humanity, a better future or

---

13. de Caussade, *Sacrament of the Present Moment*, 101.

The Evocation of Saints

a just civilization. But since the language of "radicalization" represents such an important part of contemporary social discourse, it is worth reflecting on saints as "radical" Christians, with a view to clarifying what saints "bring to the table."

In J. R. R. Tolkien's tale *The Hobbit*, when asked "Why the halfling?" the wizard Gandalf replied:

> Saruman [falsely] believes that it is only great power that can hold evil in check. That is not what I have found. I have found that it is the small things, every day deeds from ordinary folk, that keeps the darkness at bay. Simple acts of kindness and love. Why Bilbo Baggins? Perhaps it is because I am afraid and because he gives me courage.[14]

In this statement, Tolkien (through Gandalf) could easily be speaking about saints. Indeed, it is possible that Tolkien was speaking about the beauty and gentleness of redeemed humanity when he spoke of the small and inconsequential nature of hobbits, and of saints in a world that has grown cold and loveless. But every age needs its heroes—many of whom are of the most unlikely kind—to change the course of history, and right its wrongs.

Referencing Edith Wyschogrod's discussion of saints and postmodernism, Martin Poorthuis and Joshua Schwarz sketch the ethical profile of the modern saint, writing:

> A holy life is a life in which compassion for the Other is central. The saint's story is extremely modern and contemporary, or can be, because it speaks of self-denial and of the primacy of the Other in such a way that readers and hearers experience the motives that impel the holy man or woman.[15]

What is most notable about saints is not the extent of their power, resources, and abilities, but rather the extent of their vulnerability and weakness. When confronted by wickedness, evil, and selfishness, saints begin to draw on the distinctive "power" that is available only to them. They break out the towel, the serving bowl, and the healing balm, and offer to the world a distinctive insignia—their love and their compassion. Their desire is always to act on behalf of the other, and to do be willing to pay out of their own lives, resources, wealth, health, time, efforts, and energy, in order that others might benefit. In this regard, saints bring a significant measure of

---

14. Jackson, dir., *The Hobbit: The Desolation of Smaug*, film.
15. Poorthuis and Schwarz, *Saints and Role Models in Judaism and Christianity*, 405.

humility, weakness, and other-centeredness to their transformative work in the world. C. S. Lewis observed, "How monotonously alike all the great tyrants and conquerors have been; how gloriously different are the saints."[16] What is "radical" about the saints is the extent to which they are like Jesus, willing to lay down their lives for others. Radical saints are willing to break company with the "spirit of the age" that is marked by selfish gain and a kind of "grasping" greed that ignores the needs of others—in order to serve the world in the name of Christ in the hope and expectation of the coming of the kingdom of God on earth.

Saints are blood-bought, love-steeped, twice-born, remade persons who nurture within themselves and others the seed of their redeemed nature, and who—because they are fully forgiven and deeply loved by God, in Christ—recognize that they are under obligation to give away their lives (Mark 8:35). Radicalized by the extreme love of God for humankind, saints exercise a ministry of selfless service and ceaseless reconciliation (2 Cor 5:18) as co-workers with Christ and his church. "After consecration . . . there is no more 'life as usual.'"[17] This calls for the perseverance of the saints. As St. Augustine inquired of himself, "If they, why not I?—If these men and women could become saints, why cannot I with the help of him who is all-powerful?"

> By the mercy of God I am a Christian; by my deeds, a great sinner; and by vocation a homeless pilgrim, a man of mean estate who wanders from place to place. These are my belongings: over my shoulders I carry a pouch of dried bread crusts, and in my breast pocket a Bible. That is all.[18]

---

16. Lewis, in Martin, *My Life with the Saints*, 6.
17. Panikkar, *Blessed Simplicity*, 91.
18. Pentkovsky, *Pilgrim's Tale*, 49.

The Evocation of Saints

A Blessing

You holy saints who live on the upward Way, close to the heart of God. You have been planted in a world in urgent need of restoring.

- Truly, yours is a life given to Christ in full and glad surrender
- Truly, you wear the family likeness of humility and beauty in your redeemed humanity
- Truly you open your hands to friends, enemies and strangers
- Truly, you give away your lives, only to receive them back pressed down and running over.

You have been blessed, chosen from among all the peoples of the earth. You are loved with a fierce, passionate and gentle love. You are embraced, anointed and called to live near to the heart of God. You are graced to go out as heaven's representatives on earth.

And now Sisters and Brothers—become who you were called to be by creation, baptism, and redemption.

Shine your light, for your time has come.

Amen.

Bibliography

à Kempis, Thomas. *Imitation of Christ*. London: Burns & Oates, 1960.
Allison, Gregg. "Toward a Theology of Human Embodiment." *Southern Baptist Journal of Theology* 13:2 (2009) 4–17.
Anderson, Ray S. *On Being Human: Essays in Theological Anthropology*. Grand Rapids: Eerdmans, 1982.
Arnold, Eberhard. *The Early Christians in Their Own Words*. Farmington, PA: Plough, 1997.
Augustine. *Confessions*. Nashville: Thomas Nelson, 1999.
Australian Anglican Prayer Book: Liturgical Resources. Alexandria, NSW: Broughton, 1995.
Baillie, John. *Our Knowledge of God*. London: Oxford University Press, 1949.
Barclay, John M. G., and J. Simon Gathercole. *Divine and Human Agency in Paul and his Cultural Environment*. London: T & T Clark, 2006.
Beck, Richard. "The Witness of the Saints." Experimental Theology (blog), http://experimentaltheology.blogspot.com.au/2013/09/the-witness-of-saints.html.
Berdyaev, Nikolai. *The End of Our Time*. Translated by Donald Attwater. London: Sheed & Ward, 1933.
Bloom, Harold, ed. *James Joyce: Comprehensive Biography and Critical Analysis*. Philadelphia: Chelsea House, 2003.
Bonhoeffer, Dietrich. *The Cost of Discipleship*. London: SCM, 1964.
Bosch, David J. *Transforming Mission: Paradigm Shifts in Theology of Mission*. Maryknoll, NY: Orbis, 1991.
Bottum, Joseph. "The Judgment of Memory." In *The Best Spiritual Writing 2010*, edited by Phillip Zaleski, 37–58. New York: Penguin, 2010.
Bouyer, Louis. *Introduction to Spirituality*. New York: Desclee, 1961.
Bradley, Ian C. *Colonies of Heaven: Celtic Models for Today's Church*. London: Darton, Longman & Todd, 2000.
Brague, Rémi. *The Legend of the Middle Ages: Philosophical Explorations of Medieval Christianity, Judaism, and Islam*. Chicago: University of Chicago Press, 2009.
Brooks, Phillips. *Visions and Tasks and Other Sermons*. 1910. Reprint. London: Forgotten, 2013.
Buechner, Frederick. *The Longing for Home: Recollections and Reflections*. San Francisco: HarperSanFrancisco, 1996.
Chesterton, G. K. *Orthodoxy*. New York: Dover, 2004.

Bibliography

Chrétien, Jean-Louis. *The Call and the Response*. New York, NY: Fordham University Press, 2004.

Christensen, Michael J. *Partakers of the Divine Nature: The History and Development of Deification in the Christian Traditions*. Grand Rapids: Baker Academic, 2007.

Chrysostom, John. "Sermon 6 on Matthew," Section 8, 2009. http://www.newadvent.org/fathers/200106.htm.

Cioran, E. M. *Tears and Saints*. Chicago: University of Chicago Press, 1995.

Clark, Francis. *Godfaring: On Reason, Faith, and Sacred Being*. Washington, DC: Catholic University of America Press, 2000.

Collins, Gregory. *Come and Receive Light: Meditations for Ministers of Christ*. Dublin: Columba, 2003.

Connell, Mary. *Updike and the Patriarchal Dilemma Masculinity in the Rabbit Novels*. Carbondale: Southern Illinois University Press, 1996.

Craughwell, Thomas J. *Saints Behaving Badly: The Cutthroats, Crooks, Trollops, Con Men, and Devil-worshippers who Became Saints*. New York: Doubleday, 2006.

Cunningham, Lawrence. *The Meaning of Saints*. London: Harper and Row, 1980.

Cupit, Tony. *Stars Lighting up the Sky: Stories of Contemporary Christian Heroes*. Falls Church, VA: Baptist World Alliance, 2003.

Dante, Alighieri. "Dante's the Inferno, Canto 1. A new translation by Mary Jo Bang. In *The Best Spiritual Writing 2010*, edited by Philip Zaleski, 9–15. New York: Penguin, 2010.

de Caussade, Jean P. *The Sacrament of the Present Moment*. San Francisco: Harper & Row, 1982.

de Chardin, P. Teilhard. *The Divine Milieu*. Sussex: Sussex Academic Press, 2004

Devenish, Stuart C. *Seeing and Believing: The Eye of Faith in a Visual Culture*. Eugene, OR: Wipf and Stock, 2012.

———. "The Contribution of Spirituality to our Understanding of Human Flourishing." In *Beyond Well-Being: Spirituality and Human Flourishing*, edited by Maureen Miner et al., 49–64. Charlotte, NC: Information Age, 2012.

Drane, John W. *Do Christians Know How to Be Spiritual?: The Rise of New Spirituality and the Mission of the Church*. London: Darton, Longman & Todd, 2005.

Eagleton, Terry. "The Nature of Evil." In *The Best Spiritual Writing 2013*, edited by Philip Zaleski, 10–20. New York: Penguin, 2013.

———. *Culture and the Death of God*. New Haven, CT: Yale University Press, 2014.

Ellsberg, Robert. *All Saints: Daily Reflections on Saints, Prophets, and Witnesses for Our Time*. New York: Crossroad, 2007.

"Experts in the Art of Dying." *Barnabas Aid Magazine*, May/June 2015, 10, https://issuu.com/barnabasfund/docs/bfaidmay_jun15.

Flescher, Andrew M. *Heroes, Saints and Ordinary Morality*. Washington, DC: Georgetown University Press, 2003.

Frank, Georgia. *The Memory of the Eyes: Pilgrims to Living Saints in Christian Late Antiquity*. Berkeley, CA: University of California Press, 2000.

Francis. "World Youth Day Address," 2013. *The British Catholic Herald*, http://www.catholicherald.co.uk/news/2013/07/28/wyd-2013-full-text-of-pope-franciss-homily-for-world-youth-days-closing-mass/.

Friedman, Maurice S. *Martin Buber and the Human Sciences*. Albany, NY: State University of New York Press, 1996.

Giblet, Freda. "Profile: Sister Ella Williams." *Faith and Freedom*, December 1992, 19.

Bibliography

Glenstal Book of Daily Prayer: A Benedictine Prayer Book. Collegeville, MN: Liturgical, 2008.
Gordon, Hayim. *Fighting Evil: Unsung Heroes in the Novels of Graham Greene.* Westport, CT: Greenwood, 1997.
Gorman, Michael J. *Inhabiting the Cruciform God: Kenosis, Justification, and Theosis in Paul's Narrative Soteriology.* Grand Rapids: Eerdmans, 2009.
Green, Joel B. *Conversion in Luke-Acts: Divine Action, Human Cognition, and the People of God.* Grand Rapids: Baker Academic, 2015.
Greene, Graham. *The Power and the Glory.* New York: Viking, 1946.
Guardini, Romano. *The Saints in Daily Christian Life.* Philadelphia: Chilton, 1966.
Guiley, Rosemary E. "Julian of Norwich." In *The Encyclopaedia of Saints*, 198–99. New York: Facts on File, 2001.
Harrison, Verna E. F. *God's Many-Splendored Image: Theological Anthropology for Christian Formation.* Grand Rapids: Baker Academic, 2010.
Hauerwas, Stanley. "Dietrich Bonhoeffer's Political Theology." *Conrad Grebel Review* 20:3 (2002) 17–39.
Hernandez, Will. *Henri Nouwen: A Spirituality of Imperfection.* Mahwah, NJ: Paulist, 2006.
Herrick, Vanessa, and Ivan Mann. *Jesus Wept: Reflections on Vulnerability in Leadership.* London: Darton, Longman & Todd, 1998.
Heschel, Abraham J. "The Spirit of Jewish Education." *Journal of Jewish Education* 24:2 (1953) 9–62.
———. *The Prophets.* New York: Harper & Row, 1962.
Hobbes, Thomas. *Leviathan.* London: Andrew Crooke, 1651.
Holder, Arthur G. *The Blackwell Companion to Christian Spirituality.* Oxford: Blackwell, 2011.
Howell, James C. *Servants, Misfits, and Martyrs: Saints and their Stories.* Nashville: Upper Room, 1999.
Hugo, Victor. *Les Misérables.* London: Penguin, 1982.
Hummel, Leonard M. *Clothed in Nothingness: Consolation for Suffering.* Minneapolis: Fortress, 2003.
Jackson, Peter, dir. *The Hobbit: An Unexpected Journey.* MGM, 2012.
James, William. *Varieties of Religious Experience.* London: Longmans, Green & Co., 1928.
Job, Rubin P., and Norman Shawchuck. *A Guide to Prayer for Ministers and Other Servants.* Nashville: Upper Room, 1983.
John Paul II. *Apostolic Letter Tertio Millennio Adveniente.* http://www.vatican.va/holy_father/john_paul_ii/apost_letters/documents/hf_jp-ii_apl_10111994_tertio-millennio-adveniente_en.html, section IV-33.
Jones, Kathleen. *Women Saints: Lives of Faith and Courage.* Maryknoll, NY: Orbis, 1999.
Kavanaugh, Kieran. *Collected Letters of St. Teresa of Avila.* Washington, DC: ICS, 2001.
Kieckhefer, Richard. *Sainthood: Its Manifestations in World Religions.* Berkeley, CA: University of California Press, 1990.
Kierkegaard, Søren. *The Journals of Kierkegaard, 1834–1854.* London: Fontana, 1958.
Koehler, Pat. *The Little Book of Contemplative Photography: seeing with wonder, respect and humility.* Intercourse, PA: Good Books, 2005.
Kreeft, Peter. "What is a Saint?" Catholic Education Resource Centre, http://www.catholiceducation.org/en/culture/catholic-contributions/what-is-a-saint.html.
Kurtz, Ernest, and Katherine Ketchum. *The Spirituality of Imperfection: Storytelling and the Journey to Wholeness.* New York: Bantam, 1994.

Bibliography

Levine, Amy-Jill. "The Most Infallible Sign." *America*, April 2, 2007. http://americamagazine.org/issue/609/article/most-infallible-sign.
Lewis, C. S. *Mere Christianity*. London: Collins/Fontana, 1970.
———. *The Weight of Glory*. London: SPCK, 1942.
———. *The Problem of Pain*. London: Fontana, 1957.
———. *They Asked Me for a Paper*. London: Geoffrey Bles, 1962.
Lewis, Sinclair. *Elmer Gantry*. New York: Harcourt, Brace and Co., 1927.
Lonergan, Bernard J. F. *The Subject*. Milwaukee: Marquette University Press, 1968.
Louf, Andre. *Way of Humility*. Kalamazoo, MI: Cistercian, 2007.
Maley, Jacqueline. "Dawkins derides sainthood as Pythonesque." *Sydney Morning Herald*, March 15, 2010. http://www.smh.com.au/national/dawkins-derides-sainthood-as-pythonesque-20100314-q676.html.
Marion, Jean-Luc. "This is Not Funny: The Quest for the Historical Bibfeldt to Bibfeldt with/without Being." *Criterion* 43:3 (2004) 18–23.
Martin, James. *Becoming Who You Are: Insights on the True Self from Thomas Merton and Other Saints*. New York: Paulist, 2006.
———. *Between Heaven and Mirth: Why Joy, Humor, and Laughter Are at the Heart of the Spiritual Life*. New York, NY: HarperOne, 2011.
———. *My Life with the Saints*. Chicago: Loyola, 2006.
Marty, Martin E., and Gerald C. Brauer, eds. *The Unrelieved Paradox: Studies in the Theology of Franz Bibfeldt*. Grand Rapids: Eerdmans, 2013.
McCarthy, David M. *Sharing God's Good Company: A Theology of the Communion of Saints*. Grand Rapids: Eerdmans, 2012.
McClay, William M. "Our Buried Sentiments." In *The Best Spiritual Writing 2010*, edited by Philip Zaleski, 151–54. New York: Penguin, 2010.
McGinlay, Hugh. *Uniting in Worship*. Melbourne: Uniting Church Press, 1988.
McGinley, Phyllis. *Saint-Watching*. New York: Viking, 1969.
McInerny, Ralph. *The Very Rich Hours of Jacques Maritain: A Spiritual Life*. Notre Dame, IN: University of Notre Dame Press, 2003.
McClendon, James W., Jr. *Biography as Theology: How Life Stories Can Remake Today's Theology*. Eugene, OR: Wipf & Stock, 2002.
Meltzer, Françoise, and Elsner, Jas. *Saints: Faith without Borders*. Chicago: University of Chicago Press, 2011.
Merton, Thomas. *Seven Storey Mountain*. San Diego: Harcourt Brace & Co., 1976.
Metzner, Ralph. "Ten Classical Metaphors of Self Transformation." *The Journal of Transpersonal Psychology* 12:1 (1980) 47–62.
Milnes, Peter, Genevieve Milnes, and Keith Truscott. "Three Australian Aboriginal Pastors Interpret Forgiveness." *National Journal of the Christian Counselors' Association of Australia*, October 2014, 38–47.
Mochulsky, Konstantin. *Dostoevsky: His Life and Work*. Translated by Michael A. Minihan. Princeton, NJ: Princeton University Press, 1971.
Moltmann, Jürgen. *The Crucified God: the Cross of Christ as the Foundation and Criticism of Christian Theology*. Minneapolis: Fortress, 1993.
———. *The Way of Jesus Christ*. Minneapolis: Fortress, 1993.
Monk Kidd, Sue. *Firstlight: Early Inspirational Writings*. New York: Guidepost, 2006.
Moyes, Gordon. "New South Wales Parliament Hansard." *Hansard*, November 12, 2003: 4791.

Bibliography

Murphy, Nancey C. *Bodies and Souls, or Spirited Bodies?* Cambridge, UK: Cambridge University Press, 2006.

Newbigin, Lesslie. *The Gospel in a Pluralist Society.* Grand Rapids: Eerdmans, 1989.

Nichols, Alan, ed. *From Every Nation: Stories of Faith and Culture Struggles by Melbourne Anglicans Who Have Been Refugees.* Melbourne: Anglican Diocese of Melbourne Multicultural Ministry Department, 2012.

Nietzsche, Friedrich. *Beyond Good and Evil.* Cambridge Texts in the History of Philosophy. Cambridge: Cambridge University Press, 2002.

Nouwen, Henri J. M. *The Wounded Healer: Ministry in Contemporary Society.* New York: Doubleday, 1972.

O'Connell, Mary. *Updike and the Patriarchal Dilemma: Masculinity in the Rabbit Novels.* Carbondale, IL: Southern Illinois University Press, 1996.

O'Connor, Flannery. *Spiritual Writings.* Maryknoll, NY: Orbis, 2013.

Oakes, Edward T. *Cambridge Companion to Hans Urs Von Balthasar.* Cambridge: Cambridge University Press, 2004.

Oden, Thomas C. *Systematic Theology.* San Francisco: HarperCollins, 1987.

Oudshoorn, Daniel. "Speaking Christianly as a Missional Activity in the Midst of Babel". *Stimulus* (February 2006) 14:1. http://imissional.org/wp-content/uploads/2010/07/Living_Xnly_in_Babel1.pdf.

Pai, Gita V. "Orwell's Reflections on Saint Gandhi." *Concentric: Literary and Cultural Studies* 40:1 (March, 2014) 51–77.

Panikkar, Raimon. *Blessed Simplicity: The Monk as Universal Archetype.* New York: Seabury, 1982.

Peck, M. Scott. *People of the Lie: The Hope for Healing Human Evil.* New York: Simon and Schuster, 1983.

Pentkovsky, Aleksei. *The Pilgrim's Tale.* New York: Paulist, 1999.

Peterson, Eugene H. *Practise Resurrection: A Conversation on Growing up in Christ.* London: Hodder & Stoughton, 2009.

———. "The Business of Making Saints." *Leadership Journal*, Spring 1997, http://www.christianitytoday.com/le/1997/spring/7l22oa.html.

Phillips, David M. *Courage in a Hostile World: The Story of Family Voice Australia.* Adelaide: Family Voice Australia, 2014.

Pool, Jeff B. *God's Wounds: Hermeneutic of the Christian Symbol of Divine Suffering.* Cambridge: James Clarke, 2009.

Poorthuis, Marcel, and Joshus Schwarz. *Saints and Role Models in Judaism and Christianity.* Jewish and Christian Perspectives Series. Edited by Marcel Poorthuis, Joshua Schwarz, and Frank Van der Steen. Volume VII. Leiden: Brill, 2004.

Range, Melissa. "Scriptorium: The Lindisfarne Gospels." In *The Best Spiritual Writing 2010*, edited by Phillip Zaleski, 172–74. New York: Penguin, 2010.

Rifkin, Lawrence. "5 Best Jewish Jokes Ever." *The Huffington Post*, http://www.huffingtonpost.com/lawrence-rifkin/5-best-jewish-jokes-ever_b_7630812.html.

Rohr, Richard. *Falling Upward: A Spirituality for the Two Halves of Life.* San Francisco: Jossey-Bass, 2011.

———. *Immortal Diamond: The Search for Our True Self.* San Francisco: Jossey-Bass, 2013.

———. *Job and the Mystery of Suffering: Spiritual Reflections.* New York: Crossroad, 1996.

Ryken, Leland, Philip G. Ryken, and Todd Wilson. *Pastors in the Classics: Timeless Lessons on Life and Ministry from World Literature.* Grand Rapids: Baker, 2012.

Bibliography

Sayers, Dorothy. *The Mind of the Maker*. San Francisco: Harper, 1987.
Scheler, Max. *Ressentiment*. New York: Free Press of Glencoe, 1961.
Scheller, Christine. "Olga Robertson: Setting Prisoners Free through Christ." *Calvary Chapel Magazine* 6 (Winter 2001) 47. http://www.calvarymagazine.org/images/stories/PDFs/Issue_25/Personal_Testimony_Olga_Robertson_25.pdf.
Schwartz, Joshua. *Saints and Role Models in Judaism and Christianity*. Leiden: Brill, 2004.
Seligman, Martin. *Flourish: A Visionary New Understanding of Happiness and Well-being*. North Sydney, NSW: Random House Australia, 2011.
Sexton, Anne. "The Earth." In *Complete Works of Anne Sexton*, 431. New York: Houghton Mifflin, 1999.
Shelley, Bruce L. *Church History in Plain Language*. Dallas: Word, 1995.
Smelik, Klaas A. D., ed. *Etty: The Letters and Diaries of Etty Hillesum, 1941–1943*. Translated by Arnold J. Pomerans. Grand Rapids: Eerdmans, 2002.
Spader, Dann. *Walking as Jesus Walked: Making Disciples the Way Jesus Did*. Chicago: Moody, 2011.
Stackhouse, John. In-class notes for "Radical Doubt, Radical Faith & Responsible Reasoning." Intensive at Tabor Adelaide, July 6–10, 2015.
Sweeney, Jon M. *The Lure of Saints: A Protestant Experience of Catholic Tradition*. Brewster, MA: Paraclete, 2005.
Sypher, Wylie. *Comedy*. Baltimore: Johns Hopkins University Press, 1956.
Szabo, Sarah. "China's Forgotten Children." *Scoop Arts & Culture Magazine*, Autumn 2014, 98–101. http://scoop-magazine.scoop.com.au/?iid=89148&startpage=98#folio=98.
Taylor, John V. *Christian Spirituality*. London: SCM, 2007.
Teresa of Avila. *The Letters of Saint Teresa*. Translated and annotated by the Benedictines of Stanbrook. London: Thomas Baker, 1921.
Tillich, Paul. *Biblical Religion and the Search for Ultimate Reality*. Chicago: University of Chicago Press, 1955.
Tolstoy, Leo. *A Confession: The Gospel in Brief, and What I Believe*. London: Oxford University Press, H. Milford, 1940.
Underhill, Evelyn. *The Spiritual Life*. New York: Harper & Brothers, 1937.
Von Balthasar, Hans Urs. *Glory of the Lord*. Vol. 1, *Seeing the Form*. San Francisco: Ignatius, 1983.
———. *Thérèsa of Liseux: The Story of a Mission*. London: Sheed and Ward, 1954.
Wangerin, Walter. *Mourning into Dancing*. Grand Rapids: Zondervan, 1992.
Webb, Stephen H. *Jesus Christ, Eternal God: Heavenly Flesh and the Metaphysics of Matter*. Oxford: Oxford University Press, 2012.
Webber, Robert E. *The Divine Embrace: Recovering the Passionate Spiritual Life*. Grand Rapids: Baker, 2006.
West, Christopher. *Theology of the Body Explained: A Commentary on John Paul II's "Gospel of the Body."* Leominster, Herefordshire: Gracewing, 2003.
Whittington, Vera. "Women of Compassion: The Sisters of the People their mission and work in Western Australia 1893–1977." Gawler, SA: unpublished.
Wiesel, Elie. *Night*. New York: Hill and Wang, 2006.
Willard, Dallas. *Renovation of the Heart: Putting on the Character of Christ*. Colorado Springs: NavPress, 2002.
Williams, Diana. *Horizon is Where Heaven and Earth Meet: A Love Story That Crossed Boundaries*. Milson's Point, NSW: Random House, 2001.

Bibliography

Williams, Donald T. *Mere Humanity: G. K. Chesterton, C. S. Lewis, and J. R. R. Tolkien on the Human Condition*. Nashville: Broadman & Holman, 2006.

Willimon, William H. *Sinning Like a Christian: A New Look at the 7 Deadly Sins*. Nashville: Abingdon, 2013.

Wink, Walter. *Engaging the Powers: Discernment and Resistance in a World of Domination*. Minneapolis: Fortress, 1992.

Wojtyla, Karol. *Love and Responsibility*. Translated by H. T. Willetts. San Francisco: Ignatius, 1981.

Wolf, Susan. "Moral Saints." *The Journal of Philosophy* (1982) 419–39.

Wuthnow, Robert. *Be Very Afraid: The Cultural Response to Terror, Pandemics, Environmental Devastation, Nuclear Annihilation, and Other Threats*. Oxford: Oxford University Press, 2010.

Wynn, Mark Robert. "Saintliness and the Moral Life." *Journal of Religious Ethics* 31:3 463–85.

Wyschogrod, Edith. *Saints and Postmodernism: Revisioning Moral Philosophy*. Chicago: University of Chicago Press, 1990.

Yancey, Philip. *What Good is God?: In Search of a Faith That Matters*. New York: Faithwords, 2010.

Zehr, Howard. *The Little Book of Contemporary Photography*. Intercourse, PA: Good Books, 2005.

Index

absolution, 37–38
Acta Sanctorum, 97
after church, 13–15
age of saints, 164, 170
agency, 78, 106–7
altruism, 46–47
anastasis, 123–24, 129
apologetic, 48, 167
Apostles Creed, 17, 78
appetite/s, 29, 35, 67, 100
Archbishop Desmond Tutu, 20, 69
Athanasius, 103, 164
atheist/atheism, 16, 45, 150, 160
Auschwitz, 91–92, 161

beauty, 1, 6, 10, 26, 31, 51, 67, 70, 74, 81–84, 88, 101, 148, 171
blessing, 48, 80, 160, 173
body/ies, 17–18, 25–26, 40, 43, 54, 62, 67, 72, 77, 81, 92, 94, 97–104, 107–8, 110–11, 125ff., 135, 145, 157, 166

C.S. Lewis, 5, 21, 85–86, 126, 147
carriers, 5
chastity, 33, 44, 97
compassion, 20, 53, 59, 71, 117, 123, 132–33, 158, 166, 169–71
consecration, 18, 36, 50, 172
consumerism, 10, 132, 166
contentment, 67
crucis, 123–24, 129

Dallas Willard, 111
Dante Alighieri, 26, 64, 149
devotion, 7, 13, 18, 32–34
Dietrich Bonhoeffer, 55–56, 169
dignity, 43, 74, 81–83, 96, 134, 139, 145, 154, 164
disciple/discipleship, 4–11, 16–19, 22, 28, 34, 38, 45, 48–50, 55, 62–65, 68, 76–78, 86, 96–97, 102, 105, 110, 117–18, 122, 124–25, 127–30, 132, 135, 140, 154, 159, 168–70
Dorothy Day, 20, 56, 64, 86, 161

Elie Wiesel, 161
Elmer Gantry, 29–30
Etty Hillesum, 89–92, 146
Eugene Peterson, 9, 77, 123, 168
Evelyn Underhill, 80
evil, 4, 8, 28–29, 33, 35, 38, 48, 68–69, 80, 97, 100–103, 110, 117, 120, 126, 133–35, 152–53, 165, 169, 171
evocation, 165, 167

flesh, 21–24, 49, 65, 71, 82, 94, 97, 101–7, 111, 124–25, 129, 140, 167
Francis of Assisi, 20, 86
Frederick Buechner, 136
Frederick Nietzsche, 44–47
freedom, 27, 44, 80–83, 96, 126–27, 129, 135, 141, 143, 166
fruit of the Spirit, 61
Fyodor Dostoevsky, 51–52, 66

Index

gallery, 13–14
generosity, 5, 9–10, 26, 49–50, 64, 129, 139, 158, 167
genius, 3, 22, 86, 163, 168
Geoff and Di Hall, 112–14
G.K. Chesterton, 80
godfaring, 12, 23
good man, 66
Good Samaritan, 49, 71
goodness, 5, 8, 22–23, 26, 38, 44, 47–48, 51, 54, 56, 61, 65–66, 68–69, 111, 115, 146, 148, 151, 169
gospel, 2–5, 7–8, 10–11, 15, 18–19, 30–31, 37, 48–49, 50, 55–56, 87, 104–5, 110, 118, 125, 136, 152, 160, 165–68, 170
gratefulness, 9, 50, 167
great-hearted, 170

Hans U von Balthasar, 48, 67, 167
Henri Nouwen, 39, 136
heretic, 27
heritage of humanity, 170
hero/es/ic, 14, 20–22, 61, 69, 71, 85, 95, 108, 118, 126, 170–71
holiness, 4, 8, 25, 27, 34–35, 38, 44, 48, 67, 81, 88, 101, 126, 133–34, 146–48, 150, 165
holy fool/s, 44, 52, 151
human persons, 22, 24, 47, 71ff., 79ff., 104–7

inauthentic self, 88
indulgence, 17
infection, 5
infighting, 3
injustice, 8, 53, 56, 116, 120–21, 126, 129
instructors, 11–12
insurrection, 162–63
invocation, 165

James Martin, 154, 159
Jimmy Swaggart, 31–32
J.R.R. Tolkien, 13, 69, 160, 171
Julian of Norwich, 20, 53–54, 86, 116
Jurgen Moltman, 70, 129, 168

Karl Barth, 18, 55, 102
kenosis, 122–24, 129
kneeling down, 90

laughter, 64, 73, 133, 149–61, 169
Les Miserables, 52–53
Life of Brian, 150, 160
Lindisfarne Gospels, 105–6

Martin Luther, 34, 164
Martyr/dom, 6, 22, 44ff., 59, 86, 96, 110–11, 133, 136, 160, 165, 169
moral teaching, 8, 86
mystery, 50, 67, 74, 76, 81, 83–85, 88, 137, 170

Nadia's face, 72–74, 82
necessity, 46, 49, 83–84
new birth, 18, 147
Nicene Creed, 76–78, 165

Paphnutius, 24–26
parable, 1–3
peak experience, 67
perform/ance, 9, 42, 85, 99, 108–11, 114–15, 128, 144, 148, 167
physical/ity, 39, 44, 54, 64, 81, 98ff., 101ff., 103, 111ff., 125, 131, 135, 144ff.
Pope Francis, 83, 105
Pope John Paul II, 40, 44, 162
Positive Psychology, 47, 128
post-Christian, 10, 12–16, 19, 22, 34, 87, 152, 165
postmodern, 15, 121, 171
Prince Myshkin, 51
proof/s, 8, 11, 19, 80, 99, 152, 165, 168
prostitution, 94–96, 98

radical Christians, 170–71
redemption, 53, 77, 79–81, 88, 102–3, 107, 120, 134, 173
repentance, 23, 32–33, 38–39, 54, 111, 132, 160,
resurrection, 7, 14, 17–18, 45–46, 80, 97, 103, 110, 122–23, 162–63
revelatory, 10, 87, 104, 106 167

Index

revitalization, 2
Richard Dawkins, 150, 159
Richard Rohr, 85
righteous/ness, 4, 7, 14, 25, 27, 39, 46, 67, 69, 77, 96, 101, 115, 119ff., 131, 151, 160, 169
Robert Webber, 35
Robert Wuthnow, 166
Roman Catholic, 13, 15–16, 33, 39, 50, 53 150, 162
Ronnie Williams, 56–57

sainthood, 6, 50, 87, 150
salvation, 3–4, 21, 29, 33, 38, 62, 76–78, 87, 97, 101, 103ff., 106, 108, 110–11, 123, 154
sanctification, 3, 147
Scott Peck, 38
secular saints, 47
sensuality, 98
servant-hearted, 5
servants, 11–12, 103, 105, 122, 129, 135
sex/sexual, 14, 27, 31, 34, 44, 62, 72, 81, 90, 94–98, 100, 116, 120, 155
Sister Ella Williams, 21, 58–59
Søren Kierkegaard, 40, 83, 121, 149
spirituality of imperfection 38–40, 144
St Augustine, 20, 36, 75, 84, 86, 97, 131, 164, 172
St Bede, 74
St Clements, 93
St Damien of Molokai, 42–44, 146
St Mary McKillop, 150, 156
submission, 7–9, 35, 50, 54, 65, 167

suffer/ing, 20, 25, 35, 39, 51, 54, 59, 63ff., 86, 91, 103, 109, 116–37, 140ff., 148, 170
Susan Wolf, 46

T.S. Eliot, 54
Terry Eagleton, 36, 153
Tertullian, 25, 108
testimony, 8, 18, 28, 86, 104, 109–11, 135
theosis, 124, 129
Thomas à Kempis, 59, 61
Thomas Merton, 32–33, 87
Tony Cupit, 108–9
transform/ation, 5, 22, 45, 52, 71, 74, 78, 83–84, 86–87, 96, 99, 108, 110, 117–19, 124, 130, 145–47, 169, 172
trophy/ies, 6, 8, 104, 163, 168
true north, 3, 7

value, 3, 8, 12, 18, 22, 26, 40, 44, 46–47, 53–54, 66, 70, 73, 81, 83–84, 98, 106, 115, 121, 128, 134, 147–48, 150, 152
venerate/veneration, 6–7, 17, 53, 164
Victor Hugo, 52–53
vocation, 6, 8, 33, 42, 84, 101, 146–48, 165, 172

Whisky Priest, 28–29
wicked/ness, 4–5, 80–81, 98, 103, 136, 153, 171
William James, 62, 99
William Willimon, 36–37, 169
witness/ses, 6, 22, 31, 34, 40, 55, 87, 97, 106–8, 110–11, 168–70

www.ingramcontent.com/pod-product-compliance
Lightning Source LLC
Chambersburg PA
CBHW030109170426
43198CB00009B/558